Financial Market Rates and Flows

JAMES C. VAN HORNE

Stanford University

Prentice-Hall, Inc. Englewood Cliffs, New Jersey 07632

Library of Congress Cataloging in Publication Data

Van Horne, James C
  Financial market rates and flows.

  Includes bibliographies and index.
  1. Interest and usury.   2. Finance.
3.   Flow of funds.   I.   Title.
HB539.V338   332.8   77-25090
ISBN 0-13-316190-0 pbk
     0-13-316182-x

Printed in the United States of America

10 9 8 7 6 5 4 3 2 1

PRENTICE-HALL INTERNATIONAL, INC., *London*
PRENTICE-HALL OF AUSTRALIA PTY. LIMITED, *Sydney*
PRENTICE-HALL OF CANADA, LTD., *Toronto*
PRENTICE-HALL OF INDIA PRIVATE LIMITED, *New Delhi*
PRENTICE-HALL OF JAPAN, INC., *Tokyo*
PRENTICE-HALL OF SOUTHEAST ASIA PTE. LTD., *Singapore*
WHITEHALL BOOKS LIMITED, *Wellington, New Zealand*

Contents

Preface

This book is an outgrowth of *Function and Analysis of Capital Market Rates* (Prentice-Hall, Inc., 1970). With the passage of time, much has changed in the theoretical and empirical consideration of interest rates. As the changes in the book are substantial—with only about one-third held over from before—the title was changed in order to better reflect the book's current emphasis.

The purpose of *Financial Market Rates and Flows* is to provide the reader with a basic conceptual understanding of the function of financial markets, of the flow of funds, of market efficiency or the lack thereof, of levels of interest rates, and of interest-rate differentials. The latter are due to differences in maturity, default risk, coupon rate, call feature, and taxability; and the effect of each is examined in detail. Another factor, the social allocation of capital, affects both interest rates and financial flows; the effect here is examined in the last chapter.

A second purpose of the book is to evaluate a rich body of empirical evidence as it bears on the various theories that are considered. The focus, then, is not only on the theoretical foundations for interest rates and interest-rate differentials, but on the "real world" conditions that affect these rates and differentials. As the book unfolds, a conceptual framework is developed for analyzing interest rates under conditions of uncertainty.

Financial Market Rates and Flows can be used as a supplement for courses in money and capital markets, money and banking, monetary policy, investments, and financial institutions. In addition, it is useful to those in the financial community, in business, and in government who are concerned with investing in or issuing fixed-income securities and with the flow of funds through financial markets.

JAMES C. VAN HORNE
Palo Alto, California

The Function of
Financial Markets

1   In this book, the underlying structure of financial markets is examined, as is the price mechanism, which brings about a balance between supply and demand. Our purpose is not to describe specific money or capital markets or the institutions involved in these markets, and it is not to provide data on financial flows; this information is available elsewhere.[1] Rather, this book provides a basis for understanding and analyzing interest rates and funds movements in financial markets. The instruments studied are financial assets. Unlike real, or tangible, assets, a *financial* asset is a claim on some other economic unit. It does not provide its owner with the physical services that a real asset does. Instead, financial assets are held as a store of value and for the return that they are expected to provide. The holding of these assets, with the exception of equity securities, indicates neither direct nor indirect ownership of real assets in the economy.

Savings-Investment Foundation

Financial assets exist in an economy because the savings of various economic units (current income less current expenditures) during a period of time differ from their investment in real assets. In this regard, an

[1]Herbert E. Dougall and Jack E. Gaumnitz, *Capital Markets and Institutions*, 3rd ed. (Englewood Cliffs, N.J.: Prentice-Hall, Inc., 1975); Roland I. Robinson and Dwayne Wrightsman, *Financial Markets: The Accumulation and Allocation of Wealth* (New York: McGraw-Hill Book Co., 1974); Murray E. Polakoff et al., *Financial Institutions and Markets* (Boston: Houghton Mifflin Company, 1970); Charles N. Henning, William Pigott, and Robert Haney Scott, *Financial Markets and the Economy* (Englewood Cliffs, N.J.: Prentice-Hall, Inc., 1974); and Raymond W. Goldsmith, *The Flow of Capital Funds in the Postwar Economy* (New York: National Bureau of Economic Research, 1965).

economic unit can be (1) a household or partnership, (2) a nonprofit organization, (3) a corporation (financial or nonfinancial), or (4) a government (federal, state, or local). There are a number of reasons why economic units invest more than they save or save more than they invest over an interval of time. These include the present income of the economic unit, expected future income, costs of goods and services, personal tastes, age, health, education, family composition, and current interest rates, as well as a number of other reasons.

The productive resources in any society, such as land, machines, buildings, natural resources, and workers, are limited. These resources may all be devoted to producing goods and services for current consumption; or a part of them may go toward things that will enhance the nation's ability to produce, and hence consume, in the future. This process might involve the production of machinery, the exploration for iron ore, or the training of workers in new technology. Capital formation can be defined as any investment which increases the productive capacity of society. If resources are fully employed, the only way to make such investments is to refrain from current consumption. If resources are less than fully employed, however, it is possible to have capital formation without necessarily foregoing current consumption.

In a broad sense, capital formation involves not only investment in tangible assets, such as buildings, equipment and inventories, but also intangible investments in such things as education, training, health, and labor mobility—all of which enhance productivity.[2] For our purposes in studying financial flows, however, we will use a narrower definition and restrict our attention to investments in tangible or real assets. Investment in human capital will be treated as consumption, not because it does not contribute to increased productivity, but because data on it are imprecise for purposes of quantifying financial flows.

Assume for the moment a closed economy in which there are no foreign transactions. If savings equal investment for all economic units in that economy over all periods of time, there would be no external financing and no financial assets. In other words, each economic unit would be self-sufficient; current expenditures and investment in real assets would be paid for out of current income. A financial asset is created only when the investment of an economic unit in real assets exceeds its savings, and it finances this excess by borrowing, issuing equity securities, or issuing money (if the economic unit happens to be a monetary institution).[3] For

[2]See John W. Kendrick, *The Formation and Stocks of Total Capital* (New York: National Bureau of Economic Research, 1976); and Selig D. Lesnox and John C. Hambor, "Social Security, Saving and Capital Formation," *Social Security Bulletin*, 38 (July, 1975), 3–15.

[3]A financial asset may be created for the purpose of financing consumption in excess of current income. Although it is possible for investment in real assets for a period to be zero, that investment would still exceed the negative savings of the economic unit.

an economic unit to finance, of course, another economic unit or other units in the economy must be willing to lend. This interaction of the borrower with the lender determines interest rates. For identification, economic units whose current savings exceed their investment in real assets are called *savings-surplus units*. Economic units whose investment in real assets exceeds their current savings are labeled *savings-deficit units*.[4] In the economy as a whole, funds are provided by savings-surplus units to the savings-deficit units. This exchange of funds is evidenced by pieces of paper representing financial assets to the holders and financial liabilities to the issuers.

If an economic unit holds existing financial assets, it is able to cover the excess of its investment in real assets over savings by means other than issuing financial liabilities. It simply can sell some of the financial assets it holds. Thus, as long as an economic unit holds financial assets, it does not have to increase its financial liabilities by an amount equal to its excess of investment over savings. The purchase and sale of existing financial assets occur in the *secondary market*. Transactions in this market do not increase the total stock of financial assets outstanding. It is possible, although unlikely, for a substantial number of savings-deficit units to exist in an economy over a period of time and for little change to occur in total financial assets outstanding. For this to happen, however, savings-deficit units must have sufficient financial assets to cover the excess of their investment in real assets over savings and, of course, must be willing to sell these assets.

Efficiency of Financial Markets

The purpose of financial markets is to allocate savings efficiently in an economy to ultimate users, either for investment in real assets or for consumption. In this section, we regard financial markets in a broad sense as including all institutions and procedures for bringing buyers and sellers of financial instruments together, no matter what the nature of the financial instrument. If those economic units which saved were the same as those which engaged in capital formation, an economy could prosper without financial markets. In modern economies, however, the economic sector most responsible for capital formation—nonfinancial corporations—invest in real assets in an amount in excess of their total savings. The household sector, on the other hand, has total savings in excess of total investment. Therefore, a balance is *not* achieved. The more diverse the patterns of desired savings and investment among economic units, the greater the need for efficient financial markets to channel savings

[4]These labels correspond to those given by Raymond W. Goldsmith, *The Flow of Capital Funds in the Postwar Economy* (New York: National Bureau of Economic Research, 1965).

to ultimate users. Their job is to allocate savings from savings-surplus economic units to savings-deficit units so that the highest level of want satisfaction can be achieved. These parties should be brought together, either directly or indirectly, at the least possible cost and with the least inconvenience.

Efficient financial markets are essential to assure adequate capital formation and economic growth in a modern economy. To appreciate this statement, imagine an economy without financial assets other than money.[5] In such an economy, each economic unit could invest in real assets only to the extent that it saved. Without financial assets, then, an economic unit would be constrained greatly in its investment behavior. If it wanted to invest in real assets, it would have to save to do so. If the amount required for investment were large in relation to current savings, the economic unit simply would have to postpone investment until it had accumulated sufficient savings. Moreover, these savings would have to be accumulated as money balances, since there would be no alternatives. Because of the absence of financing, many worthwhile investment opportunities would have to be postponed or abandoned by economic units lacking sufficient savings.[6]

In such a system, savings in the economy would not be channeled to the most promising investment opportunities; and, accordingly, capital would be less than optimally allocated. Those economic units which lacked promising investment opportunities would have no alternative except to accumulate money balances. Likewise, economic units with very promising opportunities might not be able to accumulate sufficient savings rapidly enough to undertake the projects. Consequently, inferior investments might be undertaken by some economic units, while very promising investment opportunities would be postponed or abandoned by others. Capital is misallocated in such a system, and total investment tends to be low relative to what it might be with financial assets. In this situation, growth in the economy is restrained, if not stagnant, and the level of want satisfaction is far from optimal. An important resource—namely, capital—is allocated inefficiently, with an adverse effect upon national income and the real standard of living for individuals in that economy. For want of a better system, financial assets must come into being.

The discussion above has been confined to the private sector of the economy. With money, however, the federal government is able to finance

---

[5]In a barter economy, without money or financial assets, each economic unit must be in balance with respect to savings and investment. It must invest in real assets in an amount equal to its savings. No economic unit could invest more than it saved.

[6]The development of this section draws on John G. Gurley and Edward S. Shaw, *Money in a Theory of Finance* (Washington, D.C.: The Brookings Institution, 1960); and John G. Gurley, "The Savings-Investment Process and the Market for Loanable Funds," reprinted in Lawrence S. Ritter, ed., *Money and Economic Activity* (Boston: Houghton Mifflin Company, 1967), pp. 50–55.

its purchases of goods and services by issuing money. If the federal government increases the supply of money, in keeping with increases in the demand for money by other economic units, purchases of goods and services by the government increase.[7] To the extent that the federal government centralizes investment and channels it into promising opportunities, capital formation in the economy is efficient. However, if the government is a large cumbersome bureaucracy, which is unresponsive to market conditions, government decisions are unlikely to result in efficient capital formation.

We turn now to the situation where there are financial assets as well as money in the economy, but no financial institutions. With financial assets, investment in real assets by an economic unit is no longer constrained by the amount of its savings. If it wants to invest more than it saves, it can do so by reducing the amount of its money balances, by selling financial assets, or by increasing its financial liabilities. When an economic unit increases its financial liabilities, it issues a *primary security*. For this to be done, however, another economic unit or other units in the economy must be willing to purchase it. In a developing economy, these transactions between borrower and lender usually take the form of direct loans. The ability of economic units to finance an excess of investment over savings improves greatly the allocation of savings in a society. Many of the problems cited earlier are eliminated. Individual economic units no longer need to postpone promising investment opportunities for lack of accumulated savings. Moreover, savings-surplus units have an outlet for their savings other than money balances—an outlet that provides an expected return. With financial assets in the form of direct loans, the overall level of want satisfaction in the economy is higher than it would be otherwise.

Still, there are degrees of efficiency. A system of direct loans may not be sufficient to assemble and "package" large blocks of savings for investment in large projects. To the extent that a single savings-surplus economic unit cannot service the capital needs of a savings-deficit unit, the latter must turn to additional savings-surplus units. If the need for funds is large, the user may have considerable difficulty in locating pockets of available savings and in negotiating multiple loans. For one thing, his communication network is limited. Consequently, there is a need to bring together ultimate savers and investors in a more efficient manner than through direct loans between the two parties.

To service this need, various loan brokers may come into existence to find savers and bring them together with economic units needing funds. Because a broker is a specialist who is continually in the business of matching the need for funds with the supply, usually he is able to do it

[7]Gurley, *op. cit.*, p. 51.

more efficiently and at a lower cost than are individual economic units themselves. One improvement is that he is able to divide a primary security of a certain amount into smaller amounts more compatible with the preferences of savings-surplus economic units. As a result, savers are able to hold their savings in a diversified portfolio of primary securities; this feature encourages savers to invest in financial assets. The resulting increased attractiveness of primary securities improves the flow of savings from savers to users of funds. In addition to performing the brokerage function involved in selling securities, investment bankers may underwrite an issue of primary securities. By underwriting, the investment banker bears the risk of selling the issue. He buys the primary securities from the borrower and resells them to savers. Since he pays the borrower for the security issue, the latter does not bear the risk of not being able to sell the securities. This guaranteed purchase makes it easier than otherwise for savings-deficit economic units to finance their excess of investment in real assets over savings.

Another innovation that enhances the efficiency of the flow of savings in an economy is the development of *secondary markets*, where existing securities can be either bought or sold. With a viable secondary market, a savings-surplus economic unit achieves flexibility when it purchases a primary security. Should it need to sell the security in the future, it will be able to do so because the security is marketable. The existence of secondary markets encourages more risk-taking on the part of savings-surplus economic units. If, in the future, they want to invest more than they save, they know that they will be able to sell financial assets as one means of covering the excess. This flexibility encourages savings-surplus economic units to make their savings available to others rather than to hold them as money balances. All the innovations discussed contribute to the efficiency of the flow of savings from ultimate savers to ultimate users through primary securities. As a result, capital allocation is more efficient: Savings are more readily channeled to the most promising investments.

The Role of Financial Intermediaries

Up until now, we have considered only the direct flow of savings from savers to users. However, the flow can be indirect if there are financial intermediaries in the economy. Financial intermediaries include such institutions as commercial banks, savings banks, savings and loan associations, life insurance companies, and pension and profit-sharing funds. These intermediaries purchase primary securities and, in turn, issue their own securities. Thus, they come between ultimate borrowers and ultimate lenders. In essence, they transform direct claims—primary securities—into indirect claims—called *indirect securities*—which differ in form from direct claims. For example, the primary security that a savings and loan association purchases is a mortgage; the indirect claim issued is a savings account or certificate of deposit. A life insurance company, on the other hand, purchases mortgages and bonds and issues life insurance policies.

Financial intermediaries transform funds in such a way as to make them more attractive.[8] On one hand, the indirect security issued to ultimate lenders is more attractive than is a direct, or primary, security. In particular, these indirect claims are well suited to the small saver. On the other hand, the ultimate borrower is able to sell its primary securities to a financial intermediary on more attractive terms than it could if the securities were sold directly to ultimate lenders. Financial intermediaries provide a variety of services and economies that make the transformation of claims attractive.

1. *Economies of scale.* Because financial intermediaries continually are in the business of purchasing primary securities and selling indirect claims, economies of scale not available to the borrower or to the individual saver are possible.

2. *Divisibility and flexibility.* A financial intermediary is able to pool the savings of many individual savers to purchase primary securities of varying sizes. In particular, it is able to tap small pockets of savings for ultimate investment in real assets. The offering of indirect securities of varying size contributes significantly to the attractiveness of financial intermediaries to the saver. The borrower achieves flexibility in dealing with a financial intermediary as opposed to a large number of lenders. He is able to obtain terms tailored to his needs more readily.

3. *Diversification and risk.* By purchasing a number of different primary securities, the financial intermediary is able to spread risk. If these securities are less than perfectly correlated with each other, the intermediary is able to reduce the risk associated with fluctuations in value of principal. The benefits of reduced risk are passed on to the indirect security holders. As a result, the indirect security provides a higher degree of liquidity to the saver than does a like commitment to a single primary security. To the extent the individual is unable, because of size or other reasons, to achieve adequate diversification on his own, the financial intermediation process is beneficial.

---

[8]See Raymond W. Goldsmith, *Financial Institutions* (New York: Random House, Inc., 1968), pp. 22–33. For an analysis of primary security divisibility as it pertains to financial intermediation, see Michael A. Klein, "The Economics of Security Divisibility and Financial Intermediation," *Journal of Finance*, 28 (September, 1973), 923–931.

4. *Maturity*. A financial intermediary is able to transform a primary security of a certain maturity into indirect securities of different maturities. As a result, the maturities on the primary and the indirect securities may be more attractive to the ultimate borrower and lender than they would be if the loan were direct.

5. *Expertise and convenience*. The financial intermediary is an expert in making purchases of primary securities and in so doing eliminates the inconvenience to the saver of making direct purchases. For example, not many individuals are familiar with the intricacies of making a mortgage loan; they have neither the time nor the inclination to learn. For the most part, they are happy to let savings and loan associations, commercial banks, savings banks, and life insurance companies engage in this type of lending and to purchase the indirect securities of these intermediaries. The financial intermediary is also an expert in dealing with ultimate savers—an expertise lacking in most borrowers.

Financial intermediaries tailor the denomination and type of indirect securities they issue to the desires of savers. Their purpose, of course, is to make a profit by purchasing primary securities yielding more than the return they must pay on the indirect securities issued and on operations. In so doing, they must channel funds from the ultimate lender to the ultimate borrower at a lower cost or with more convenience or both than is possible through a direct purchase of primary securities by the ultimate lender. Otherwise, they have no reason to exist.

To illustrate this notion, suppose that without financial intermediaries the rate of interest to a borrower would be 10 per cent. In addition, he must incur the indirect costs of searching for lenders and arranging for the loan. Suppose that these costs approximate 1 per cent per annum. Therefore, the effective cost of borrowing via the direct loan is 11 per cent. The rate of interest to the lender, of course, is 10 per cent. However, search costs are incurred by the lender. In addition, the amount of the funds he has available may not correspond to the amount that the potential borrower wishes to obtain. As a result, it may be necessary to pool the funds of several potential lenders, and this involves time and energy. Also, there is the cost of administrating the loan and attending to the numerous details involved. The amount that some individuals are required to loan may be so great, relative to their total financial assets, that it precludes adequate diversification. Such lenders must be compensated for the greater risk. Finally, the lumpiness of the loan may result in pockets of unusable funds. For example, an individual may have $2,700 to lend, but his participation in the loan amounts to only $2,500. As a result, there is an idle $200.

Suppose that all of these costs correspond to an annual interest rate of 6 per cent. When this is deducted from the gross interest rate of 10 per cent, the "net" interest rate to the lender becomes 4 per cent. Thus, we have the following:

Borrower:	
Total cost to borrower	11 per cent
Less search costs	1 per cent
Interest rate charged	10 per cent
Lender:	
Gross interest rate received	10 per cent
Less costs of search, administration,	
pooling, and diversification constraints	6 per cent
Net interest return	4 per cent

Therefore, the differential between the total cost to the borrower and the net return to the lender is 11 per cent less 4 per cent, which equals 7 per cent.

Suppose now that financial intermediation is possible, and that a deposit-type intermediary stands ready to accept longer-term deposits at a 6 per cent rate with no inconvenience to the saver. It also will lend to the borrower in question at a 9 per cent rate. The 3 per cent spread between the two rates covers the expenses of the intermediary and provides it with a profit. We see then that the ultimate borrower is able to borrow at a lower effective rate—9 per cent as opposed to 11 per cent. Moreover, the net return to the lender is higher—6 per cent as opposed to 4 per cent. The spread between the effective borrowing and lending rates has been narrowed from 7 per cent to 3 per cent. This is possible for all of the reasons stated above. As a result, the presence of financial intermediaries is beneficial both to ultimate borrowers and to ultimate lenders.

Thus, financial intermediaries tend to make financial markets more efficient. By transforming primary securities into indirect securities, they lower the cost to the ultimate borrower and provide a security better suited to the ultimate lender. The yield differential, as represented by the difference in yield between the borrower's cost and the net yield to the saver on an equivalent loan, is narrowed by their presence. In our example, it is narrowed from an 11–4 per cent spread to a 9–6 per cent spread. One of the marks of efficient financial markets is that when opportunities for profit exist or arise, financial intermediaries and other financial innovations come into being to exploit the opportunity. By entering the market, they tend to narrow the differential, as defined above. Thus, they facilitate the movement of savings from ultimate savers to ultimate borrowers at a lower cost and with less inconvenience. The result is that a higher proportion of income tends to be saved in a society, and interest costs to borrowers tend to be lower than they would be in the absence of these intermediaries. The development of financial intermediaries has been an important factor contributing to capital formation and the growth of the economy. In turn, this has contributed to a higher level of want satisfaction.

With the introduction of financial intermediaries, we have four main sectors in an economy: households, nonfinancial business firms, governments, and financial institutions. These four sectors form a matrix of claims against one another. This matrix is illustrated in Fig. 1-1, which shows hypothetical balance sheets for each sector. Financial assets of each sector include money as well as primary securities. Households, of course,

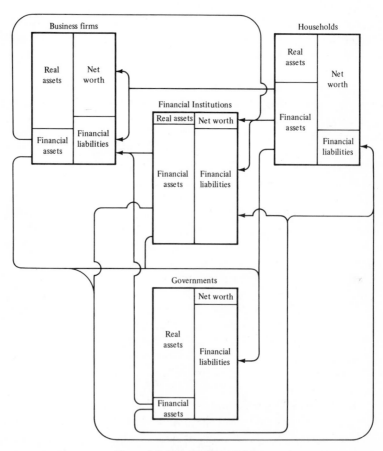

Figure 1-1. Relationship of claims.

are the ultimate owners of all business enterprises, whether they are nonfinancial corporations or private financial institutions. The figure illustrates the distinct role of financial intermediaries. Their assets are predominantly financial assets; they hold a relatively small amount of real assets. On the right-hand side of the balance sheet, financial liabilities are predominant. Financial institutions, then, are engaged in transforming direct claims into indirect claims that have a wider appeal. The relationships of financial to real assets and of financial liabilities to net worth distinguishes them from other economic units.[9]

The more varied the vehicles by which savings can flow from ultimate savers to ultimate users of funds, usually the more efficient the financial markets of an economy. With efficient financial markets, there can be sharp differences between the pattern of savings and the pattern of investment for economic units in the economy. The result is a higher level of capital formation, growth, and want satisfaction. Individual economic units are not confined either to holding their savings in money balances or to investing them in real assets. Their alternatives are many; each contributes to the efficient channeling of funds from ultimate savers to users.

The Implications of Savings

Having outlined the reason for financial assets in an economy and traced through the efficiency of financial markets, we now consider the implications of savings, individually and collectively, for economic units. Recall that savings represent current income less current consumption.

For the *individual*, savings represent expenditures foregone out of current income, and they may be the result of a number of acts. One of the most familiar is spending less than one's discretionary income, with the difference going into a savings account. The build-up in a savings account, in itself, does not represent an act of savings but, rather, is the result of it. Other aspects of savings for the individual are less familiar. For example, savings may be the result of repayment of principal in a mortgage payment. Another means by which net worth may be increased is through contributions, either voluntary or involuntary, to a pension or profit-sharing plan or both. In addition, an individual may save through the payment of a premium on a life insurance policy.

For the *corporation*, *net* savings represent earnings retained during the period being studied—that is, profits after taxes and after the payment of dividends on preferred and common stock. *Gross* savings for corporations

---

[9]For an analysis of the sources and uses of funds of financial intermediaries, see Raymond W. Goldsmith, *Financial Institutions*, (New York: Random House, Inc., 1968), Chapter 3.

include capital-consumption allowances (mainly depreciation) in addition to retained earnings. Finally, savings for a *government* unit represent a budget surplus, and dissavings a budget deficit.

For a given period of time, the total uses of funds by an economic unit must equal its total sources. Thus,[10]

$$RA + MT + L + E = S + D + IM + B + IE \qquad (1\text{-}1)$$

where RA = gross change in real assets
MT = change in money held
L = lending (change in fixed-income securities held)
E = equity investment (change in equity securities held)
S = net savings
D = capital-consumption allowance
IM = issuance of money
B = borrowing
IE = issuance of equity securities

All the symbols represent net flows over a period of time, and they can be positive or negative. Depending upon the type of economic unit involved, however, some of the variables may not be applicable. As only monetary institutions can issue money, IM is applicable only to the central bank and commercial banks. Similarly, only corporations can issue equity securities, so IE applies only to them. For the economic unit, the total uses of funds on the left side of the equation must equal total sources on the right side.

For purposes of financial-market analysis, net savings for the economic unit usually are defined as[11]

$$S = (MT + L + E) \; - \; (IM + B + IE) \; + \; (RA - D) \qquad (1\text{-}2)$$

gross savings   financing   net savings
through   through
financial assets   real assets

net savings through
financial assets

For the economy as a whole, *ex post* savings for a given period of time

---

[10]This equation is a modification of an equation developed by Goldsmith in *The Flow of Capital Funds in the Postwar Economy*, p. 59. For simplicity, we assume a closed economy with no foreign transactions.

[11]Again, this equation is a modification of Goldsmith, *The Flow of Capital Funds in the Postwar Economy*.

must equal *ex post* investment in real assets for that period. Consequently,

$$\sum_j S = \sum_j (RA - D) \qquad (1\text{-}3)$$

where j is the jth economic unit in the economy. Thus, changes in financial assets for a period cancel out when summed for all economic units in the economy.

$$\sum_j (MT + L + E) - \sum_J (IM + B + IE) = 0 \qquad (1\text{-}4)$$

As a result, savings for the economy as a whole must correspond to the increase in net real assets in that economy. There is no such thing as savings through financial assets for the economy as a whole. However, individual economic units can save through financial assets, and this is the process we wish to study. The fact that financial assets wash out when they are totaled for all economic units in the economy is a recognizable identity. It is the interaction between the issuers of financial claims and the potential holders of those claims that is important. Also, we must recognize that desired or *ex ante* savings for the economy as a whole need not equal *ex ante* investment. The equilibrating process has implications not only for interest rates in general but for the interactions among individual economic units.

Liquidity and Financial Markets

All financial instruments have a common denominator in that they are expressed in terms of money—the accepted medium of exchange. Thus, financial flows occur in terms of money. Money, the most liquid of assets, is the measure against which various types of financial instruments are compared as to their degree of substitution. In this regard, *liquidity* may be defined as the ability to realize value in money. As such, it has two dimensions: (1) the length of time and transaction cost required to convert the asset into money, and (2) the certainty of the price realized. The latter represents the stability of the ratio of exchange between the asset and money—in other words, the degree of fluctuation in market price. The two factors are interrelated. If an asset must be converted into money in a very short period of time, there may be more uncertainty as to the price realized than if there were a reasonable time period in which to sell the asset.

Financial markets tend to be efficient relative to other markets. As the good involved is a claim, evidenced by a piece of paper, it is transportable at little cost and is not subject to physical deterioration. Moreover, it can be defined and classified easily. For most financial markets, information is readily available, and geographical boundaries are not a great problem. By their very nature, then, financial markets are fairly efficient when compared with the full spectrum of markets.

Frequently, these markets are classified according to the final maturity of the particular instrument involved. On one hand, *money* markets usually are regarded as including financial assets that are short term, are highly marketable, and, accordingly, possess low risk and a high degree of liquidity. These assets are traded in highly impersonal markets, where funds move on the basis of price and risk alone. Thus, a short-term loan negotiated between a corporation and a bank is not considered a money-market instrument. Examples of money markets include the markets for short-term government securities, bankers' acceptances, and commercial paper. *Capital* markets, on the other hand, include instruments with longer terms to maturity. These markets are somewhat more diverse than money markets. Examples include markets for government, corporate, and municipal bonds; corporate stocks; and mortgages. The maturity boundary that divides the money and capital markets is rather arbitrary. Some regard it as one year, while others maintain that it is five years. Because the foundation for their existence is the same, we have not concerned ourselves in this chapter with the breakdown between the two markets.

Financial Flows and Interest Rates

In studying financial markets, we are interested in the flow of savings from ultimate savers to ultimate users. These flows can be analyzed with *flow-of-funds* data. Flow of funds is a system of social accounting that enables one to evaluate savings flows among various sectors in the economy. This system and its usefulness are examined in Chapter 2. The actual allocation, or channeling, of savings in an economy is accomplished primarily through interest rates. Presumably, economic units with the most promising investment opportunities will pay more for the use of funds on a risk-adjusted return basis than those with higher opportunities. To the extent that the former bid funds away from the latter, savings tend to be channeled to the most efficient uses. Interest rates adjust continually to bring changing supply and demand in each market into balance. The movement toward equilibrium occurs not only in an individual financial market but also across financial markets. The role of interest rates in the equilibrating process is studied in Chapter 3.

Subsequent chapters are devoted to an analysis of relative yields for various financial instruments. In Chapters 4 through 8, we investigate reasons for differences in the level of interest rates among fixed-income securities. These differences are called *yield differentials*. In each case, the theoretical reasons for a yield differential are considered first, followed by an examination of relevant empirical evidence. In Chapter 4, we see how the length of time to maturity affects the yield. Known as the *term structure of interest rates*, this topic is qualified slightly in Chapter 5 for the effect of differences in coupon rates, which, in turn, affect the duration of a financial instrument. In Chapter 6, the effect of differences in default risk on yields is analyzed. Chapter 7 is devoted to the effect of a call feature on the value of a financial instrument. The presence of a call provision usually results in the possibility that *actual maturity* will be less than *stated maturity*. In Chapter 8, the effect of taxes on yields is explored. If market equilibration occurs in terms of after-tax rates of return, the impact of whether or not interest income is taxed, the differential tax on interest and capital gains, estate tax considerations, and the impact of depreciation and the investment tax credit have important influences on relative yields.

Much of our analysis is in terms of nominal yields. However, in Chapter 5 we consider the market equilibration process in terms of real rates of return. Inflation expectations are found to have an important influence on the interest rates we observe in the marketplace. While the allocation of savings in an economy occurs primarily through interest rates, it is affected also by institutional imperfections and by government restrictions. The effects of various institutional imperfections are taken up in Chapters 4 through 8, as they bear on a particular problem. The effect of government restrictions is addressed in Chapter 9; here we consider attempts by the government to socially allocate capital in an economy and/or to lower the interest-rate cost for certain borrowers. The various methods for socially allocating capital are presented and are analyzed as to their effectiveness and cost.

Summary

A financial asset is a claim against some economic unit in an economy. It is held for the return it provides and as a store of value—reasons that differentiate it from a real asset. Financial assets and markets exist because during a period of time some economic units save more than they invest in real assets, while other economic units invest more than they save. To cover an excess of investment over savings for a period, an economic unit can reduce its holdings of existing financial assets, increase its financial liabilities, or undertake some combination of the two. When it increases its financial liabilities, a new financial instrument is created in the economy. The existence of financial markets permits investment for economic units to differ from their savings.

The purpose of financial markets is to allocate efficiently savings in an economy to ultimate users of funds. For the economy as a whole, *ex post* investment must equal *ex post* savings. However, this is not true for individual economic units; they can have considerable divergence between savings and investment for a particular period of time. The more vibrant the financial markets in an economy, the more efficient the allocation of savings to the most promising investment opportunities, and the greater the capital formation in that economy. A number of innovations make financial markets efficient. Among the most important are financial intermediaries. A financial intermediary transforms the direct claim of the ultimate borrower into an indirect claim, which is sold to ultimate lenders. Intermediaries channel savings from ultimate savers to ultimate borrowers at a lower cost and with less inconvenience than is possible on a direct basis.

All financial flows occur in terms of money, the most liquid of assets. Liquidity may be defined as the ability to realize value in money. Generally, financial markets are efficient relative to other markets. In the chapters that follow, we shall investigate in depth both the flow of savings and the price mechanism—namely, interest rates—which bring about a balance between supply and demand in the various financial markets. Our concern is with both the level of interest rates and the differentials between interest rates for different financial instruments.

SELECTED REFERENCES

Dougall, Herbert E., and Jack E. Gaumnitz, *Capital Markets and Institutions*, 3rd ed. Englewood Cliffs, N.J.: Prentice-Hall, Inc., 1975.

Goldsmith, Raymond W., *Financial Institutions*. New York: Random House, Inc., 1968.

_____, *Financial Intermediaries in the American Economy since 1900*. Princeton, N.J.: National Bureau of Economic Research, 1958.

_____, *The Flow of Capital Funds in the Postwar Economy*, Chapter 1. New York: National Bureau of Economic Research, 1965.

Gurley, John G., "The Savings-Investment Process and the Market for Loanable Funds," reprinted in Lawrence S. Ritter, ed., *Money and Economic Activity*, pp. 50–55. Boston: Houghton Mifflin Company, 1967.

_____, and Edward S. Shaw, *Money in a Theory of Finance*. Washington, D.C.: The Brookings Institution, 1960.

_____, "Financial Intermediaries and the Saving-Investment Process," *Journal of Finance*, 11 (May, 1956), 257–266.

Henning, Charles N., William Pigott, and Robert Haney Scott, *Financial Markets and the Economy*. Englewood Cliffs, N.J.: Prentice-Hall, Inc., 1975.

Jacobs, Donald P., Loring C. Farwell, and Edwin Neave, *Financial Institutions*, 5th ed. Homewood, Ill.: Richard D. Irwin, Inc., 1972.

Kaufman, George G., *Money, the Financial System, and the Economy*, Part II. Chicago: Rand McNally & Co., 1973.

Moore, Basil J., *An Introduction to the Theory of Finance*, Chapters 1, 3, and 4. New York: The Free Press, 1968.

Polakoff, Murray E. et al., *Financial Institutions and Markets*. Boston: Houghton Mifflin Company, 1970.

Pyle, David H., "On the Theory of Financial Intermediation," *Journal of Finance*, 26 (June, 1971), 737–747.

Ritter, Lawrence S., and William L. Silber, *Principles of Money, Banking and Financial Markets*, Part 5. New York: Basic Books, Inc., 1974.

Robinson, Roland I., and Dwayne Wrightsman, *Financial Markets: The Accumulation and Allocation of Wealth*. New York: McGraw-Hill Book Co., 1974.

Smith, Paul F., *Economics of Financial Institutions and Markets*. Homewood, Ill.: Richard D. Irwin, Inc., 1971.

Woodworth, G. Walter, *The Money Market and Monetary Management*, 2nd ed. New York: Harper & Row, Publishers, 1972.

The Flow-of-Funds
System

2 An indispensable tool of the financial-market analyst is the flow-of-funds framework. This framework enables him to analyze the movement of savings through the economy in a highly structured, consistent, and comprehensive manner. He is able not only to evaluate the complex interdependence of financial claims throughout the economy but also to identify various pressure points in the system. The insight gained from studying these pressure points is valuable when it comes to analyzing possible changes in market rates of interest. In addition, the flow-of-funds framework makes possible an analysis of the interaction between the financial and the real segments of the economy. Such analysis was not possible before flow-of-funds data were available.

The flow of funds itself is a system of social accounting developed only in recent years. Its foundation was Morris A. Copeland's celebrated work in 1952.[1] The Board of Governors of the Federal Reserve System first began to publish data on the flow of funds in 1955[2] and published a revised and quarterly presentation of data in 1959.[3] Since 1959, quarterly data have been published regularly by the Federal Reserve System. Whereas the national-income accounting system deals with goods and services, flow-of-funds data provide information on the financial segment of the economy, thereby complementing the information provided in the national-income accounts. For example, national-income accounts provide

[1]Morris A. Copeland, *A Study of Moneyflows in the United States* (New York: National Bureau of Economic Research, 1955).

[2]*Flow of Funds in the United States, 1939–1953* (Washington, D.C.: Board of Governors of the Federal Reserve System, 1955).

[3]See "A Quarterly Presentation of Flow of Funds and Savings," *Federal Reserve Bulletin,* 45 (August, 1959), 828–859.

data on the amount of savings, but they give no information on how savings are used. The process by which funds flow from savings to investment is omitted. One must turn to flow-of-funds data to obtain this information. In this chapter, we will discuss the structure of the flow-of-funds accounting system, examine the interrelationship of sources and uses of funds for various sectors in the economy, and, finally, investigate the uses of this information.

The Structure of the System

Flow-of-funds data for an economy are derived for a specific period of time by (1) preparing source-of-funds and use-of-funds statements for each sector in the economy, (2) totaling the sources and uses for all sectors, and (3) presenting the information in a flow-of-funds matrix for the entire economy.[4] The time span studied usually is either a quarter of a year or a full year.

Sectoring

The starting point in any flow-of-funds accounting system is the division of the economy into a workable number of sectors; the idea is to lump together those economic units with similar behavior. Because funds movements through sectors are being analyzed, economic units in a sector must be relatively homogeneous decision-making units if the analysis is to be meaningful. For this reason, sectors are defined along institutional lines according to the similarity of their asset and liability structures. The number of sectors used depends upon the purpose of the analysis, the availability of data, and the cost involved in collecting the data. The maximum possible number of sectors, of course, is the total number of economic units in the economy; in the United States, this would be over 80 million. The minimum number is two, for there can be no flow of funds with only one sector—the economy as a whole.

If there are too few sectors, significant relationships among various groups of economic units are likely to be hidden. On the other hand, if there are too many sectors, the analysis of the interaction among sectors becomes very cumbersome. Here, the problem is that important relationships, although not hidden, may be overlooked. Needless to say, the number of sectors finally employed usually represents a compromise. In

---

[4]See Lawrence S. Ritter, *The Flow of Funds Accounts: A Framework for Financial Analysis* (New York: Institute of Finance, New York University, 1968), for an exposition on the preparation of a flow-of-funds system of social accounting.

the sectoring of the economy, it is absolutely necessary that all economic units be included. Moreover, if foreign transactions are considered, a sector must be included for the rest of the world.

The four main sectors used in the United States flow-of-funds system are households, governments, business enterprises, and financial institutions. For reporting purposes, the Federal Reserve has subdivided some of these sectors, breaking them down into the following categories:

1. Households, personal trusts, and nonprofit organizations.
2. Nonfinancial business (subsectors: farm; nonfarm; noncorporate; and corporate).
3. Governments (subsectors: state and local governments; U.S. government; and federally sponsored credit agencies).
4. Banking system (subsectors: monetary authorities; and commercial banks).
5. Nonbank finance (subsectors: savings and loan associations; mutual savings banks; credit unions; life insurance companies; private pension funds; state and local government retirement funds; other insurance; finance companies; real estate investment trusts; open-end investment companies; and security brokers and dealers).
6. Rest of the world.

The last sector comprises all residents and governments outside the United States. Essentially, it serves to net together all external inflows and outflows so that the flow-of-funds system can be brought into balance. As the Federal Reserve is the principal source of flow-of-funds data, the analyst must settle for this breakdown of the economy.

Source and Use Statements

Once the economy has been divided into sectors, the next step is to prepare a source- and use-of-funds statement for each sector.[5] The starting point here is a balance sheet for each sector at the beginning of the period being studied:

	SECTOR A	
	JANUARY 1, 19 __	
Assets	*Liabilities and Net Worth*	
Money	Financial liabilities	
Other financial assets		
Real assets	Net worth	
Total assets	Total liabilities and net worth	

[5]The development of the immediate presentation draws upon Ritter, *op. cit.*

Most of the assets in the above balance sheet are reported at their market values. It is important to recognize that the presence of financial assets on the balance sheet for one sector means that financial liabilities of the same amount appear on the balance sheets of other sectors in the economy. In other words, financial assets represent claims against someone else and consequently must be shown as a liability on that party's balance sheet. In contrast, real assets appear on only one balance sheet, namely that of the owner.

Also, we must recognize that financial assets and liabilities among economic units in a particular sector are netted out. The financial-asset figure for the sector includes only claims against economic units in other sectors. By the same token, the financial-liability figure includes only claims held by economic units in other sectors against economic units in the sector being studied. As long as at least one economic unit in a sector holds a financial claim against another economic unit in that sector, the financial-asset figure and the financial-liability figure shown on the balance sheet for the sector will be less than the sum of financial assets and the sum of financial liabilities for all economic units in that sector. This statement does not hold for real assets, however. Because a real asset appears on the balance sheet only of the economic unit which owns it, the real-asset figure shown on the balance sheet for a sector is the sum of real assets for all economic units in the sector.

By definition, a balance sheet shows the stocks of assets, liabilities, and net worth of a sector at a moment in time. By taking the change which occurs in stocks between two balance sheets at different points in time, we obtain the net flows for the sector over the time span. These net flows can be expressed in a source- and use-of-funds statement for the sector:

SECTOR A
SOURCES AND USES OF FUNDS, 19—

Uses	Sources
Δ Money	Δ Financial liabilities
Δ Other financial assets	Δ Net worth
Δ Real assets	
Δ Total assets	Δ Total liabilities and net worth

For the period, the net change in total assets for a sector must equal the net change in total liabilities and net worth. The change in net worth represents savings for the period—that is, the difference between current income and current expenditures. Positive savings imply an increase in total assets, a decrease in total liabilities, or both. A savings-deficit sector, with investment in real assets greater than its savings, must reduce its money holdings, sell other financial assets, increase its liabilities, or perform some combination of these actions. Conversely, a savings-surplus sector must show an increase in its holdings of financial assets (including money), a reduction in its financial liabilities, or some combination.

The Preparation of a Matrix
and its Use

Once source- and use-of-funds statements have been prepared for all sectors, these statements can be combined into a matrix for the entire economy. A hypothetical example of such a matrix is shown in Table 2-1. In the table, a closed economy consisting of four sectors—households, business firms, financial institutions, and governments—is assumed. We see that the matrix forms an interlocking system of flows of funds for the period. For each sector, the total uses of funds equal the total sources. Because the system is self-contained, the total uses of funds for all sectors must equal the total sources for these sectors. More important, total savings for all sectors during the period must equal the total increase in real assets for that period. Likewise, the total change in financial assets, including money, must equal the total change in financial liabilities. Again, we see that financial assets and financial liabilities cancel out for the economy as a whole.

The value of the matrix is that it allows analysis of the flow of funds through various sectors of the economy in a manner similar to that of an input-output analysis. For the individual sector, savings need not equal investment in real assets, and the change in financial assets need not equal the change in financial liabilities. For example, business firms represent a savings-deficit sector in Table 2-1. For this sector, the excess of investment in real assets over savings was financed by an increase in financial

Table 2-1. Matrix of Flow of Funds of Entire Economy 19__

	HOUSEHOLDS		BUSINESS FIRMS		FINANCIAL INSTITUTIONS		GOVERNMENTS		ALL SECTORS	
	U	S	U	S	U	S	U	S	U	S
Net worth (savings)		101		77		4		−3		179
Real assets (investment)	82		96		1				179	
Money	2		2			5	1		5	5
Other financial assets	37		18		60		17		132	
Financial liabilities		20		39		52		21		132
	121	121	116	116	61	61	18	18	316	316

liabilities in excess of the increase in financial assets. The existence of this rather large savings-deficit sector means that there must be one or more savings-surplus sectors in the economy for the period being studied. When we analyze the matrix, we see that households, the sector primarily responsible for financing the business sector on a net basis, is the largest savings-surplus sector. In addition, however, financial institutions are a savings-surplus sector, although the excess of savings over investment for this sector is small. This sector acts almost entirely as a financial inter-mediary; it increases its financial assets by issuing financial liabilities to finance the increase in financial assets. Because the sector contains com-mercial banks and the monetary authorities, it provides money to other sectors in the economy. The $5 source of money for this sector represents an increase in demand deposits and currency held by the public and governments as claims against commercial banks and the monetary authorities. Therefore, the total increase in money held by households, business firms, and governments must equal the increase in money-balance claims against the financial-institutions sector.

The last sector in our example, governments, is a savings-deficit sector. This means that, collectively, federal, state, and local governments ran a budget deficit for the period. Although governments made substan-tial expenditures for real assets, their expenditures are not shown because of the lack of reliable estimates. Unfortunately, then, this rather important effect must be omitted from any analysis. A budget deficit for the govern-ments sector must be financed by an increase in financial liabilities in excess of the increase in financial assets. The matrix in Table 2-1 illustrates the fundamental aspects of flow of funds in an economy over a period of time. The example is kept purposely simple, with only four sectors in the economy.

It is important to recognize that certain information is destroyed in the final presentation of the results. As mentioned earlier, the change in financial assets and liabilities for a sector reflects changes that occur only with other sectors. No information is given about financial transactions among economic units in a given sector. Financial claims among these economic units simply cancel out. As a result, we do not know how much net financing occurs within the sector. The need for this information decreases, of course, as the number of sectors used in the flow-of-funds system increases. With aggregation of economic units into a sector, no information is given about the distribution of investment-savings behavior for economic units in that sector. Only the total for all economic units is reported.

Another problem is that the flow of funds for a period represents the net rather than the gross flow between two points in time. For example, the change in financial assets for a sector is simply beginning financial assets less ending financial assets. During the period, there may have been numerous changes in claims against economic units in other sectors. However, no information is given about the magnitude of these changes. For example, financial institutions may purchase $140 billion in mortgages over the period, while principal payments on existing mortgages held and the sale of existing mortgages amounts to $80 billion. The net change in mortgages reported in flow-of-funds data for the financial-institutions sector is $60 billion. Although it may be revealing to know the gross funds flow over time, we are constrained to the information available—namely, the net flow between the two dates. This problem, however, occurs in any source- and use-of-funds analysis.[6] Although all flows are netted, financial assets and liabilities for single transaction categories are not netted out. For example, a household may borrow to purchase a house. In this case, the asset and liability are not netted; both are shown.[7] These shortcomings, together with the problem of appropriate sectoring of the economy discussed previously, should be recognized when interpreting the published data. In certain cases, they may have an important influence upon the conclusions reached.

Federal Reserve Flow-of-Funds Data

The basic source of data on the flow of funds is the Federal Reserve System. Quarterly, the Flow-of-Funds Section of the Division of Research and Statistics compiles extensive data on net funds flows. This publication is available upon request. It contains information that allows one to construct a matrix of the flow-of-funds accounts.

An example of the type of information provided by the Federal Reserve is shown in Table 2-2 on page 26. Here the household sector is illustrated. The gross savings for this sector are shown in row 11. For 1975, they were $258.5 billion and for the first quarter of 1976, $271.5 billion, on an annual basis. These figures should be compared with capital expenditures, line 13, to determine whether or not the sector was a savings-surplus or a savings-deficit sector. We see that it was a substantial savings-surplus sector. The difference between gross savings and capital expenditures should be reflected in a build-up of financial assets, line 18, less the net increase in financial liabilities, line 37.

Thus, for 1975 we see that gross savings of $258.5 billion, less capital expenditures of $170.6 billion, is $87.9 billion. The build-up in financial assets of $152.1 billion, less the net increase in financial liabilities of $48.4 billion, equals $103.7 billion, which is shown in row 17 and labeled net financial investment. Obviously $87.9 billion does not equal $103.7 billion;

[6]See James C. Van Horne, *Financial Management and Policy*, 4th ed., (Englewood Cliffs, N.J.: Prentice-Hall, Inc., 1977), Chapter 26.

[7]"A Quarterly Presentation of Flow of Funds and Savings," *op. cit.*, 832.

there is a discrepancy. This discrepancy of $15.8 billion is reflected in row 48. Although the flow of funds is an interlocking accounting system which should balance in principle, unfortunately discrepancies occur. These are due to inconsistencies in timing, valuation, classification, coverage, and statistical errors in data collection. As a result, we must work with this shortcoming and allow for errors and discrepancies in balancing.

With the information in Table 2-2, together with that for other sectors, we are able to construct a matrix of actual funds flows for a period of time. This construction is illustrated in Table 2-3 for the first quarter of 1976. As reflected here, households were the most important savings-surplus sector, while the U.S. government was a substantial savings-deficit sector. Nonfinancial business also was a savings-deficit sector, with capital expenditures exceeding gross savings. This pattern is typical, although the federal deficit is extremely large by historical standards. For the period under review, the federal government was the dominant user of savings in the United States. In the table, we see that financial institutions were primarily conduits for savings; that is, the direct impact of their activities on the real economy was relatively unimportant. However, substantial savings flows occurred through them, particularly for the nonbank finance sector.

Because of foreign transactions, the rest of the world sector account is necessary. In this sector, all foreign economic units are lumped together. The sector records transactions only between economic units in foreign countries and economic units in the United States. For example, a transaction between a business firm in France and one in West Germany would not be shown. In the last column, the all sectors summary, the items for the various sectors are added together. In this regard, we know that gross savings should equal the investment in real assets, and that the increase in financial assets should equal the increase in financial liabilities. Because of discrepancies, however, this does not occur, although there is almost a balance for the period.

Credit Flows

In addition to the information provided on ultimate sources and uses of funds, the Federal Reserve provides a wealth of information on the specific financial instruments through which savings flow. This information is of particular interest to the capital market analyst. It tells him what sectors finance with what types of instruments, and what sectors hold these instruments. In order to illustrate the usefulness of this information, we examine three sectors in more detail—households; corporate, nonfinancial business; and nonbank finance. The information for households is in Table 2-2, whereas the data for the other two sectors are shown in Tables 2-4 and 2-5 (pages 30–33), respectively.

Table 2-2. Flow of Funds: Household Sector 1970–1976
(billions of dollars)

SEASONALLY ADJUSTED ANNUAL RATES

HOUSEHOLDS, PERSONAL TRUSTS, AND NONPROFIT ORGANIZATIONS

#		1970	1971	1972	1973	1974	1975	1975 I	1975 II	1975 III	1975 IV	1976 I	#
1	PERSONAL INCOME	801.3	859.1	942.5	1054.3	1154.7	1245.9	1203.6	1223.8	1261.7	1294.5	1324.4	1
2	− PERSONAL TAXES + NONTAXES	115.3	116.3	141.2	151.2	171.2	169.2	179.6	142.1	174.6	180.5	184.4	2
3	= DISPOSABLE PERSONAL INCOME	685.9	742.8	801.3	903.1	983.6	1076.7	1024.0	1081.7	1087.1	1114.0	1140.0	3
4	= PERSONAL OUTLAYS	635.4	685.5	751.9	830.4	909.5	987.8	950.4	974.2	1001.3	1025.4	1053.6	4
5	= PERSONAL SAVING, NIA BASIS	50.6	57.3	49.4	72.7	74.0	88.9	73.6	107.5	85.9	88.6	86.3	5
6	+ CREDITS FROM GOVT.INSURANCE	8.8	9.2	11.1	11.5	15.1	15.4	11.2	31.5	6.9	11.8	11.0	6
7	+ CAPITAL GAINS DIVIDENDS	.9	.8	1.4	.9	.5	.5	−.3	.5	.7	−.2	−.1	7
8	+ NET DURABLES IN CONSUMPTION	7.9	13.9	21.5	24.4	11.2	3.5	−.6	.5	5.4	8.9	14.3	8
9	= NET SAVING	68.2	81.2	83.4	109.5	100.8	108.0	84.0	140.1	98.9	109.0	111.6	9
10	+ CAPITAL CONSUMPTION	92.2	99.4	107.2	118.8	133.8	150.5	144.4	149.0	152.7	155.7	159.4	10
11	= GROSS SAVING	160.3	180.7	190.6	228.3	234.6	258.5	228.4	289.1	251.6	264.7	271.5	11
12	GROSS INVESTMENT	168.0	185.2	206.4	239.8	249.5	274.3	247.4	300.6	281.0	281.0	287.1	12
13	CAPITAL EXPEND.—NET OF SALES	113.6	134.0	157.3	173.7	165.7	170.6	159.1	163.3	174.5	185.5	199.2	13
14	RESIDENTIAL CONSTRUCTION	23.4	31.3	40.0	44.5	37.7	36.8	34.2	33.4	37.0	42.3	46.9	14
15	CONSUMER DURABLE GOODS	84.9	97.1	111.2	122.9	121.9	128.1	118.9	123.8	131.0	137.6	146.5	15
16	NONPROFIT PLANT + EQUIP.	5.3	5.6	6.0	6.3	6.3	5.7	5.9	5.8	5.7	5.6	5.8	16
17	NET FINANCIAL INVESTMENT	54.4	51.2	49.1	66.1	83.6	103.7	88.3	137.3	93.6	95.5	87.0	17
18	NET ACQ. OF FINANCIAL ASSETS	76.9	94.3	118.1	135.4	126.5	152.1	125.6	180.9	136.3	165.6	154.1	18
19	DEP.+ CR.MKT. INSTR.(1)	54.4	72.3	93.7	110.5	91.3	115.7	91.1	129.8	105.8	136.3	130.9	19
20	DEMAND DEP.+ CURRENCY	11.2	11.0	11.8	13.1	8.5	8.1	−18.7	44.1	8.8	−1.7	.7	20
21	TIME + SAVINGS ACCOUNTS	44.4	70.3	75.4	67.7	59.6	91.1	103.4	87.9	61.9	111.1	128.2	21
22	AT COMMERCIAL BANKS	27.5	29.8	29.5	39.5	37.9	31.7	36.9	16.6	10.5	62.8	45.0	22
23	AT SAVINGS INST.	16.9	40.4	45.9	28.2	21.8	59.4	66.5	71.3	51.5	48.3	83.2	23
24	CREDIT MKT. INSTRUMENTS	−1.1	−9.0	6.5	29.8	23.1	16.6	6.4	−2.2	35.1	26.9	2.1	24
25	U.S. GOVT. SECURITIES	−9.7	−14.4	.6	20.4	14.5	1.4	−23.7	−14.9	20.0	24.5	−8.2	25
26	S. + O. OBLIGATIONS	−.8	−.2	1.0	4.3	10.0	7.0	11.8	9.2	7.6	−.4	3.7	26
27	CORPORATE + FGN. BONDS	10.7	−9.3	5.2	1.1	−1.7	9.0	14.6	8.5	10.6	−2.5	4.7	27
28	COMMERCIAL PAPER	−1.5	−.2	1.5	3.5	−.5	−2.5	3.1	−6.8	−4.1	−2.2	−1.4	28
29	MORTGAGES	−.1	−.1	−1.8	.5	.8	1.5	−.7	−1.1	1.1	2.4	3.2	29
30	INVESTMENT COMPANY SHARES	−2.8	1.3	−.5	−1.6	1.0	1.6	6.8	−1.4	2.2	−1.2	−3.4	30
31	OTHER CORPORATE EQUITIES	−4.4	−6.5	−4.7	−6.5	−2.0	−2.8	−8.3	−.2	2.1	−4.7	−8.4	31
32	LIFE INSURANCE RESERVES	5.2	6.2	6.6	7.3	7.3	7.3	7.2	7.2	7.3	7.6	7.5	32
33	PENSION FUND RESERVES	19.1	21.6	23.8	24.4	31.7	34.0	28.7	48.9	25.8	32.7	31.1	33
34	NET INV. IN NONCORP. BUS.	−1.9	−3.3	−3.5	.1	−4.6	−6.1	−3.7	−5.6	−7.9	−7.5	−8.1	34
35	SECURITY CREDIT	−.9	.5	.7	−.2	−.3	.1	1.6	*	−1.4	.2	2.3	35
36	MISCELLANEOUS ASSETS	2.6	2.3	2.7	1.5	2.2	2.2	2.2	2.2	2.2	2.3	2.3	36
37	NET INCREASE IN LIABILITIES	22.5	43.1	68.9	69.3	42.9	48.4	37.3	43.6	42.7	70.1	66.2	37
38	CREDIT MARKET INSTRUMENTS	17.6	39.8	63.1	72.8	40.0	45.2	34.9	37.5	43.4	64.8	58.3	38
39	HOME MORTGAGES	12.5	24.2	38.4	44.2	32.6	34.6	29.1	33.7	33.0	42.6	38.1	39
40	OTHER MORTGAGES	5.0	5.1	4.4	1.4	1.3	1.3	.9	1.3	1.3	1.3	5.3	40
41	INSTALMENT CONS. CREDIT	1.1	9.2	16.0	20.1	8.7	9.1	−2.7	−1.6	9.1	10.1	15.9	41
42	OTHER CONSUMER CREDIT	1.1	2.0	2.8	1.8	1.3	1.6	1.2	1.5	1.1	1.2	1.2	42
43	BANK LOANS N.E.C.	−.9	1.4	2.8	1.8	−2.5	2.0	3.9	1.5	−4.1	2.6	−.2	43
44	OTHER LOANS	2.6	2.3	1.3	2.5	2.9	1.9	2.6	1.9	1.9	1.4	1.9	44

SEASONALLY ADJUSTED ANNUAL RATES

#		C1	C2	C3	C4	C5	C6	C7	C8	C9	C10	C11
45	SECURITY CREDIT	7.0	4.3	-1.7	5.1	1.4	2.2	-2.1	-4.6	4.7	2.6	-1.8
46	TRADE DEBT	.5	.5	.5	.6	.6	.6	.6	.4	.5	.3	.5
47	MISCELLANEOUS	.4	.4	.4	.4	.4	.4	.4	.4		.3	.4
48	DISCREPANCY	-15.6	-16.3	-16.5	-11.5	-19.0	-15.8	-14.9	-11.5	-15.8	-4.5	-7.6

(1) EXCLUDES CORPORATE EQUITIES.

MEMORANDA:

NET PHYSICAL INVESTMENT:

(A) RESIDENTIAL CONSTRUCTION

#		C1	C2	C3	C4	C5	C6	C7	C8	C9	C10	C11
49	EXPENDITURES	46.9	42.3	37.0	33.7	34.2	36.8	37.7	44.5	40.0	31.3	23.4
50	MOBILE HOMES	3.0	2.5	2.5	2.2	2.0	2.3	3.2	4.4	4.0	3.3	2.5
51	OTHER	43.9	39.8	34.5	31.4	32.2	34.5	34.5	40.1	36.0	28.1	20.9
52	- CAPITAL CONSUMPTION	23.5	22.9	22.3	21.7	21.1	22.0	19.5	17.1	14.7	13.7	12.8
53	- HOME MORTGAGES	38.1	42.6	33.0	33.7	29.1	34.6	32.6	44.2	38.4	24.2	12.5
54	= EXCESS NET INVESTMENT	-14.7	-23.3	-18.3	-21.7	-15.9	-19.8	-14.4	-16.8	-13.1	-6.5	-1.9

(B) CONSUMER DURABLES

#		C1	C2	C3	C4	C5	C6	C7	C8	C9	C10	C11
55	EXPENDITURES	146.5	137.6	131.8	123.8	118.9	128.1	121.9	122.9	111.2	97.1	84.9
56	- CAPITAL CONSUMPTION	132.2	128.7	126.4	123.4	119.6	124.5	110.8	98.6	89.7	83.2	77.0
57	= NET INVESTMENT	14.3	8.9	5.4	.5	-.6	3.5	11.2	24.4	21.5	13.9	7.9
58	- CONSUMER CREDIT	17.1	12.7	11.3	-1.0	-2.0	5.3	9.6	22.9	19.2	11.2	6.0
59	= EXCESS NET INVESTMENT	-2.8	-3.9	-5.9	1.4	1.4	-1.8	1.5	1.5	2.3	2.7	1.9

(C) NONPROFIT PLANT + EQUIP.

#		C1	C2	C3	C4	C5	C6	C7	C8	C9	C10	C11
60	EXPENDITURES	5.8	5.6	5.7	5.8	5.9	5.7	6.3	6.3	6.0	5.6	5.3
61	- CAPITAL CONSUMPTION	4.2	4.1	4.0	3.9	3.8	3.9	3.5	3.1	2.8	2.6	2.3
62	- NONPROFIT MORTGAGES	1.3	1.3	1.3	1.3	1.4	1.3	1.4	1.4	1.4	1.2	1.4
63	= EXCESS NET INVESTMENT	.3	.2	.4	.5	.8	.5	1.4	1.7	1.8	1.8	1.6

PER CENT RATIOS:

#		C1	C2	C3	C4	C5	C6	C7	C8	C9	C10	C11
64	EFFECTIVE TAX RATE	13.9	13.9	13.8	11.6	14.9	13.6	14.8	14.3	15.0	13.5	14.4
65	SAVING RATE, NIA BASIS	7.6	8.0	7.9	9.9	7.2	8.3	7.5	8.0	6.2	7.7	7.4

PER CENT OF DISPOSABLE INCOME ADJ. (2):

#		C1	C2	C3	C4	C5	C6	C7	C8	C9	C10	C11
66	GROSS SAVING	23.6	23.5	23.0	26.0	22.1	23.7	23.5	24.9	23.4	24.0	23.1
67	CAPITAL EXPENDITURES	17.3	16.5	15.9	14.7	15.4	15.6	16.6	19.0	19.3	17.8	16.3
68	ACQUISITION OF FINAN. ASSETS	13.4	14.7	12.4	16.2	12.1	13.9	12.7	14.8	14.5	12.5	11.1
69	NET INCREASE IN LIABILITIES	5.8	6.2	3.9	2.9	3.6	4.4	4.4	7.6	8.5	5.7	3.2
70	CREDIT MARKET BORROWING	5.1	5.8	4.0	3.4	3.4	4.1	4.4	8.0	7.8	5.3	3.4
71	DISPOSABLE INCOME ADJ. (2)	1150.9	1125.6	1094.8	1113.8	1035.0	1092.3	999.2	915.6	813.8	752.8	695.6

(2) DISPOSABLE INCOME ADJ.
(NIA DISPOSABLE INCOME + GOVT. INSURANCE CREDITS + CAPITAL GAINS DIVID.)

1/76 BASED ON INCOMPLETE AND PRELIMINARY INFORMATION.

Source: Flow of Funds Accounts, 1st Quarter, 1976 (Washington, D.C.: Federal Reserve System, Division of Research and Statistics).

Table 2-3. *Matrix of Flow of Funds, First Quarter, 1976, Seasonally Adjusted Annual Rate*
(billions of dollars)

ASSETS AND LIABILITIES	HOUSE-HOLDS U	HOUSE-HOLDS S	NON-FINANCIAL BUSINESS U	NON-FINANCIAL BUSINESS S	STATE AND LOCAL GOVERNMENT U	STATE AND LOCAL GOVERNMENT S	U.S. GOVERNMENT AND FEDERALLY SPONSORED AGENCIES U	U.S. GOVERNMENT AND FEDERALLY SPONSORED AGENCIES S	MONETARY AUTHORITIES U	MONETARY AUTHORITIES S	COMMERCIAL BANKS U	COMMERCIAL BANKS S	NON-BANK FINANCE U	NON-BANK FINANCE S	REST OF WORLD U	REST OF WORLD S	ALL SECTORS U	ALL SECTORS S
1. Gross savings		271.5		156.5		3.3		−70.0		0.1		4.6		6.3		−1.2		371.1
2. Capital expenditures	199.2		168.7						0.1		4.7		3.4				376.0	
3. Net financial investments (5–6)	87.9			20.0		2.1		69.2			3.9		2.7			2.0	1.3	
4. Gross investment (2 and 3)		287.1	148.7		−2.1		−69.2		0.1		8.6		6.1		−2.0		377.3	
5. Financial assets increase	154.1		55.6		11.1		38.9		7.6		25.8		143.6		13.2		449.9	
6. Financial liabilities increase		66.2		75.6		13.2		108.1		7.5		21.9		140.9		15.2		448.6
7. Sector discrepancy (1–4)	15.6		7.8		5.4			0.8				4.0	0.2		0.8			6.2

Source: *Flow of Funds, 1st Quarter, 1976* (Washington, D.C.: Board of Governors of the Federal Reserve System, May 10, 1976).

For households, we find that mortgages and consumer credit—in that order—represent the largest single increase in financial liabilities. Turning to Table 2-5, we can see that the nonbank finance sector was a large acquirer of home mortgages. This was largely accounted for by savings and loan associations, a subsector in this category. The nonbank finance sector also was the most important provider of consumer credit. Here credit unions and finance companies were the most important subsectors.

The principal means of financing corporations (Table 2-4) was through bonds, followed by mortgages as the secondary means. Although bank loans usually are an important source of funds for corporations, they actually were reduced during the first quarter of 1976. New equity issues also were a significant source of funds for the period. Returning to Table 2-5, we see that the nonbank finance sector was an important investor in corporate bonds as well as in mortgages. Finally, nonbank finance was the principal sector involved with investing in corporate equities. Whereas the household sector liquidated corporate equities on a net basis for the period under review, the nonbank finance sector absorbed an amount *in excess of the net amount issued by corporations*. The principal subsectors involved were life insurance companies, private pension funds, and state and local government retirement funds. The pattern of net liquidation by the household sector and net accumulation by the nonbank finance sector has existed for a number of years. Increasingly, through these intermediaries, individuals are becoming *indirect* rather then *direct owners* of common stocks.

The analysis of the interlocking nature of financial claims can be extended to all of the sectors and subsectors included in the information provided by the Federal Reserve. We have illustrated such an analysis for only three sectors. A more penetrating analysis would involve the tracing of each financial liability to find out what sectors had acquired it as a financial asset. While flow-of-funds data will not permit analysis of the behavior of individual economic units or small groups of economic units, it does enable one to evaluate economic units which are reasonably homogeneous in their behavior, as well as to trace the interaction of the financial system and the real system of the economy in a systematic and consistent manner. It tells the financial-market analyst how various sectors financed the excess of their investment in real assets over savings and how these sectors changed their holdings of financial assets. The flow-of-funds framework provides a structured, interlocking means by which to analyze what has happened in the capital markets. The interrelation of sources and uses among sectors enables the analyst to trace the movement of funds through various sectors of the economy for the period of time under review.

Given the breakdown of financial assets and liabilities provided by the Federal Reserve, a fairly detailed analysis of specific types of financial

Table 2-4. *Flow of Funds: Nonfinancial Corporate Sector, 1970–1976 (billions of dollars)*

SEASONALLY ADJUSTED ANNUAL RATES

	1970	1971	1972	1973	1974	1975	SEASONALLY ADJUSTED ANNUAL RATES, 1975–76 I	II	III	IV	I		
							NONFINANCIAL CORPORATE BUSINESS						
1	55.1	63.2	75.6	92.1	103.2	94.0	72.7	86.4	108.1	108.9	114.2	PROFITS BEFORE TAX	1
2	27.2	29.8	33.4	38.9	42.5	35.7	27.0	31.9	41.5	42.3	43.4	– PROFITS TAX ACCRUALS	2
3	19.8	20.0	21.6	24.3	30.4	30.7	30.0	30.6	31.2	30.7	28.8	– NET DIVIDENDS PAID	3
4	8.1	13.4	20.6	28.9	30.3	27.7	15.7	23.9	35.3	35.9	42.0	= UNDISTRIBUTED PROFITS	4
5	1.6	1.9	1.9	3.7	10.9	4.0	3.8	3.8	4.2	4.1	1.9	+ FOREIGN BRANCH PROFITS	5
6	-5.1	-5.2	-6.8	-18.4	-38.7	-10.8	-13.7	-6.6	-9.9	-13.1	-11.0	+ INV. VALUATION ADJUSTMENT	6
7	1.5	.3	2.6	1.6	-2.4	-5.6	-4.5	-5.0	-6.6	-6.6	-7.6	+ CAP. CONSUMPTION ADJUSTMENT	7
8	52.7	57.7	62.0	68.1	77.6	88.6	84.6	86.9	90.6	92.5	94.8	+ CAPITAL CONSUMPTION ALLOW.	8
9	58.7	68.0	80.2	83.8	77.7	103.8	85.9	103.0	113.7	112.8	120.0	= GROSS INTERNAL FUNDS	9
10	50.7	58.5	65.5	72.5	66.0	95.1	72.1	94.8	106.0	107.6	112.3	GROSS INVESTMENT	10
11	82.1	87.9	104.0	123.2	124.0	96.7	90.7	81.2	106.0	108.9	129.0	CAPITAL EXPENDITURES	11
12	77.0	82.7	93.3	107.7	113.4	111.3	110.6	107.8	110.9	115.8	119.7	FIXED INVESTMENT	12
13	73.2	77.0	86.9	101.7	109.2	107.8	108.4	104.7	106.6	111.6	116.0	PLANT + EQUIPMENT	13
14	.2	1.2	.8	-.5	-.6	.9	-1.0	.7	2.1	1.8	1.2	HOME CONSTRUCTION	14
15	3.6	4.5	5.6	6.5	4.7	2.6	3.3	2.4	2.2	2.4	2.4	MULTI-FAMILY RESIDENTIAL	15
16	5.0	5.2	10.7	15.5	10.6	-14.6	-20.0	-26.6	-5.0	-6.9	9.3	CHANGE IN INVENTORIES	16
17	-31.3	-29.4	-38.5	-50.7	-58.0	-1.6	-18.6	13.7	*	-1.3	-16.7	NET FINANCIAL INVESTMENT	17
18	12.9	23.1	30.8	40.9	43.8	38.5	-17.9	44.2	49.7	77.9	52.3	NET ACQ. OF FINANCIAL ASSETS	18
19	-.4	10.6	4.0	6.9	13.2	19.1	7.9	25.8	11.8	30.6	12.1	LIQUID ASSETS	19
20	.9	.5	-.1	-.3	.3	2.0	2.8	1.9	1.5	1.7	2.9	DEMAND DEP. + CURRENCY	20
21	1.7	3.6	3.1	1.4	6.6	-.3	-4.7	.5	5.6	-2.4	-16.8	TIME DEPOSITS	21
22	.5	2.2	-2.4	-1.8	3.5	14.7	-2.9	26.9	4.9	29.8	19.9	U.S. GOVT. SECURITIES	22
23	-.6	1.0	1.0	-.1	.6	-.2	1.6	-.2	-1.2	-.9	-2.3	S. + L. OBLIGATIONS	23
24	.5	2.4	.8	5.2	4.9	.6	6.2	-3.3	-5.0	4.4	6.0	COMMERCIAL PAPER	24
25	-3.4	.8	1.6	2.6	-2.8	2.2	5.0	-.1	6.0	-1.9	2.5	SECURITY R.P.'S	25
26	.7	.6	1.6	2.0	1.2	1.1	.2	.7	.7	3.0	.2	CONSUMER CREDIT	26
27	8.4	5.7	20.0	24.1	20.8	10.4	-30.3	8.5	30.9	32.3	34.4	TRADE CREDIT	27
28	4.2	6.2	5.2	7.9	8.6	8.0	4.2	9.3	6.5	11.9	5.7	MISCELLANEOUS ASSETS	28
29	3.6	3.8	1.5	3.6	7.2	5.5	2.3	8.5	3.0	8.3	.1	FOREIGN DIR. INVEST. (1)	29
30	-.4	1.4	1.8	2.6	-.2	.8	.3	-.8	1.8	2.0	4.0	FOREIGN CURRENCIES	30
31	.9	1.0	1.9	1.6	1.6	1.6	1.6	1.6	1.6	1.6	1.6	INSURANCE RECEIVABLES	31
32	.1	*	*	*	*	*	–	–	*	*	*	EQUITY IN SPONSORED AGS.	32
33	44.2	52.5	69.3	91.6	101.8	40.1	.6	30.6	49.7	79.2	69.0	NET INCREASE IN LIABILITIES	33
34	39.5	46.8	55.3	67.2	77.1	35.8	30.9	36.4	31.5	44.7	32.3	NET FUNDS RAISED IN MKTS.	34
35	5.7	11.4	10.9	7.4	4.1	9.9	7.7	12.9	6.9	12.2	7.2	NET NEW EQUITY ISSUES	35
36	33.8	35.4	44.4	59.7	73.0	25.9	23.1	23.5	24.7	32.5	25.1	DEBT INSTRUMENTS	36
37	–	.1	.5	1.8	1.6	2.6	1.7	3.2	2.4	3.0	1.2	TAX-EXEMPT BONDS (2)	37
38	19.8	18.8	12.2	9.2	19.7	27.2	40.1	30.5	14.6	23.6	18.5	CORPORATE BONDS (1)	38
39	5.2	11.4	15.6	16.1	10.9	10.1	6.6	9.2	11.1	13.6	12.0	MORTGAGES	39
40	.2	1.0	.6	-.4	-.4	.7	-.8	.6	1.7	1.4	1.0	HOME MORTGAGES	40
41	1.5	2.6	3.0	2.5	2.2	.7	1.0	.5	.7	.6	1.1	MULTI-FAMILY	41
42	3.6	7.9	12.0	14.1	9.1	8.7	6.4	8.1	8.6	11.6	9.9	COMMERCIAL	42
43	5.6	4.4	13.5	30.6	29.9	-13.2	-26.8	-15.7	-5.1	-5.1	-15.2	BANK LOANS N.E.C.	43
44	2.2	-1.7	-.6	-.2	4.1	-2.4	1.7	-5.8	1.0	-6.4	2.8	COMMERCIAL PAPER	44
45	.4	.3	*	-.1	1.3	.2	.9	-.4	-1.2	1.3	1.3	ACCEPTANCES	45
46	.4	1.9	2.8	2.0	4.5	1.3	-1.1	2.1	1.9	2.3	4.6	FINANCE COMPANY LOANS	46
47	.3	.2	.2	.3	1.1	.1	*	.2	.1	*	*	U.S. GOVERNMENT LOANS	47

SEASONALLY ADJUSTED ANNUAL RATES

48	-3.7	2.0	-.1	2.3	4.4	-5.7	-14.2	-11.4	.2	2.4	2.5	PROFIT TAXES PAYABLE	48
49	7.4	3.8	13.7	19.6	18.1	8.1	-17.4	2.9	18.3	28.1	32.2	TRADE DEBT	49
50	1.0	-.1	.4	2.5	2.2	1.9	1.4	2.7	-.4	4.0	2.0	MISCELLANEOUS LIABILITIES	50
51	8.0	9.5	14.7	11.2	11.8	8.7	13.8	8.2	7.7	5.2	7.8	DISCREPANCY	51
52	.9	1.9	6.3	4.5	2.8	2.3	-12.9	5.6	12.6	4.2	2.1	MEMO: NET TRADE CREDIT	52
53	30.3	27.9	33.8	37.6	41.5	41.9	42.1	43.9	42.0	39.5	41.8	PROFITS TAX PAYMENTS	53
												DEBT SUBTOTALS: (3)	
54	27.0	31.1	33.2	39.8	44.6	33.9	38.6	36.1	24.3	36.8	24.6	LONG-TERM DEBT	54
55	6.7	4.2	11.2	20.0	28.4	-8.0	-15.5	-12.6	.4	-4.3	.6	SHORT-TERM DEBT	55
56	10.5	10.0	24.8	41.9	50.9	-5.7	-47.1	-21.1	18.9	26.2	35.3	TOTAL S-T LIABILITIES	56
												PER CENT RATIOS:	
57	49.4	47.2	44.1	42.2	41.2	37.9	37.1	36.9	38.4	38.9	38.0	EFFECTIVE TAX RATE	57
58	139.7	129.2	129.6	147.2	159.5	93.1	105.6	78.8	93.2	96.6	107.4	CAPITAL OUTLAYS/INTERNAL FUNDS	58
59	41.2	40.2	42.6	48.5	58.9	26.8	25.5	28.9	23.3	29.8	19.5	CR. MKT. BORROWING/CAP. EXP.	59
												CASH FLOW AND CAPITAL EXPENDITURES ON BOOK BASIS	
60	52.7	57.7	62.0	68.1	77.6	88.6	84.6	86.9	90.6	92.5	94.8	CAP. CONS. ALLOWANCE, N I A	60
61	1.5	.3	2.6	1.6	-2.4	-5.6	-4.5	-5.0	-6.6	-6.6	-7.6	PLUS: CAP. CONS. ADJUSTMENT	61
62	54.2	58.0	64.6	69.7	75.2	83.0	80.1	81.9	84.0	85.9	87.2	EQUALS: BOOK DEPRECIATION	62
63	5.0	5.2	10.7	15.5	10.6	-14.6	-20.0	-26.6	-5.0	-6.9	9.3	INVENTORY CHANGE, N I A	63
64	-5.1	-5.2	-6.8	-18.4	-38.7	-10.8	-13.7	-6.6	-9.9	-13.1	-11.0	LESS: INV. VAL. ADJUSTMENT	64
65	10.1	10.4	17.5	34.0	49.4	-3.8	-6.2	-20.1	4.9	6.2	20.3	EQUALS: INVENTORY CHG., BOOK	65
66	8.1	13.4	20.6	28.9	30.3	27.7	15.7	23.9	35.3	35.9	42.0	UNDISTRIBUTED PROFITS	66
67	1.6	1.9	1.9	3.7	10.9	4.0	3.8	3.8	4.2	4.1	1.9	+ FOREIGN BRANCH PROFITS	67
68	54.2	58.0	64.6	69.7	75.2	83.0	80.1	81.9	84.0	85.9	87.2	+ BOOK DEPRECIATION	68
69	63.8	73.3	87.0	102.2	116.5	114.7	99.6	109.6	123.6	125.9	131.0	= GROSS INTERNAL FUNDS,BOOK	69
70	55.8	63.7	72.3	91.0	104.7	105.9	85.8	101.4	115.9	120.7	123.3	GROSS INVESTMENT, BOOK	70
71	87.1	93.1	110.8	141.7	162.7	107.5	104.4	87.8	115.9	122.0	140.0	CAPITAL EXPENDITURES	71
72	77.0	82.7	93.3	107.7	113.4	111.3	110.6	107.8	110.9	115.8	119.7	FIXED INVESTMENT	72
73	10.1	10.4	17.5	34.0	49.4	-3.8	-6.2	-20.1	4.9	6.2	20.3	INVENTORY CHG., BOOK	73
												EXCESS OF CAPITAL EXPENDITURES	
74	23.3	19.9	23.7	39.5	46.3	-7.2	4.8	-21.8	-7.7	-3.9	8.9	OVER GROSS INTERNAL FUNDS	74

(1) FOREIGN INVESTMENT EXCLUDES AMOUNTS FINANCED BY BOND ISSUES ABROAD, AND BOND ISSUES OUTSIDE THE U.S. ARE EXCLUDED FROM FINANCIAL SOURCES OF FUNDS ABOVE.

(2) INDUSTRIAL POLLUTION CONTROL REVENUE BONDS. THESE ARE FORMALLY ISSUED BY STATE AND LOCAL GOVERNMENT AUTHORITIES, BUT THEY FINANCE PRIVATE INVESTMENT AND ARE SECURED IN INTEREST AND PRINCIPAL BY THE INDUSTRIAL USER OF THE FUNDS.

(3) MATURITY SPLIT ON DEBT IS APPROXIMATE: L-T IS BONDS, M-F + COMMERCIAL MORTGAGES, AND 40% OF BANK LOANS. S-T DEBT IS OTHER CREDIT MARKET BORROWING. TOTAL S-T LIABILITIES IS S-T BORROWING + TAX LIABILITIES + TRADE DEBT.

I/76 BASED ON INCOMPLETE AND PRELIMINARY INFORMATION.

Source: *Flow of Funds Accounts, 1st Quarter, 1976* (Washington, D.C.: Federal Reserve System Division of Research and Statistics).

Table 2-5. Flow of Funds: Nonbank Finance Sector, 1970–1976
(billions of dollars)

SEASONALLY ADJUSTED ANNUAL RATES

PRIVATE NONBANK FINANCIAL INSTITUTIONS – TOTAL

#		1970	1971	1972	1973	1974	1975	1975 I	1975 II	1975 III	1975 IV	1975-76 I
1	CURRENT SURPLUS	2.1	4.8	5.0	5.3	4.7	5.2	5.3	4.7	4.8	6.0	6.3
2	PHYSICAL INVESTMENT	1.2	1.8	2.1	2.0	2.6	4.8	4.8	6.0	5.1	3.4	3.4
3	NET ACQ. OF FINANCIAL ASSETS	55.2	84.9	107.5	87.6	78.0	109.4	111.3	116.9	91.7	117.0	143.6
4	DEMAND DEPOSITS + CURRENCY	1.0	1.1	1.6	2.0	2.7	-.3	-1.1	-2.3	-.2	2.5	-2.2
5	TIME DEPOSITS (MSB)	.2	.2	.2	.1	-.2	.1	.9	-.1	-.1	-.2	2.5
6	S+L SHARES (CREDIT UNION)	.1	.1	-.2	*	.4	.4	.9	1.1	-.8	.4	.3
7	CORPORATE EQUITIES	11.3	19.3	15.9	13.3	6.1	8.4	11.3	9.4	12.1	12.8	12.1
8	CREDIT MARKET INSTRUMENTS	39.8	60.1	82.8	72.2	66.9	95.8	95.5	101.8	87.4	97.4	121.7
9	U.S. GOVERNMENT SECURITIES	3.8	2.6	7.1	3.6	5.7	25.5	30.4	32.5	24.7	14.2	35.1
10	S.L. OBLIGATIONS	1.8	4.4	5.1	3.6	1.1	5.5	2.5	4.2	6.7	8.6	2.6
11	CORPORATE + FOREIGN BONDS	11.6	14.0	13.2	10.8	22.6	25.4	32.6	29.1	26.7	29.4	25.5
12	HOME MORTGAGES	7.6	17.8	30.7	26.5	13.5	20.7	13.5	22.0	22.8	24.6	23.7
13	OTHER MORTGAGES	10.1	14.6	16.8	15.4	10.8	10.5	9.4	10.5	10.1	12.2	11.7
14	CONSUMER CREDIT	1.8	3.3	6.4	9.0	4.8	3.6	1.6	1.0	5.6	5.4	10.6
15	OTHER LOANS	3.1	3.5	3.5	5.9	8.4	4.6	5.2	2.5	7.6	3.2	7.9
16	SECURITY CREDIT	-1.3	2.5	3.9	-4.6	-1.8	2.5	2.2	5.2	1.7	.9	6.5
17	TRADE CREDIT	.5	.3	1.2	.7	.6	.3	.3	.3	.3	.2	.5
18	MISCELLANEOUS ASSETS	3.6	1.4	1.7	3.9	3.1	2.3	2.0	1.3	2.8	2.9	4.9
19	NET INCREASE IN LIABILITIES	55.1	82.4	103.7	82.3	75.3	107.7	110.6	116.3	91.5	112.6	140.9
20	TIME + SAVINGS ACCOUNTS	17.0	40.6	46.1	28.1	22.1	59.8	67.4	72.4	50.7	46.7	83.6
21	INSURANCE + PENSION RESERVES	21.8	24.8	27.1	29.5	36.1	37.6	34.5	41.3	34.8	39.8	38.5
22	CORPORATE EQUITY ISSUES (1)	4.6	2.8	1.4	-.4	-.7	.8	4.8	-2.6	1.8	-.8	-3.0
23	CREDIT MARKET INSTRUMENTS	4.7	6.2	15.9	21.0	11.8	-3.0	-13.5	-6.3	5.0	2.6	2.3
24	CORPORATE BONDS	3.0	4.2	5.8	2.3	1.3	3.0	1.8	4.0	3.4	2.7	2.7
25	MORTGAGE LOANS IN PROCESS	.6	2.0	1.2	-1.5	-1.5	1.9	.9	2.3	3.2	1.3	1.6
26	OTHER MORTGAGES	.1	.1	.5	.3	.1	.4	.9	2.3	-.3	-.3	
27	BANK LOANS N.E.C.	-.6	1.4	5.9	8.4	4.6	-5.0	-10.4	-7.5	-2.1	-.3	-1.2
28	OTHER LOANS N.E.C.	1.5	-1.5	2.5	11.5	7.2	-3.4	-10.3	-5.6	-.1	-2.2	2.9
29	OPEN-MARKET PAPER	.2	1.2	2.5	4.3	-.5	-.6	-10.5	-5.7	.3	1.6	2.9
30	FHLB LOANS	1.3	-2.7	*	7.2	6.7	-4.0	-10.5	-5.7	-.2	.6	-4.0
31	SECURITY CREDIT	1.0	1.1	4.1	-3.4	-2.5	2.2	9.2	4.1	-12.7	8.0	7.8
32	PROFIT TAXES PAYABLE	.2	-.1	.2	.1	*	.2	.2	-.1	-.2	.2	.6
33	MISCELLANEOUS LIABILITIES	5.8	7.0	8.8	7.4	7.1	10.2	8.0	7.3	11.6	14.1	11.1
34	DISCREPANCY	.8	.4	-.9	-2.0	-.6	-1.3	-.3	-1.9	-.5	-1.8	-.2

SAVINGS AND LOAN ASSOCIATIONS

#		1970	1971	1972	1973	1974	1975	1975 I	1975 II	1975 III	1975 IV	1975-76 I
1	CURRENT SURPLUS	1.2	1.5	1.8	2.2	1.9	1.8	1.8	1.8	1.8	1.9	2.0
2	NET ACQ. OF FINANCIAL ASSETS	14.1	29.8	37.1	29.2	23.7	42.9	37.0	48.0	45.5	40.9	60.4
3	DEMAND DEPOSITS + CURRENCY	.3	.5	.6	.6	.6	.6	-.7	.7	1.4	.9	1.9
4	CREDIT MARKET INSTRUMENTS	11.6	29.2	30.4	27.1	21.0	40.5	34.4	46.3	43.9	37.0	58.7
5	U.S. GOVERNMENT SECURITIES	2.9	5.2	4.3	2.*	3.3	11.1	17.0	15.3	10.5	15.3	21.7
6	HOME MORTGAGES	7.0	17.3	24.8	22.0	13.8	23.1	13.7	25.2	25.5	28.2	28.0
7	OTHER MORTGAGES	3.0	6.6	7.2	4.9	6.2	6.2	6.2	5.8	7.8	7.5	8.9
8	CONSUMER CREDIT	.3	.1	.2	.2	.2	*	-.2	*	.1	.1	.1
9	MISCELLANEOUS ASSETS	2.2	.1	.1	1.5	2.1	1.7	3.4	1.0	.7	1.9	2.6

SAVINGS AND LOAN ASSOCIATIONS

#												
10	NET INCREASE IN LIABILITIES	58.8	35.1	44.5	46.4	36.2	41.5	22.3	27.4	35.5	29.0	13.3
11	SAVINGS SHARES	59.4	36.8	38.0	51.2	46.4	43.1	15.9	20.5	32.6	27.8	10.9
12	CREDIT MARKET INSTRUMENTS	-2.2	2.2	5.3	-4.7	-11.2	-2.1	6.3	6.0	2.0	2.0	1.8
13	MORTGAGE LOANS IN PROCESS	1.6	1.3	3.2	-2.3	-2.3	1.9	-1.5	-1.5	1.2	-.1	.6
14	BANK LOANS N.E.C.	-.2	.6	2.4	-2.3	-1.7	-.1	1.1	.3	.7	-.7	-.1
15	FHLB ADVANCES	-4.0	*	-.2	-5.7	-10.5	-4.0	6.7	7.2	*	-2.7	1.3
16	PROFIT TAXES PAYABLE	.6	-.1	.1	-.2	.1	-.1	*	*	*	*	*
17	MISCELLANEOUS LIABILITIES	1.4	*	1.1	1.1	.9	.4	.1	.9	.9	1.2	.6
18	DISCREPANCY	.4	*	.4	.8	1.0	.5	.5	.3	.1	.6	.5

MUTUAL SAVINGS BANKS

#												
1	CURRENT SURPLUS	.5	.4	.4	.4	.4	.4	.5	.6	.1	.4	.3
2	NET ACQ. OF FINANCIAL ASSETS	17.5	9.1	9.3	14.1	13.6	11.5	3.8	6.0	11.0	10.4	4.7
3	DEMAND DEPOSITS + CURRENCY	-1.0	1.4	-.7	-.2	*	.1	*	-.2	.1	.1	.1
4	TIME DEPOSITS	-	-.2	-	-.2	.2	.1	.2	.1	.2	.2	.2
5	CORPORATE EQUITIES	*	*	*	.3	.2	.2	.4	.4	.6	.5	.3
6	CREDIT MARKET INSTRUMENTS	16.2	6.9	8.8	13.3	12.3	10.3	3.1	5.0	9.8	9.6	3.8
7	U.S. GOVERNMENT SECURITIES	4.8	3.5	3.9	5.6	2.1	3.7	*	-.5	1.4	.9	.3
8	STATE + LOCAL OBLIGATIONS	1.3	.2	1.0	.6	.7	*	1.0	*	.2	*	.3
9	CORPORATE BONDS	3.8	2.4	1.4	5.6	4.9	3.5	1.0	-1.1	2.1	3.9	1.2
10	HOME MORTGAGES	1.0	1.7	1.5	1.5	.6	1.3	.7	2.6	3.0	1.3	.9
11	OTHER MORTGAGES	.7	1.1	1.0	1.0	.4	.9	1.5	3.1	2.6	2.7	.9
12	CONSUMER CREDIT	1.8	-.5	.1	.1	1.2	.2	.2	-.2	-.3	.1	.1
13	COMMERCIAL PAPER	.8	-.2	.8	*	-.5	-.1	-.3	-.1	-.2	.2	.2
14	SECURITY RP'S	4.0	-1.6	-.9	-.9	3.0	-.1	-.3	-.7	-.1	.2	.1
15	MISCELLANEOUS ASSETS	.3	.9	1.1	.5	.8	.9	.2	.3	.4	.2	.3
16	SAVINGS DEPOSITS	17.1	6.8	8.9	14.6	14.3	11.2	3.1	4.7	10.2	9.9	4.4
17	MISCELLANEOUS LIABILITIES	.1	1.8	.2	-1.3	-1.2	-.1	.3	.6	.2	.1	.1
18	DISCREPANCY	.2	*	.3	-.4	-.1	-.1	-.1	-.1	-.2	.1	.1

CREDIT UNIONS

#												
1	NET ACQ. OF FINANCIAL ASSETS	7.0	5.1	3.8	6.7	6.6	5.5	3.0	2.9	3.4	2.9	1.7
2	DEMAND DEPOSITS + CURRENCY	*	*	-.8	1.1	-.1	*	*	*	.1	.1	.2
3	SAVINGS + LOAN SHARES	.3	.4	.6	5.6	.9	.4	.4	*	.1	.1	.1
4	CREDIT MARKET INSTRUMENTS	6.6	4.6	4.6	5.6	5.8	5.2	2.7	2.9	3.1	2.6	1.5
5	U.S. GOVERNMENT SECURITIES	1.3	.6	.4	3.1	3.4	1.9	.2	.2	.8	.8	.4
6	HOME MORTGAGES	.1	.1	*	.4	.4	.9	.2	.2	.2	.4	.1
7	CONSUMER CREDIT	5.3	4.0	4.1	2.4	2.4	3.2	2.5	2.7	2.1	1.8	1.0
8	CREDIT UNION SHARES	7.0	5.1	3.8	6.7	6.6	5.5	3.0	2.9	3.4	2.9	1.7

1/76 BASED ON INCOMPLETE AND PRELIMINARY INFORMATION.

.(1) INCLUDES INVESTMENT COMPANY SHARES.

Source: *Flow of Funds Accounts, 1st Quarter, 1976* (Washington, D.C.: Federal Reserve System Division of Research and Statistics).

instruments and markets is possible. For particular instruments, we are able to evaluate which sectors are important in the market and the magnitude of their purchases. When this analysis is extended over time, one is able to evaluate the degree of pressure in the various markets. Pressure arises whenever a traditional source of financing curtails its investment in the financial instrument. The curtailment of investment should be related to the savings and investment in real assets for the sector involved. Thus, a study of the behavior of individual sectors with respect to investment in financial assets and issuance of financial liabilities over time is useful in determining the impact of that sector on the capital markets.

Other Funds-Flow Information

In addition to the Federal Reserve, various private organizations provide useful data on the source and use of funds. Among these organizations are Bankers Trust Company and Salomon Brothers, which publish information on the "final" sources and uses of funds according to the institutions providing the funds, and the instrument in which the funds are used. This information differs from that provided by the Federal Reserve in that a flow-of-funds matrix for the entire economy cannot be constructed. The ultimate sources and uses of funds by sectors are not shown—only the final sources and uses. Although the former is sometimes implied, it is very difficult to evaluate savings-surplus and savings-deficit sectors on the basis of the information provided. The users shown may or may not be the ultimate investors in real assets. By the same token, the suppliers of funds may or may not be ultimate savers. Where financial institutions are the suppliers, for the most part they are not the ultimate savers. Thus, only a portion of the flow-of-funds matrix of the entire economy is revealed.

Although the Federal Reserve provides a great deal of information on "final" sources and uses of funds, additional insight can be obtained from such "outside-of-government" annual publications as *Credit and Capital Markets* of the Bankers Trust Company and the *Supply and Demand for Credit* of Salomon Brothers. Considerable in-depth information about the major sources and uses of funds for the various capital and credit markets is provided. In addition, these annual publications provide written commentary on economic and other factors which affect interest rates and funds flows for the various sectors. As a result, it is possible to make a penetrating analysis of the final sources and uses of funds as they relate to the various financial markets.

So far we have considered only *ex post* data, whether they be flow of funds or source and use statements. Although these data are valuable in appraising past trends and in forming expectations of the future, we often need forecasts of the future involving *ex ante* estimates. To this aspect we now turn.

Forecasts of Future Funds Flows

In addition to flows that have actually occurred, estimates of future funds flows are important in financial-market analysis. These estimates indicate likely strains in the system and the resulting pressure on interest rates. In this way, the analyst is able to get a better feel for desired demand and supply and for the change in interest rates necessary to bring about a balance between the two. He is interested both in the expected absolute change in interest rates for a particular market and in the change relative to changes in interest rates in other markets. Bankers Trust Company, Salomon Brothers, as well as certain others, make forecasts of future funds flows. In the preparation of these forecasts, independent estimates are made of the expected need for funds, classified according to the type of financial instrument, and of the expected funds available for investment by various financial institutions and by individuals.

Once independent estimates of supply and demand have been made, one benefit of the forecast comes in analyzing how supply and demand will come into balance. We know, of course, that on an *ex post* basis supply must equal demand. The first step is simply to match the independently prepared estimates to determine the size and direction of any imbalance. This imbalance indicates pressures that are likely to develop. Knowing these pressures, the analyst is able to estimate in an approximate way the change in market interest rates necessary to bring about a balance in supply and demand. For example, suppose the need for mortgage funds is estimated to be $40 billion in the forthcoming year, but the supply of funds into this market is estimated at only $32 billion. As a result of this imbalance, there would likely be upward pressure on interest rates in order to bring about a balance between supply and demand for mortgages.

By analyzing imbalances across capital markets, the analyst can estimate whether interest rates in one segment of the financial markets are likely to rise or fall relative to interest rates in other segments. In this way, he may be able to forecast relative changes in interest rates. However, one must be careful not to lose sight of the interrelated nature of financial markets. Supply and demand forces in one market are not independent of those in other markets. Therefore, interest-rate changes in the various markets cannot be estimated independently.

In the published forecasts, a balance is always shown between estimated sources of funds and estimated uses. In other words, adjustments are made until a balance is achieved. Consequently, certain valuable information is not available to the reader—namely, the independent estimates of supply and demand by the forecasters and the resulting *ex ante* gap. However, a residual category is shown, and this category gives us some information about any imbalance between supply and demand. To illustrate, an example of a source- and use-of-funds statement, prepared by Salomon Brothers, is shown in Table 2-6. Historical sources and uses and also a forecast for 1977 are shown. In the table, the residual for households is reflected in the next to last line. In a certain sense, this residual can be regarded as a balancing factor in the forecast and can be used in judging strains in particular markets.[8] The larger the residual, the more "gap" there is for individuals to fill; and the higher interest rates would be expected to go in order to bring about a balance between supply and demand. In our example, the large residuals in 1973 and 1974 would suggest that interest rates rose during this period. This was indeed the case during the latter part of 1973 and virtually all of 1974, when interest rates rose to new heights. Similar experiences have been recorded in the past when the portion of total funds supplied by residual investors was relatively large. Because of the correlation between the residual and the level of interest rates, analysts may be able to use, with perhaps some degree of success, the estimate of the residual as a basis for forecasting interest rates.

A forecast of sources and uses of funds differs from a forecast of the flow of funds for the entire economy. Whereas the former takes account of the final sources and uses of funds for various financial instruments, a flow-of-funds forecast takes account of the source and use of funds for each sector of the economy. Because a simultaneous balance must be reached for each sector and across all sectors, a flow-of-funds forecast forces a tighter analysis than does a forecast of sources and uses. The idea of having to force projections into the flow-of-funds framework may cause the analyst to be less conservative in his final estimates. To achieve a balance which satisfies the interlocking structure of the flow of funds, he must sometimes make fairly extreme estimates.[9] These estimates, however, may well be warranted by the conditions projected. A less rigorous framework encourages the tendency to project only moderate changes and not to predict extreme changes and turning points. The flow-of-funds

[8]See William C. Freund and Edward D. Zinbarg, "Application of Flow of Funds to Interest-Rate Forecasting," *Journal of Finance*, 18 (May, 1963), 236–248.

[9]See Stephen Taylor, "Uses of Flow-of-Funds Accounts in the Federal Reserve System," *Journal of Finance*, 18 (May, 1963), 249–258.

Table 2-6. Salomon Brothers' Summary of Supply and Demand for Credit
(billions of dollars)

	See Table	ANNUAL NET INCREASES IN AMOUNTS OUTSTANDING							AMOUNTS OUTSTANDING
		1971	1972	1973	1974	1975	1976e	1977p	12/31/76e
Net Demand									
Privately held mortgages	II	44.3	68.8	68.7	42.8	38.5	61.3	69.5	760.1
Corporate bonds	III	24.7	18.9	13.5	27.5	32.7	27.6	24.1	334.3
Domestically held foreign bonds	III	0.9	1.0	1.0	2.2	6.3	9.3	10.4	34.2
Subtotal long-term private		69.9	88.7	83.2	72.5	77.5	98.2	104.0	1,128.6
Business loans	VIII	7.7	24.8	38.4	34.3	-14.5	-1.1	14.0	236.6
Consumer installment credit	VIII	9.3	15.6	19.7	9.0	6.9	16.0	21.0	178.2
All other bank loans	VIII	7.7	11.0	7.4	3.2	2.8	10.0	12.0	89.4
Open market paper	VII	-0.1	1.6	8.3	16.6	-1.3	5.6	7.0	72.0
Subtotal short-term private		24.6	53.0	73.8	63.1	-6.1	30.5	54.0	576.2
Privately held treasury debt	V	19.0	15.2	-2.0	10.2	75.8	61.8	49.5	406.7
Privately held federal agency debt	VI	2.7	9.0	21.2	17.9	7.7	13.1	18.5	119.5
Subtotal federal		21.7	24.2	19.2	28.1	83.5	74.9	68.0	526.2
State and local tax-exempt bonds	IV	16.4	14.1	13.3	11.9	16.9	17.8	19.0	228.6
State and local tax-exempt notes	IV	5.3	-1.3	0.8	2.6	-1.2	-4.1	-2.0	13.8
Subtotal tax-exempt		21.7	12.8	14.1	14.5	15.7	13.7	17.0	242.4
Total Net Demand for Credit		137.9	178.7	190.3	178.2	170.6	217.3	243.0	2,473.4
Net Supply[a]									
Mutual savings banks	IX	9.0	8.8	5.3	3.1	10.4	11.9	11.9	121.1
Savings and loan associations	IX	30.2	37.1	27.5	21.7	42.0	51.0	53.0	362.7
Credit unions	IX	2.0	2.9	3.5	3.3	5.1	6.9	8.0	38.9

Table 2-6. (Cont.)

	See Table	ANNUAL NET INCREASES IN AMOUNTS OUTSTANDING							AMOUNTS OUTSTANDING
		1971	1972	1973	1974	1975	1976e	1977p	12/31/76e
Life insurance companies	IX	7.2	8.8	10.0	10.3	15.2	18.0	18.6	228.1
Fire and casualty companies	IX	3.7	3.8	3.5	4.6	5.4	4.1	4.5	55.3
Private noninsured pension funds	IX	-1.7	-0.7	2.0	5.8	7.9	7.4	7.6	59.0
State and local retirement funds	IX	3.6	3.1	3.4	8.0	7.0	8.8	9.0	82.3
Personal and common bank trust funds	IX	3.9	2.7	4.1	2.0	3.6	4.0	4.7	52.3
Foundations and endowments	IX	1.7	-0.1	0.6	0.9	1.1	1.2	1.5	18.2
Closed-end corporate bond funds	IX	0.2	1.2	1.1	0.2	0.0	0.0	0.0	2.8
Money market funds	IX	0.0	0.0	0.0	1.0	0.6	0.3	0.4	1.8
Municipal bond funds	IX	0.3	0.4	0.7	1.1	2.1	2.8	4.5	8.9
Open-end stock funds	IX	0.0	0.0	-0.2	-0.4	0.7	0.4	-0.3	8.0
Real estate investment trusts	IX	2.3	4.1	5.6	0.2	-4.6	-4.6	-2.2	6.2
Finance companies	IX	4.2	7.5	8.8	2.4	0.5	8.1	10.1	84.4
Total nonbank institutions	X	66.6	79.6	75.9	64.2	97.0	120.3	131.3	1,130.0
Commercial banks[b]	X	50.9	73.3	77.6	59.8	31.0	44.5	58.0	785.9
Business corporations	XI	2.4	0.9	3.4	8.0	10.6	7.1	8.1	74.2
State and local governments	XI	-3.5	5.5	3.3	1.2	2.5	6.7	7.7	44.1
Foreigners	XI	26.4	9.1	2.1	10.9	4.5	14.2	15.7	100.4
Subtotal		142.8	168.4	162.3	144.1	145.6	192.8	220.8	2,134.6
Residual: Households direct	XII	-4.9	10.3	28.0	34.1	25.0	24.5	22.2	338.8
Total net supply of credit		137.9	178.7	190.3	178.2	170.6	217.3	243.0	2,473.4

Source: *Prospects for the Credit Markets in 1977* (New York: Salomon Brothers, 1976).

[a]Excludes funds for equities, cash, and miscellaneous demands not tabulated above.
[b]Includes loans transferred to nonoperating holding and other bank-related companies.

matrix forces the use of estimates that are consistent and in keeping with the initial assumptions. Therefore, they may tend to be more realistic.

The flow-of-funds framework and the source- and use-of-funds statement, which we have examined, provide a basis for analyzing financial markets. By comparing estimates of supply and demand, the analyst obtains insight into the likely strains in the system. Given these likely strains, he then is able to interpret their effect upon interest rates. Within either of these frameworks, the analysis of interest rates is likely to be far more rigorous, consistent, and comprehensive than it is if estimates are made on a market-by-market basis.

Summary

The flow of funds is a system of social accounting that permits the financial-market analyst to evaluate the flow of savings through various sectors of the economy. A sector consists of a grouping of economic units that are relatively homogeneous in their behavior. By combining source- and use-of-funds statements for all sectors, we may obtain a matrix for the entire economy. This matrix shows the interlocking nature of financial assets and liabilities among various sectors. It enables us to analyze savings-deficit sectors and the means by which they finance the excess of their investment in real assets over savings, together with the behavior of savings-surplus sectors and the way they invest in financial assets. Subject to certain limitations, the flow-of-funds data give the financial-market analyst rich insights. By tracing through the sources of funds for investment in a particular financial instrument, one gains much information about strains in the financial system and about interest rates.

In addition to the Federal Reserve flow-of-funds data, various source and use statements are published by several private organizations. However, these data do not show the interaction between the real and the financial segments of the economy. They are concerned only with the final supply and demand for funds. Nevertheless, source and use statements provide detailed information on financial markets and are very valuable to the financial-market analyst.

The analyst gains insight not only from a study of flows that have occurred in the past but also from forecasts of the future. Here, independent forecasts should be made of the demand for and the supply of funds. If there is an imbalance, the analyst studies the change in interest rates necessary to bring about a balance. In the published forecasts, there usually is a residual category for individuals and other investors. The amount of the residual tends to vary directly with the level of interest rates in financial markets. Consequently, the residual is useful in estimating future interest rates.

SELECTED REFERENCES

Cohen, J., "Copeland's Moneyflows after Twenty-Five Years: A Survey," *Journal of Economic Literature*, Vol. 2 (March, 1972), 1–25.

Credit and Capital Markets, 1976. New York: Bankers Trust Company, 1976.

The Flow-of-Funds Approach to Social Accounting. New York: National Bureau of Economic Research, 1962.

Freund, William C., and Edward D. Zinbarg, "Application of Flow of Funds to Interest-Rate Forecasting," *Journal of Finance*, 18 (May, 1963), 231–248.

Goldsmith, Raymond W., *Capital Market Analysis and the Financial Accounts of the Nation.* Morristown, N.J.: General Learning Press, 1972.

_____, *The Flow of Capital Funds in the Postwar Economy*, Chapter 2. New York: National Bureau of Economic Research, 1965.

Moore, Basil J., *An Introduction to the Theory of Finance*, Appendix to Chapter 1. New York: The Free Press, 1968.

Prospects for the Credit Markets in 1977. New York: Salomon Brothers, 1976.

"A Quarterly Presentation of Flow of Funds and Savings," *Federal Reserve Bulletin*, 45 (August, 1959), 828–859.

Ritter, Lawrence S., *The Flow of Funds Accounts: A Framework for Financial Analysis.* New York: Institute of Finance, New York University, 1968.

Taylor, Stephen, "Uses of Flow-of-Funds Accounts in the Federal Reserve System," *Journal of Finance*, 18 (May, 1963), 249–258.

Foundations for
Interest Rates

3 As we showed in Chapter 1, the function of financial markets is to facilitate the flow of savings from savings-surplus economic units to savings-deficit ones. The allocation of these savings occurs primarily on the basis of price, expressed by interest rates. Economic units in need of funds must outbid others for the use of these funds. Although the allocation process is affected somewhat by capital rationing and government restrictions, interest rates are the primary mechanism whereby supply and demand are brought into balance for a particular financial instrument across financial markets. Those economic units willing to pay the highest interest rate for the use of funds, holding risk constant, are the ones entitled to their use. If rationality prevails, the economic units bidding the highest prices are the ones with the most promising investment opportunities. As a result, savings are allocated to the most efficient uses, and capital formation and want satisfaction in the economy tend toward optimality. In this chapter, we analyze how the price mechanism works to bring the supply of a financial instrument into balance with its demand. In subsequent chapters, the focus is on explaining relative yields or yield differentials among various financial instruments.

Definition of Yield

Before we proceed, a brief discussion of the measurement of yields is in order. The yield on a financial instrument is the discount rate that equates the present value of expected cash inflows to the investor with the current market price of the security. If these inflows are assumed to occur at the end of the year, the yield can be determined by solving the following equation for r:

$$P_0 = \frac{C_1}{(1+r)} + \frac{C_2}{(1+r)^2} + \cdots + \frac{C_n}{(1+r)^n} \tag{3-1}$$

where P_0 is the current market price of the instrument
C_t is the expected cash inflow to the investor in period t
n is the final period in which a cash inflow is expected
r is the yield to maturity for which we solve

C_t may be interest payments, repayment of principal, or dividend payments, depending upon the security being analyzed.

To illustrate the use of the equation, suppose that the current market price of a $1,000 face-value bond with 20 years to maturity were $894 and that this bond had a 6 per cent coupon, i.e., that it paid $60 in interest to the investor at the end of each of the next 20 years. The yield to maturity for this bond can be determined by solving the following equation for r:

$$894 = \frac{60}{(1+r)} + \frac{60}{(1+r)^2} + \cdots + \frac{60}{(1+r)^{20}} + \frac{1,000}{(1+r)^{20}} \tag{3-2}$$

When the equation is solved for the discount rate that equates the current market price with the stream of interest payments plus the final redemption value of $1,000, it is found to be 7 per cent. Thus, the bond would yield 7 per cent to maturity.

If interest were paid more than once a year, Eq. (3-1) is modified to

$$P_0 = \frac{C_1}{\left(1+\frac{r}{m}\right)} + \frac{C_2}{\left(1+\frac{r}{m}\right)^2} + \frac{C_3}{\left(1+\frac{r}{m}\right)^3} + \cdots + \frac{C_n}{\left(1+\frac{r}{m}\right)^{mn}} \tag{3-3}$$

where m is the number of times in the year interest is compounded. If interest were paid semiannually on a $1,000 face-value bond with 20 years to final maturity, a coupon rate of 5 per cent, and a current market price of $1,032, the yield to maturity would be found by solving the following equation for r:

$$1,032 = \frac{25}{\left(1+\frac{r}{2}\right)} + \frac{25}{\left(1+\frac{r}{2}\right)^2} + \frac{25}{\left(1+\frac{r}{2}\right)^3} + \cdots$$
$$+ \frac{25}{\left(1+\frac{r}{2}\right)^{40}} + \frac{1,000}{\left(1+\frac{r}{2}\right)^{40}} \tag{3-4}$$

In this equation, r is 4.75 per cent. Fortunately, one need not solve for yield to maturity mathematically. Elaborate bond-value tables permit one to look up the yield, given the market price of the bond, the coupon rate, and the date of final maturity.

The yield to maturity, as calculated above, may differ from the holding-period yield on that security if the security is sold prior to maturity. The holding-period yield is the rate of discount that equates the present value of cash inflows (interest payments or dividends) plus the present value of terminal value at the end of the holding period with the price paid for the security. For example, suppose a share of stock were bought for $50 on a net basis and sold three years later for $70 net. Moreover, assume that the stock paid a $1 cash dividend at the end of each year. The holding-period yield, or annual return, would then be found by solving the following equation for r:

$$50 = \frac{1}{(1+r)} + \frac{1}{(1+r)^2} + \frac{1}{(1+r)^3} + \frac{70}{(1+r)^3} \qquad (3\text{-}5)$$

where r is found to be 13.67 per cent. In the ensuing discussion, both yield to maturity and holding-period yield will be considered. They facilitate the comparison of returns for different financial instruments. While commonly used because of their general natures, both measures have certain drawbacks. These drawbacks relate primarily to oversimplification and will become apparent as we explore the meaning of return in greater depth. For now, however, they will suffice.

The Interest Rate in an Exchange Economy

Interest rates in financial markets are determined by a complex interaction of supply and demand forces. In order to understand these forces we will simplify the problem by looking at it in varying degrees of abstraction. Essentially, we will focus on the choice of individual economic units between consumption and investment. In market equilibrium, of course, there must be a balance between investment and the restraint from consumption—that is, savings. We begin by looking at the consumption-savings phenomenon for the individual and then move on to consider the equilibrating process among individuals. We assume initially a world of certainty and analyze the determination of the rate of interest in such a world—namely, the riskless rate. Following this presentation, we will consider the determination of interest rates when risk exists.

The Individual Choice

Consider an individual with a two-point time horizon—now and one year from now. Moreover, suppose the individual is concerned only with a single commodity—call it corn. While the example could be

extended to a "basket" of consumption commodities, for ease of compre-
hension we simplify and consider only one commodity. The initial question
is "What is the individual's preference for present consumption vis à vis
future consumption?" This can be visualized with the help of Fig. 3-1.
Along the horizontal axis we have *present consumption*, whereas along the
vertical we have consumption at time 1, or *future consumption*. The curves
depict the individual's tradeoff between present and future consumption
and are called *indifference curves*. Along a curve, an individual is indifferent as to present or future consumption. To part with present consumption, that is, to save, the individual must be promised increasing amounts
of future consumption, C_1. Each curve upward and to the right represents
a higher level of satisfaction or utility. The object then is to strive for the
highest indifference curve, because it represents the highest level of present
and future want satisfaction. The indifference curves give us the *preference
function* of the individual.

Imagine now a situation where individuals can produce corn but
there is no exchange. That is, they cannot exchange the commodity they
produce for something else or for corn in the future. The corn just
harvested can either be consumed now or saved for the next planting.
Suppose that the production opportunity situation for the individual is
depicted by the $X'X$ curve in Fig. 3-2. Point X on the horizontal axis
represents the individual's present endowment of corn—the harvest just
past; it can be entirely consumed and nothing saved for next year's
planting. In that case, consumption at time 1 will be zero. Alternatively,
part or all of the present endowment can be saved as seed corn for next

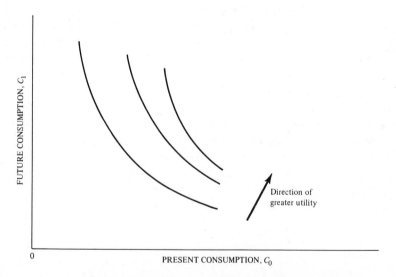

Figure 3-1. Indifference curves for an individual.

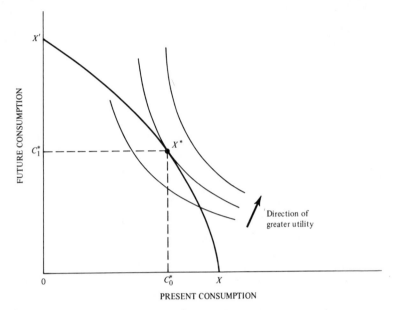

Figure 3-2. Production and consumption optimum without exchange.

year's planting. In our world of certainty we know the yield of corn at time 1, given an amount of seed corn held over at time 0. If all corn is held over as seed corn, consumption at time 1 will be X'. The $X'X$ curve shows the combinations of present and future consumption that are possible. Starting with the present endowment of X, note that each increment of corn saved for seed increases future consumption but at a decreasing rate. In other words, production increases but at a diminishing rate as more seed is planted in a given plot of land.

The optimum present consumption and hence the savings of the individual is represented by the point of tangency of the production opportunity curve with the highest indifference curve. This is depicted in Fig. 3-2 by X^*. Given this equilibrium point, the individual would consume C_0^* of corn presently and withhold $X - C_0^*$ for seed. This would result in future production and consumption of C_1^*.

Optimum with Exchange

What happens if there exists the possibility of exchange? By exchange we mean opportunities for the exchange of present and future claims to consumption—in this case to corn—with other economic units. In general, this possibility allows the individual economic unit to obtain a

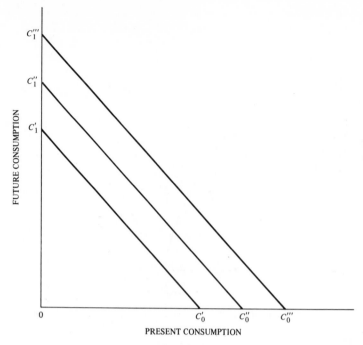

Figure 3-3. Market exchange lines.

higher level of present and future want satisfaction.[1] Suppose that the market exchange opportunities are depicted by the diagonal lines shown in Fig. 3-3. The slope of these lines describes the exchange ratio between present and future consumption. The graph shows that to obtain a number of units of present consumption, it is necessary to give up an even greater number of units of future consumption. This implies a preference in the market for present consumption vis à vis future consumption. The ratio of exchange for the first line and, because they are parallel, for all other lines, is

$$\frac{C_1'}{C_0'} = 1 + r \tag{3-6}$$

Thus, r represents the rate of interest for the sacrifice of current consumption for future consumption. At this rate, trading in the market is possible between present and future consumption claims. While the interest rate is

[1]The approach presented was formulated many years ago by Irving Fisher, *The Theory of Interest* (New York: The Macmillan Co., 1930). For analyses of Fisher's work, which place it in perspective with respect to the theory of interest rates, see Joseph W. Conard, *An Introduction to the Theory of Interest* (Berkeley: University of California Press, 1959), Chapter IV; and Friederich A. Lutz, *The Theory of Interest* (Dordrecht, Holland: D. Reidel Publishing Co., 1967), Chapter 7.

positive in this case, it need not be. Time preferences could be such as to favor future consumption vis à vis present consumption. In this case, the slope of the lines in Fig. 3-3 would be less than 45 degrees and a negative interest rate would prevail.

Each line in the figure represents a level of endowment of present and future consumption. The further upward and to the right, the higher the level of endowment. The endowment can be thought of as a constraint, in that it limits the opportunities for consumption. If the initial endowment in present consumption were C_0'', for example, only opportunities along the C_0''-C_1'' line would be possible. If C_0'' were consumed now, nothing would be exchanged for future consumption. At the other extreme, all of C_0'' could be exchanged for C_1'' of future consumption. Any combination between these two extremes is possible and connotes some exchange of present consumption for future consumption at an exchange ratio of $1 + r$. This corresponds to *lending*. In constrast, if one's endowment were entirely in a claim to future consumption, any exchange of future for present consumption would occur at an exchange ratio of $1/(1 + r)$. This corresponds to *borrowing*. Thus, the initial endowment can be in terms of present consumption claims, future consumption claims, or, as is likely, some combination of the two.

Combined Effect

Whereas we have analyzed separately the productive optimum, in the absence of exchange, and the exchange of present and future consumption claims (borrowing–lending), in the absence of production opportunities, we wish now to consider both simultaneously. For the individual economic unit, the derivation of production and consumption optimums can be pictured by the example in Fig. 3-4. The productive opportunity set is denoted by the curve $X'X$, as it was in Fig. 3-2. However, in this case the production optimum is not determined by the point of tangency of the production opportunity curve with the highest indifference curve. The situation is altered by the possibility of exchange. Optimal behavior by the individual is determined by the point of tangency between the production opportunity curve and the highest market exchange line. We see that this is point X^* in Fig. 3-4.

Having determined a production optimum, the individual then would undertake borrowing or lending along the market exchange line $C_1 - C_0$ until a point of tangency with the highest indifference curve was reached. We see in the figure that this is at point C^*, which is below and to the right of X^*, the production optimum. This means that the individual would exchange future consumption claims for present ones. In other words, the individual would borrow. If the point of tangency were above X^* and to the left, the individual would have to lend to obtain an optimal balancing of present and future consumption claims.

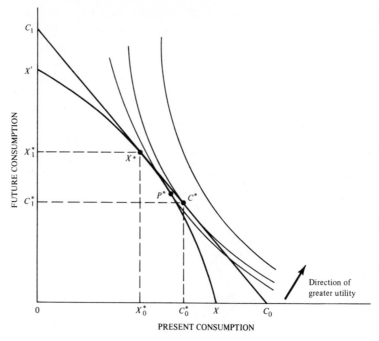

Figure 3-4. Production and consumption optimum with exchange.

To recapitulate, the individual should seek the productive opportunity along curve $X'X$ where a point of tangency exists between this curve and the highest market exchange ratio line. This is point X^*, and it implies that $X - X_0^*$ units of corn (along the horizontal axis) will be withheld as seed corn. It also implies X_1^* of future production, on the vertical axis. Given a productive optimum of X^*, the individual then would borrow against his future production in order to obtain the highest level of present and future want satisfaction. This is attained at C^*. It represents borrowing in the sense of giving up $X_1^* - C_1^*$ of claim to future consumption (vertical axis) for $C_0^* - X_0^*$ of additional present consumption (horizontal axis). Thus, the individual would move upward and to the left along line $X'X$ to point X^* and then downward and to the right along line C_1C_0 until point C^* was reached.

Note that the overall level of want satisfaction of C^* with production *and* exchange opportunities is higher than that obtained with production opportunities alone. The latter optimum would occur at P^*, where the productive opportunity curve is tangent with an indifference curve. With exchange opportunities, a higher level of want satisfaction is usually possible.

Also, we should emphasize that with production *and* exchange opportunities, determination of the production optimum, point X^* in Fig. 3-4, is

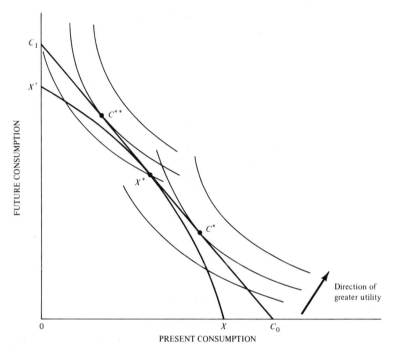

Figure 3-5. Illustration of the separation theorem.

independent of the individual's utility preferences. This is illustrated in Fig. 3-5, where we draw another set of indifference curves. The lower set of indifference curves depicts borrowing to obtain C^*, whereas the upper set depicts lending to obtain C^{**}. In both cases, determination of the productive optimum is distinct from the utility preferences of the individual. Put another way, the individual's utility preferences can change but this will not affect the production optimum. This condition is known as the *separation theorem*. It derives from our underlying assumption that the individual can both borrow and lend at the market rate r. Under such circumstances the intertemporal production decision is based solely on the point of tangency of the productive opportunity curve with the highest market exchange line.

Market Equilibrium

Up until now we have assumed a given value for the slope of the market exchange line—that is, the rate of interest. In effect, the individual has been viewed as a price taker with the exchange ratio as the price. However, the market is comprised of many individuals and the equilibrium rate of interest is determined by their interaction. In order to borrow, for example, there must be one or more individuals who are willing to lend at an agreed upon exchange ratio. To illustrate, suppose that the production-consumption optimum for individual 1 is that shown in Fig. 3-4. In the figure the individual is seen to want to exchange $X_1^* - C_1^*$ in future consumption claims for $C_0^* - X_0^*$ of present consumption.

Suppose that the market is comprised of only one other individual whose productive-consumptive equilibrium is illustrated in Fig. 3-6. The slope of the market exchange line is the same as that in Fig. 3-4. The productive optimum for this individual is X^* and, given his utility preference, he would strive to lend $X_0^* - C_0^*$ of present consumption claims for $C_1^* - X_1^*$ of future consumption claims. However, the amount the second individual desires to lend at the prevailing rate of interest is less than that which the first individual desires to borrow. This creates a disequilibrium situation.

The forces in this situation work in the direction of a higher rate of interest—thus there is a greater slope in the market exchange line. With a greater slope, the second individual's productive optimum will be downward and to the right. This is depicted in the lower panel of Fig. 3-7. Instead of X^* being the optimum production opportunity, given a market exchange line of $C_1 C_0$, the optimum becomes X^{**} with a market exchange line of $C_1' C_0'$. Moreover, the individual is able to attain a higher indif-

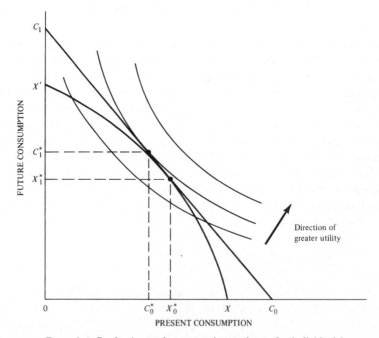

Figure 3-6. Production and consumption optimum for individual 2.

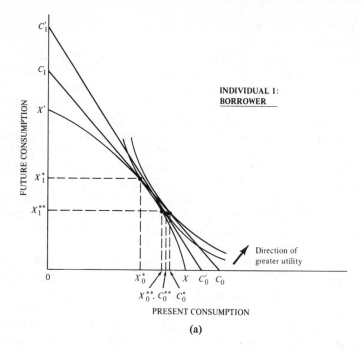

(a)

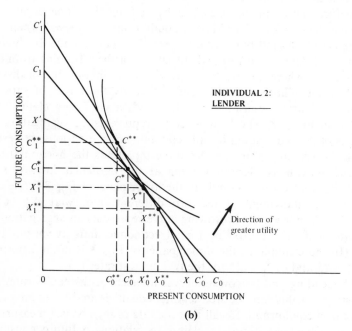

(b)

Figure 3-7. Illustration of upward shift in the interest rate.

ference curve in lending owing to the greater slope of the market exchange line. The import of all this is that at the new rate of interest the individual is willing to lend more than before, $X_0^{**} - C_0^{**}$ as opposed to $X_0^* - C_1^*$.

The shift in slope of the market exchange line also affects the behavior of the first individual. His production optimum also shifts downward and to the right, as shown in the upper panel of Fig. 3-7. Moreover, the higher rate of interest results in his being able to achieve only a lower indifference curve. The overall effect is a dramatic lessening in his desire to borrow for current consumption, $C_0^{**} - X_0^{**}$ as opposed to $C_0^* - X_0^*$ before. In fact, the first individual wishes to borrow much less than the second individual desires to lend at the higher interest rate. Therefore, a lower rate of interest is in order. The interest rate, or slope of the market exchange line, will continue to adjust until the amount the first individual wishes to borrow equals the amount the second individual desires to lend. In an earlier vernacular, "it takes two to tango."

Now obviously the "market" is comprised of more than two individuals. However, the equilibrating process works in the way illustrated when we have multiple economic units. As the rate of interest changes, some individuals will want to borrow more or less, while others will want to lend less or more. In fact, as the interest rate rises some economic units previously wanting to borrow will want to lend and as the interest rate declines some economic units will wish to borrow although they wanted to lend before. This can be visualized by shifting the slope of the market exchange lines in Fig. 3-7. Market equilibrium is achieved when desired lending equals desired borrowing across all economic units. In the context of Chapter 1, lending corresponds to saving, or the refraining from current consumption, whereas borrowing corresponds to investment, or dissavings.

Market equilibrium then is determined by the forces of supply and demand for current consumption claims vis à vis future claims. This is depicted in Fig. 3-8. The lending curve represents an aggregation of the amounts of desired lending for all economic units at various interest rates. In other words, any point on the curve represents the horizontal sum of different individuals' desired lending at the particular interest rate involved. In terms of our example in the lower panel of Fig. 3-7, the desired loans of the individual at the two different rates were $X_0^* - C_0^*$ and $X_0^{**} - C_0^{**}$. Similarly, the borrowing curve represents an aggregation of the amounts of desired borrowing for all economic units at various interest rates. (In the example in the upper panel of Fig. 3-7, desired borrowings are $C_0^* - X_0^*$ and $C_0^{**} - X_0^{**}$ for the two interest rates.)

The lending and borrowing curves intersect at the equilibrium rate of interest, r^*. At this rate, desired lending equals desired borrowing and the market is in equilibrium. Recall that the rate of interest is a measure of the price of current consumption claims in relation to future consumption claims. The curves in Fig. 3-8 represent an aggregation of production-con-

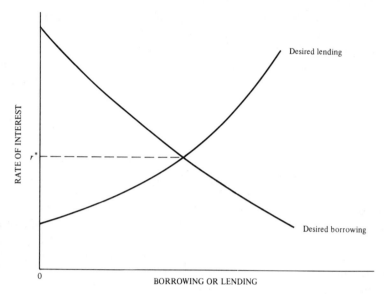

Figure 3-8. Market equilibrium.

sumption optimums for all individuals under varying interest rates, as illustrated in Fig. 3-7 and earlier figures. Thus, the equilibrium market rate of interest embodies the desired lending and borrowing behavior of all economic units according to their productive opportunity sets and their utility preferences. Shifts in these factors will cause shifts in desired lending or borrowing and in the equilibrium rate of interest.

At the beginning of this section, we invoked the assumption of certainty with respect to the future. As a result, our problem was reduced to showing the determination of the riskless rate of interest. Assuming no transaction costs or other market impediments, this then became the rate at which all individual economic units could either borrow or lend. When we leave the world of certainty, necessarily we must consider risk. In the remainder of this chapter and in the Appendix, we present an overall framework for determining interest rates under conditions of risk. In subsequent chapters, we extend this analysis to consider the factors that give rise to risk and their impact on market rates of interest. In other words, we proceed from the general to the sepcific.

Interest Rates in a World with Risk

When we leave the riskless world assumed in the previous section, the determination of interest rates is altered. With risk, for example, we can and do have multiple financial instruments. This contrasts with the previous section where there was but one financial instrument—a riskless contract between the borrower and lender. This contract bore an interest rate that was the same for all such contracts in the market. Stated in another way, only one rate of interest prevailed, the risk-free rate. In a world characterized by risk, different interest rates occur. This is the topic we wish to study.

Behavior of Individual Economic Units

Interest rates in risky financial markets cannot be analyzed in isolation. They are dependent not only upon interest rates in other financial markets but also upon the real sector of the economy and upon consumption. All these factors interact to determine an equilibrium structure of interest rates. In this section we study the behavior of individual economic units in choosing assets and issuing financial liabilities. An understanding of this behavior allows us later to examine how economic units interact to determine interest rates in the economy.

As recalled from Chapter 2, the balance sheet for an economic unit at any moment is

Assets	Liabilities and Net Worth
Money	Financial liabilities
	#1
Other financial assets	#2
#1	.
#2	.
.	.
.	#n
.	
#n	
Real assets	
#1	
#2	
.	
.	Net worth
.	
#n	

It is assumed that the economic unit adjusts its balance sheet toward a desired, or preferred, mix of assets and liabilities in keeping with changes in interest rates, investment opportunities, wealth, and other factors. It may increase its total asset holdings only if its net worth increases, it issues additional financial liabilities, or both. In turn, a change in net worth can be the result of two occurrences: (1) current expenditures less than or more than current income and (2) capital gains or losses on financial assets and liabilities and on real assets over the period.

Consumption clearly represents an alternative to holding assets or issuing financial liabilities and, accordingly, influences the desired totals in the balance sheet for the economic unit. A household, for example, has several choices to make in the allocation of its wealth and income. To purchase a house, it may have to save, by consuming less than its income, until it has accumulated sufficient funds for a downpayment. The alternative to purchasing a house in this case would be increased consumption. If the household were already consuming less than its current income, the alternative might be increasing its financial assets. A household must decide not only on the proportion of income to save but also on where these savings are to be employed—that is, what type of asset is to be increased (money, other financial assets, or real assets) or what type of financial liability is to be paid off. A business corporation, on the other hand, may purchase a piece of capital equipment by retaining its earnings, by reducing its financial assets, or by increasing its financial liabilities.

These examples are sufficient to illustrate the complexities that face the individual economic unit in determining the total amount and composition of financial assets it holds and the amount and composition of financial liabilities it issues. How does the individual economic unit adjust its holdings of assets, its financial liabilities, and its consumption to achieve a preferred position? It does so on the basis of maximizing total utility. At a moment in time, the economic unit increases its financial liabilities to finance its holding of money, other financial assets, and real assets as long as it can increase its total utility by doing so. Over time the economic unit can increase or decrease its marginal propensity to consume. Changes in net worth affect and are affected by consumption, the holdings of various assets, and the financial liabilities issued. Thus, all of these factors are interdependent with respect to the utility preferences of an economic unit and its behavior.

Utility for Financial Assets

Assuming that economic units attempt to maximize their total utility, we must consider now the utility derived from holding various assets and from issuing financial liabilities. This consideration is fundamental to understanding how economic units in an economy interact to determine interest rates. For financial assets other than money, we assume that the preferences of economic units are based upon a two-parameter utility function; these parameters are (1) the expected return from the instrument and (2) the risk involved in holding it.[2] If the future were known, no risk would be involved in holding a financial asset. The income stream would be certain. Because utility is associated positively with return, all economic units would try to maximize their total return from the holding of financial assets by investing in that financial asset which promised the greatest return. With certainty about the future and perfect capital markets, however, arbitrage would assure that every financial asset yielded no more than the risk-free rate, as determined in the previous section.

When the future is *not* known, the utility function of an economic unit is more complex. The economic unit must consider the range of possible returns. To reduce the problem to manageable proportions, we assume that an individual is able to summarize his beliefs about the probability distribution of possible returns from a financial asset or portfolio of financial assets in terms of two parameters of the distribution. These parameters are the expected value and the standard deviation of the distribution.

The expected value of the probability distribution is calculated by

$$\bar{R} = \sum_{x=1}^{n} R_x P_x \tag{3-7}$$

where $\bar{R}$ is the expected value, R_x is the return for the xth possibility, P_x is the probability of occurrence of that return, and n is the total number of possibilities. It is assumed that investors associate risk with the dispersion of the probability distribution. The greater the dispersion, the more risky the financial asset, and vice versa. The conventional measure of dispersion of a probability distribution is the standard deviation, which is calculated by

$$\sigma = \sqrt{\sum_{x=1}^{n} \left(R_x - \bar{R} \right)^2 P_x} \tag{3-8}$$

Equation (3-8) gives only the standard deviation for a single financial asset. However, an economic unit usually has more than one investment opportunity available. Rather than evaluate the expected value of return and the standard deviation for a single financial asset, one must evaluate them for a portfolio of financial assets. It is implied that economic units maximize the utility arising from holding a portfolio of financial assets. The expected value of return for a portfolio is simply the sum of the

[2]For a justification of this approach, see James Tobin, "Liquidity Preference as Behavior Towards Risk," *Review of Economic Studies*, XXV (February, 1958), 65–86.

expected values of return for the financial assets making up the portfolio. The standard deviation, however, is not the sum of the individual standard deviations, but

$$\sigma = \sqrt{\sum_{j=1}^{m} \sum_{k=1}^{m} A_j A_k r_{jk} \sigma_j \sigma_k} \qquad (3\text{-}9)$$

where m is the total number of financial assets under consideration, A_j is the proportion of total funds invested in financial asset j, A_k is the proportion invested in financial asset k, r_{jk} is the expected correlation between returns for financial assets j and k, σ_j is the standard deviation about the expected value of return for financial asset j, and σ_k is the standard deviation for financial asset k. These standard deviations are calculated with Eq. (3-8). The correlation between returns may be positive, negative, or zero, depending upon the nature of the association. A correlation coefficient of 1.00 indicates that the returns from two financial assets vary positively, or directly, in exactly the same proportions; a correlation coefficient of -1.00 indicates that they vary inversely in exactly the same proportions; and a zero coefficient indicates an absence of correlation.

By diversifying its holdings to include financial assets with less than perfect positive correlation among themselves, the risk averse economic unit is able to reduce the dispersion of the probability distribution of possible returns for its portfolio in relation to the expected value of return for that portfolio. In so doing, it reduces the risk of holding financial assets. However, this diversification must be among the right financial assets. It is not enough for an economic unit simply to spread its endowment among a number of financial assets; diversification must be among financial assets not possessing high degrees of positive correlation among themselves.[3] It is evident from Eq. (3-9) that the dispersion of the probability distribution for a portfolio could be reduced to zero if financial assets with negative correlation could be found. The objective of diversification, however, is not to reduce dispersion per se but to obtain the best combination of expected value of return and standard deviation.

The individual economic unit is assumed to have a preference function with respect to the expected value of return and risk from holding a portfolio of financial assets. In other words, it is assumed to make optimal portfolio decisions on the basis of these two parameters. If an economic

---

[3] For a much more detailed analysis of diversification, see, among others, William F. Sharpe, *Investments* (Englewood Cliffs, N.J.: Prentice-Hall, Inc. 1978), Chapter 6; John Lintner, "Security Prices, Risk and Maximal Gains for Diversification," *Journal of Finance*, 20 (December, 1965), 587–615; and Franco Modigliani and Gerald A. Pogue, "An Introduction to Risk and Return," *Financial Analysts Journal*, 30 (March–April, 1974). All of the work along this line is an outgrowth of the classic work of Harry M. Markowitz, *Portfolio Selection: Efficient Diversification of Investments* (New York: John Wiley & Sons, Inc., 1959).

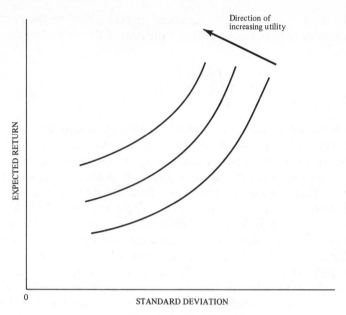

Figure 3-9. Hypothetical indifference curves.

unit is averse to risk and associates risk with divergence from expected return, its utility schedule may be similar to that shown in Fig. 3-9. The expected value of return is plotted on the vertical axis, while the standard deviation is along the horizontal. As before, the curves are known as *indifference curves*; in this case the individual is indifferent between any combination of expected value of return and standard deviation on a particular curve. In other words, a curve is defined by those combinations of expected return and standard deviation that result in a fixed level of expected utility.[4] The greater the slope of the indifference curves, the more averse the investor is to risk. As we move upward and to the left in Fig. 3-9, each successive curve represents a higher level of expected utility.

The individual will want to hold that portfolio of financial assets that places him on the highest indifference curve, choosing it from the opportunity set of available portfolios. An example of an opportunity set, based upon the subjective probability beliefs of an individual economic unit, is shown in Fig. 3-10. This opportunity set reflects all possible portfolios of securities as envisioned by the individual. The line at the top of the set is the line of efficient combinations, or the efficient frontier. It depicts the tradeoff between risk and expected value of return. According to the Markowitz mean-variance maxim, an economic unit should seek a

---

[4]For further discussion and proof that indifference curves for a risk-averse investor are concave, see Eugene F. Fama and Merton H. Miller, *The Theory of Finance* (New York: Holt, Rinehart and Winston, 1972), pp. 226–228.

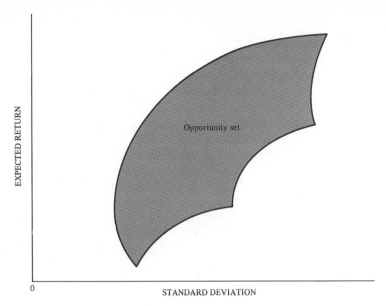

Figure 3-10. Hypothetical opportunity set.

portfolio of securities that lies on the efficient frontier.[5] A portfolio is not efficient if there is another portfolio with a higher expected value of return and a lower standard deviation, a higher expected value and the same standard deviation, or the same expected value but a lower standard deviation. If an individual's portfolio is not efficient, he can increase the expected value of return without increasing the risk, decrease the risk without decreasing the expected value of return, or obtain some combination of increased expected value and decreased risk by switching to a portfolio on the efficient frontier.

As can be seen, the efficient frontier is determined on the basis of dominance. Portfolios of securities tend to dominate individual securities because of the reduction in risk obtainable through diversification. As discussed before, this reduction is evident when one explores the implications of Eq. (3-9). The objective of the economic unit is to choose the best portfolio from those that lie on the efficient frontier. The portfolio with the maximum utility is the one at the point of tangency of the opportunity set with the highest indifference curve. This tangency is illustrated in Fig. 3-11, and the portfolio represented by the point of tangency is the optimal one for an economic unit with those expectations and utility function.[6]

[5]Markowitz, *Portfolio Selection: Efficient Diversification of Investments* (New York: John Wiley & Sons, Inc., 1959), Chapters 7 and 8.

[6]For a more sophisticated and mathematical discussion of the point of tangency, see Fama and Miller, *op. cit.*, pp. 223–226 and 243–250. For ease of understanding, we have purposely kept the presentation graphical.

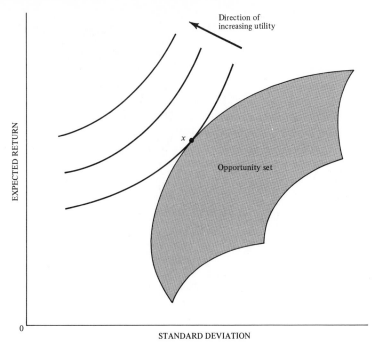

Figure 3-11. Selection of optimal portfolio.

Presence of Risk-Free Security

If a risk-free security exists that yields a certain future return, the portfolio selection process described above must be modified. Suppose for now that the economic unit is able not only to lend at the risk-free rate but to borrow at it as well. To determine the optimal portfolio under these conditions, we first draw a line from the risk-free rate, i, through its point of tangency with the opportunity set of portfolio returns, as illustrated in Fig. 3-12. This line then becomes the new efficient frontier. Note that only one portfolio of risky financial assets—namely, m—would be considered. In other words, this portfolio now dominates all others, including those on the efficient frontier of the opportunity set.

Any point on the straight line tells us the proportion of the risky portfolio, m, and the proportion of loans or borrowings at the risk-free rate. To the left of point m the economic unit would hold both the risk-free security and portfolio m. To the right, it would hold only portfolio m and would borrow funds in order to invest in it. The optimal behavior is determined by the point of tangency between the straight line in Fig. 3-12 and the highest indifference curve. As shown in the figure, this point is portfolio x and it consists of an investment in both the risk-free financial asset and the risky portfolio, m.

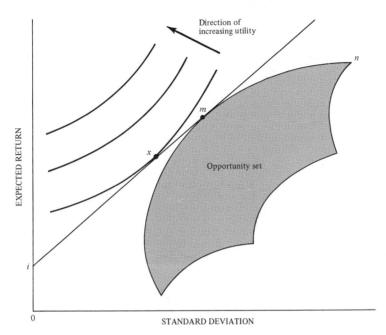

Figure 3-12. Selection of optimal portfolio when risk-free asset exists.

The theory underlying this notion could be developed in much more detail. For example, if homogeneous expectations are assumed on the part of all economic units, one can determine the expected rate of return for an individual financial asset, given the risk-free rate and the incremental riskiness of that financial asset with respect to an efficiently diversified portfolio of financial assets. Development of this line of thought, known as the capital-asset pricing model, is well advanced in literature and is available elsewhere.[7] Our focus in this chapter is somewhat broader in sketching a theory of general equilibrium in financial and other markets. While this approach does not provide much in the way of predictive ability (owing to the generality involved), it does afford an overall insight into the market equilibrating process.

In this regard, we assume that all economic units select portfolios of financial assets in such a way as to maximize their expected utility. In turn, utility preferences are assumed to be formulated on the basis of the expected value and the standard deviation of the probability distribution of possible returns. It is important to point out that we allow for heterogeneous expectations on the part of individual economic units. As we will

---

[7]See, for example, William F. Sharpe, *Portfolio Analysis and Capital Markets* (New York: McGraw-Hill Book Co., 1970); Fama and Miller, *op. cit.*; Sharpe, *op. cit.*; James C. Van Horne, *Financial Management and Policy*, 4th ed. (Englewood Cliffs, N.J.: Prentice-Hall, Inc., 1977), Chapters 2 and 3; or numerous other books and articles dealing with the topic.

discuss in the latter part of this chapter and in the Appendix, heterogeneous expectations, together with differences in utility preferences among economic units, have a major bearing upon the structure of interest rates.

Utility for Financial Liabilities

We asume also that the issuance of financial liabilities can be analyzed on the basis of a two-parameter utility function. Because an economic unit must pay the return on a financial liability, it would have a negative utility for doing so, all other things the same. Consequently, $\partial U/\partial e < 0$, where e is the expected value of return on the financial liability. If an economic unit is a risk averter, it would prefer less variance to more variance, holding constant the expected value of return, so $\partial U/\partial v < 0$, where v is the standard deviation for the financial liability. For the risk seeker, $\partial U/\partial v > 0$.

For a financial liability, variance pertains to the dispersion of the probability distribution of possible future market prices. For fixed-income financial liabilities, the issuer knows with certainty its contractual obligation to meet interest and principal payments. After issuance, however, the instrument fluctuates in market price because of changes in the overall level of interest rates and because of changes in perceived risk by investors. To the extent that a borrower is unconcerned with the future market price of its financial liability, it would have a one-parameter utility function. In other words, its preferences would be governed only by the yield to be paid at the time of issuance. In this case e, the expected value of return, would correspond to the intitial yield.

Utility for Other Assets

In the previous discussion, we considered the effect of holding financial assets and issuing financial liabilities on the utility of an economic unit. We now must consider the utility arising from the holding of other assets. Because our primary interest is in financial instruments, however, our examination necessarily will be brief. Afterward, the maximization of utility for an economic unit in its holdings of assets, in its issuance of financial liabilities, and in its consumption will be considered. Having established these building blocks, we will deal in the remainder of the chapter and in the Appendix with how economic units interact to determine interest rates in an economy.

Because money is a medium of exchange and other financial assets are not, it was not included in our previous discussion. For purposes of analysis, we use the "narrow" definition of money—currency in circulation and demand deposits. If it were not for money, of course, trading would have to be done on the basis of exchanging one good for another. Such a barter system allows little or no store of purchasing power, no common unit of account in which different goods can be expressed, and little divisibility. Because of these obvious inefficiencies, money has come to serve as the accepted medium of exchange in acquiring goods and services. In addition, it serves as the unit of account, or common denominator, in the pricing of goods and services. For example, a good or service does not have to be priced in terms of so many units of other goods and services. It can be priced in terms of units of money. Although money additionally serves as a store of value, other assets, of course, also serve this function.

Keynes has identified three motives for holding money—the transactions motive, the precautionary motive, and the speculative motive.[8] The transactions motive is the desire to hold money to pay for goods and services. This need tends to rise with the level of income and expenditures of an economic unit. The precautionary motive for holding money involves maintaining a cushion, or buffer, to meet unexpected contingencies. The more predictable the money needs of an economic unit, the less precautionary balances are needed. If an economic unit is able to borrow on short notice to meet emergency money drains, the need for this balance also is reduced. The last motive, the speculative one, means holding money to take advantage of expected changes in security prices. When interest rates are expected to rise and security prices to fall, this motive would suggest that the economic unit should hold money until the rise in interest rates ceases, in order to avoid a loss in security value. When interest rates are expected to fall, money may be invested in securities; the economic unit will benefit by any subsequent fall in interest rates and rise in security prices.

The marginal utility for holding money can be related to these three motives, and it is assumed that economic units formulate utility preferences for money on these bases. The expected value of return for holding paper money is zero. However, no risk is involved, for the future price is known. To be sure, there may be an opportunity loss in the form of eroded purchasing power. However, there is no dispersion of the probability distribution of possible monetary returns. X dollars of paper money held today will be worth X dollars tomorrow. With demand deposits, a commercial bank may possibly fail, and the depositor may suffer a loss. However, with deposit insurance and a central bank, the probability for actual loss is rather small if not negligible. Consequently, we will regard money as having no uncertainty as to future price.

Unlike financial assets, real assets are held for the physical services they provide the owner. These assets may be productive, such as a machine

[8]John Maynard Keynes, *The General Theory of Employment Interest and Money* (New York: Harcourt, Brace & World, Inc., 1936), pp. 170–174.

tool, or may be designed to satisfy the wants of economic units, such as a house or a consumer durable. Real assets are tangible; they cannot be produced instantaneously but only over time. The marginal utility arising from owning a real asset must be related to the services it provides. In the case of a productive asset, it usually is related to the marginal profitability of another unit of input. In analyzing profitability, one must take account of the interdependence of inputs in the production function. It is the partial derivative of profitability with respect to the asset that is important. The marginal utility of consumer durables and dwellings is much more difficult to measure. Here, marginal utility must be related to the want satisfaction the asset provides the owner.

The holding of certain real assets can be explained in terms of the overall portfolio of the owner. Business firms, on the one hand, hold capital assets for the return they are expected to provide. Households, on the other hand, do not appear to acquire consumer durables on the basis of portfolio considerations. However, the acquisition of a home seems to have portfolio implications, for generally it is the largest asset holding of the household. Although the model developed in this chapter implies an independence of the utility function for real assets from that for financial assets, the holding of certain real assets can be explained in terms of an expected return-risk tradeoff for the economic unit as a whole. In these cases, the interdependence of real and financial assets must be recognized in the final determination of an optimal portfolio.

Market Equilibrium

The amount of money, financial assets, and real assets held, the amount of financial liabilities issued, and consumption are determined by an economic unit on the basis of maximizing its total utility, subject to net worth and income constraints. In equilibrium, the marginal utility derived from holding each asset is the same. *Marginal utility* is defined as the change in total utility that accompanies an increase of one dollar in a particular asset. Thus, the marginal utility derived from the last dollar increase in financial asset 1 must equal the marginal utility derived from the last dollar increase in money, in financial assets 2, 3, and n, and in real assets $1, 2, \ldots, n$. In equilibrium, the following equation holds:

$$\frac{MU \text{ money}}{P \text{ money}} = \frac{MU \text{ } FA_1}{P FA_1} = \frac{MU \text{ } FA_2}{P FA_2} = \frac{MU \text{ } FA_n}{P FA_n}$$
$$= \frac{MU \text{ } RA_1}{P RA_1} = \frac{MU \text{ } RA_2}{P RA_2} = \frac{MU \text{ } RA_n}{P RA_n} \qquad (3\text{-}10)$$

Here MU stands for marginal utility, P for price per unit, FA_n for financial asset n, and RA_n for real asset n. In other words, maximum satisfaction occurs at the point at which the marginal utility of a dollar's worth of money equals the marginal utility of a dollar's worth of financial asset n and the marginal utility of a dollar's worth of the other assets held. If this equation is not satisfied, an economic unit can increase its total utility by shifting from an asset with a lower ratio of marginal utility to price to one with a higher ratio. By such shifting, equilibrium will eventually be achieved where the ratios of marginal utility to price are all equal to some constant λ. If the price of money is 1, $\lambda = MU$ money$/1$, or the marginal utility of money.

For simplicity in analysis, we hold constant the effect of consumption by considering the balance sheet of an economic unit at only a moment in time. Over time, of course, an economic unit can have current expenditures. Then, in equilibrium, the marginal utility derived from a dollar's worth of current expenditures must equal that derived from a dollar's worth of each asset held. In other words, consumption competes with the holding of assets in the maximization of total utility. This implies that the marginal utility of savings (current income less current expenditures) must be evaluated in relation to the satisfaction derived from the assets into which savings are put. To facilitate later analysis, however, we hold constant the effect of savings and consumption and assume that an economic unit will not sell assets, use money, or issue financial liabilities for consumption.

Financial liabilities represent a negative marginal utility to the issuer. An economic unit does not issue a financial liability for its own sake but rather to acquire assets. As long as the positive marginal utility from an additional dollar's worth of assets exceeds in absolute magnitude the negative marginal utility from the issuance of an additional dollar of financial liabilities, the economic unit will issue financial liabilities. In equilibrium, the negative marginal utility per dollar's worth of each financial liability should be the same. Moreover, the ratio of marginal utility to price for each financial liability should equal the ratio of marginal utility to price for each asset (if we ignore the sign of the ratio). For the risk averter, we would expect the negative ratio of marginal utility to price to increase at an increasing rate as a financial liability is increased beyond some point. This occurrence is a result not only of the utility preferences of the economic unit but also of possible increases in the interest rate as more financial liabilities are issued. Because of the decreasing positive ratio of marginal utility to price for acquiring additional assets and the increasing negative ratio of marginal utility to price for issuing financial liabilities, an equilibrium will be achieved for the individual economic unit.

Maximizing Utility for the Economic Unit

At any moment in time, the holding of financial assets and the issuance of financial liabilities are constrained by the net worth of the individual economic unit.

$$
\begin{aligned}
M + \mathrm{FA}_1 P_{\mathrm{FA1}} + \mathrm{FA}_2 P_{\mathrm{FA2}} \\
+ \cdots + \mathrm{FA}_n P_{\mathrm{FA}n} + \mathrm{RA}_1 P_{\mathrm{RA1}} + \mathrm{RA}_2 P_{\mathrm{RA2}} \\
+ \cdots + \mathrm{RA}_n P_{\mathrm{RA}n} - \mathrm{FL}_1 P_{\mathrm{FL1}} - \mathrm{FL}_2 P_{\mathrm{FL2}} \\
- \cdots - \mathrm{FL}_n P_{\mathrm{FL}n} = NW
\end{aligned}
\tag{3-11}
$$

where FA_1 is the quantity of financial asset n, $P_{\mathrm{FA}n}$ is the price per unit of that asset, FL_n is the quantity of liability n, and $P_{\mathrm{FL}n}$ is the price per unit of that financial liability. The individual economic unit will try to maximize its total utility by changing its asset holdings and liabilities issued, subject to its net worth constraint. Its objective function is

$$
\operatorname{Max} X = U(M, X, R, Y) \tag{3-12}
$$

subject to

$$
M + \sum_i P_i x_i + \sum_k P_k r_k - \sum_j P_j y_j = NW \tag{3-13}
$$

where X = a column vector of x_i, where x_i is the quantity of the ith financial asset
P_i = price per unit of the ith financial asset
R = a column vector of r_k, where r_k is the quantity of the kth real asset
P_k = price per unit of the kth real asset
Y = a column vector of y_j, where y_j is the quantity of the jth financial liability
P_j = price per unit of the jth financial liability

Recall that the utility to an economic unit of holding financial assets and issuing financial liabilities was assumed to be based upon the expected value and standard deviation of the probability distributions of possible returns. Each economic unit forms expectations about possible returns from all feasible portfolios of financial assets and all feasible combinations of financial liabilities. We recognize, however, that an economic unit is limited in the number of financial assets it can consider at one time. It simply is unable to form expectations about the universe of financial assets available to it for investment; consequently, the number of feasible portfolios is restricted. Once the optimal portfolio of financial assets and the optimal combination of financial liabilities are determined by an economic unit, it then increases or decreases them to maximize its total utility, in keeping with Eqs. (3-12) and (3-13).

In summary, the individual economic unit maximizes its utility according to Eq. (3-12) by varying M, X, R, and Y, subject to the net worth constraint. In equilibrium, the marginal utility per dollar of money equals the marginal utility per dollar of the optimal financial-asset portfolio, which, in turn, equals the marginal utility per dollar of real assets held. In addition, the negative marginal utility per dollar of the optimal combination of financial liabilities must equal the ratio for the assets (if we ignore the sign). If it were less, an economic unit could increase its total utility by increasing its financial liabilities and increasing its holdings of assets.

The Action of All Economic Units

The action of all economic units in an economy maximizing their utility according to Eq. (3-12) determines market prices for real and financial assets in that economy. Whereas prices in Eq. (3-13) are assumed to be given for the individual economic unit, they are not given for economic units collectively. These economic units act to maximize their individual utilities, and in doing so, they determine market prices and interest rates in the economy. For the economy as a whole, financial assets equal financial liabilities. Accordingly, market prices must adjust so that in equilibrium there is no excess demand or excess supply.

The equilibrium structure of financial-asset prices and interest rates is the result of a complex blending of the expectations, net worths, incomes, and utility functions of all economic units in an economy. This structure is affected by the utility preferences of economic units regarding money, real assets, financial assets, and financial liabilities. For example, an increase in the marginal utility of all economic units toward holding real assets would lead, ceteris paribus, to a greater aggregate demand for real assets, higher prices for these assets, a lower aggregate demand for financial assets, and a greater aggregate supply of financial liabilities. For equilibrium to be achieved, prices of financial instruments would have to decline and interest rates rise.

Equilibrium in financial markets requires that the total quantity of a financial instrument demanded equal the total quantity an economic unit desires to issue. The relative influence of an economic unit on market price depends on its net worth, its utility preferences, its expectations, and its existing holdings of assets and liabilities. On the supply side of the market, the quantity of a particular financial liability that an economic unit desires to issue also depends on these factors. In a modern economy, most economic units exert at least some influence on interest rates. Differing expectations, net worths, and utility functions of economic units, however, make determination of equilibrium prices of financial instruments in an economy an extremely complex process involving the interaction of all economic units in the economy. Perhaps the key element in this process is expectations. On the basis of expectations as to return, variance, and covariance, different financial instruments are perceived differently by different economic units. Economic units in need of funds must compete for them on the basis of the expected return paid. (Actually, the need for funds and the expected return paid are determined simultaneously.) Through the interaction of the various economic units, interest rates are determined and savings are allocated in the economy. Because of the mathematical complexity of the process, it is examined in detail in the Appendix to this chapter.

Summary

Savings in an economy are allocated primarily through interest rates. The *yield* on a financial instrument is the discount rate that equates the present value of expected future cash inflows, including the redemption price, with the current market price. The yield to maturity on an instrument differs from its *holding-period yield* in that the latter encompasses both the cash inflows and the capital gain or loss for the holding period.

In a riskless world, individuals maximize their utility by first seeking a productive optimum between *current* consumption claims and *future* consumption claims. This optimum occurs at the point of tangency between their production opportunity curve and the market exchange line. The individual then moves up (lends) or down (borrows) the line until a point of tangency is reached with the highest indifference curve. At this point, present and future want satisfaction is maximized. When all economic units behave in this manner, the slope of the market exchange line, which represents the interest rate, shifts until the amount of desired lending equals the amount of desired borrowing at the particular interest rate involved. Thus the equilibrium rate of interest embraces the productive opportunity sets and utility preferences of all economic units.

In a risky world, there is not one but many interest rates. A general equilibrium framework is necessary to understand their determination. The individual economic unit continually adjusts its asset holdings and liabilities toward a preferred mix of assets, liabilities, and consumption. At the preferred mix, the wealth and income of the unit are allocated optimally. The economic unit adjusts its mix to maximize its total utility. In equilibrium, the marginal utilities of each dollar of money, each dollar of each financial asset, and each dollar of each real asset are the same. These ratios are equal also to the negative marginal utility of each dollar of each financial liability (if we ignore the sign).

The utility preferences for holding financial assets and issuing financial liabilities are assumed to be based upon the expected value and the dispersion of the probability distribution of possible returns. In either case, it is the portfolio of assets or liabilities that is important, for an economic unit can reduce dispersion of its portfolio through diversification. The behavior of risk averters and risk seekers with respect to an optimal portfolio was examined. Individual economic units maximize their total utility arising from holding money, financial assets, and real assets; from issuing financial liabilities; and from consuming, subject to wealth and income constraints. The behavior of all economic units in a closed economy maximizing their total utility in this manner determines interest rates on financial instruments in that economy. In equilibrium, the total amount of financial assets demanded must equal the total amount supplied; there can be no excess demand or excess supply in financial markets. Interest rates adjust to clear these markets and are the result of a complex interaction of all economic units in the economy.

SELECTED REFERENCES

Bierwag, G. O., and M. A. Grove, "On Capital Asset Prices: Comment," *Journal of Finance*, 20 (March, 1965), 89–93.

———, "Slutzky Equations for Assets," *Journal of Political Economy*, 76 (January–February, 1968), 114–127.

Conard, Joseph W., *An Introduction to the Theory of Interest*. Berkeley: University of California Press, 1959.

Fama, Eugene F., and Merton H. Miller, *The Theory of Finance*. New York: Holt, Rinehart and Winston, 1972.

Fisher, Irving, *The Theory of Interest*. New York: The Macmillan Co., 1930.

Hirshleifer, J., *Investment, Interest and Capital*. Englewood Cliffs, N.J.: Prentice-Hall, Inc., 1970.

Keynes, John Maynard, *The General Theory of Employment Interest and Money*. New York: Harcourt, Brace & World, Inc., 1936.

Lintner, John, "Security Prices, Risk and Maximal Gains from Diversification," *Journal of Finance*, 20 (December, 1965), 587–615.

Lutz, Friedrich A., *The Theory of Interest*. Dordrecht, Holland: D. Reidel Publishing Co., 1967.

Markowitz, Harry M., *Portfolio Selection: Efficient Diversification of Investments*. New York: John Wiley & Sons, Inc., 1959.

Sharpe, William F., *Investments*. Englewood Cliffs, N.J.: Prentice-Hall, Inc., 1978.

APPENDIX:
THE EQUILIBRIUM PRICES
OF FINANCIAL ASSETS*

The purpose of this Appendix is to develop a model of financial-asset prices in a closed economy. We begin by assuming that at a moment in time an individual economic unit may hold money, financial assets, and real assets. In addition, it may issue a variety of financial liabilities to finance its holding of assets. Consider a simplified situation with only one financial asset—a fixed-income security—in which an individual economic unit may invest and with only one type of financial liability which it may issue—also a fixed-income security. The asset and the liability are assumed to have a zero coupon rate with interest expressed as a discount. Moreover, we assume no transaction costs, no short sales, and no taxation. The economic unit will attempt to maximize its total utility arising from holding money, the financial asset, and real assets, and from issuing the financial liability. The amounts of the various assets are constrained by the net worth of the economic unit at time t plus the amount of the financial liability it issues.[1] The relationship for the individual economic unit may be expressed as

$$\max Z = U(M, x, R, y) + \lambda(N - M - P_x x - R + P_y y) \qquad (3A\text{-}1)$$

where M = money, expressed in units of one dollar,
and assumed to be nonnegative[2]
x = quantity of the financial asset held at time t
P_x = price of the financial asset at time t
R = market value of real assets held at time t, expressed in units of one dollar, and assumed to be nonnegative
y = quantity of the issued financial liability at time t
P_y = price of the financial liability at time t
N = net worth of economic unit at time t, expressed in units of one dollar
λ = a Lagrangian multiplier

It is evident from Eq. (3A-1) that the individual economic unit will increase its financial liability to finance its holdings of money, the financial asset, and real assets as long as it can increase its total utility by doing so. Assuming no short sales, so that $x \geqslant 0$ and $y \geqslant 0$, the equilibrium conditions

---

*I am grateful to Professor Robert Wilson for helpful comments in the development of this Appendix.

[1]The net worth of an individual economic unit is assumed to be constant. We assume that it will not sell assets, use money, or borrow to consume.

[2]We assume that the economic unit analyzed is not able to issue money.

for the financial asset and liability are

$$\frac{\partial U}{\partial x} - \lambda P_x \leqslant 0, \qquad x \geqslant 0, \qquad x\left[\frac{\partial U}{\partial x} - \lambda P_x\right] = 0 \qquad \text{(3A-2)}$$

$$\frac{\partial U}{\partial y} + \lambda P_y \leqslant 0, \qquad y \geqslant 0, \qquad y\left[\frac{\partial U}{\partial y} + \lambda P_y\right] = 0 \qquad \text{(3A-3)}$$

We assume a one-period horizon and that the future price of the financial asset and the future price of the financial liability at time $t+1$ are subjective random variables.[3] We also assume that the individual economic unit knows the mean and variance of the probability distributions. Thus, the value of the financial asset to rule at time $t+1$ is a random variable with a mean of

$$E = \bar{\rho}_x x \qquad \text{(3A-4)}$$

and a variance of

$$V = \sigma_x^2 x^2 \qquad \text{(3A-5)}$$

where $\bar{\rho}_x$ is the mean of the probability distribution of possible prices one period hence, σ_x^2 is the variance, and x is the quantity of the asset held.

Similarly, the value of the financial liability to rule at time $t+1$ is also a random variable with a mean of

$$e = \bar{\rho}_y y \qquad \text{(3A-6)}$$

and a variance of

$$v = \sigma_y^2 y^2 \qquad \text{(3A-7)}$$

where $\bar{\rho}_y$ is the mean of the probability distribution, σ_y^2 is the variance, and y is the quantity of the liability issued.

We assume that individual economic units may be analyzed as though their utilities with respect to holding and issuing a financial asset and a liability were governed by the mean and variance of the respective probability distributions. We also assume that the price of money and the prices of real assets at time $t+1$ are known with certainty and that these prices are the same as those that prevailed at time t. Thus, we consider only a subset of prices of financial assets and liabilities within which equilibrium can occur. Moreover, we assume that the prices of the financial asset and the financial liability are stochastically independent.

Under conditions (3A-4) through (3A-7), Eqs. (3A-2) and (3A-3) become

---

[3]The immediate subsequent analysis draws upon G. O. Bierwag and M. A. Grove, "On Capital Assets Prices: Comment," *Journal of Finance*, 20 (March, 1965), 89–93; and J. R. Hicks, "Liquidity," *The Economic Journal*, LXXII (December, 1963), 795, 798–802.

$$\frac{\partial U}{\partial E}\frac{\partial E}{\partial x} + \frac{\partial U}{\partial V}\frac{\partial V}{\partial x} - \lambda P_x \leqslant 0, \qquad x \geqslant 0,$$

$$x\left[\frac{\partial U}{\partial E}\frac{\partial E}{\partial x} + \frac{\partial U}{\partial V}\frac{\partial V}{\partial x} - \lambda P_x\right] = 0 \quad (3A\text{-}8)$$

or $\dfrac{\partial U}{\partial E}\bar\rho_x + \dfrac{\partial U}{\partial V}2x\sigma_x^2 - \lambda P_x \leqslant 0, \qquad x \geqslant 0,$

$$x\left[\frac{\partial U}{\partial E}\bar\rho_x + \frac{\partial U}{\partial V}2x\sigma_x^2 - \lambda P_x\right] = 0$$

and $\dfrac{\partial U}{\partial e}\dfrac{\partial e}{\partial y} + \dfrac{\partial U}{\partial v}\dfrac{\partial v}{\partial y} + \lambda P_y \leqslant 0, \qquad y \geqslant 0,$

$$y\left[\frac{\partial U}{\partial e}\frac{\partial e}{\partial y} + \frac{\partial U}{\partial v}\frac{\partial v}{\partial y} + \lambda P_y\right] = 0 \quad (3A\text{-}9)$$

or $\dfrac{\partial U}{\partial e}\bar\rho_y + \dfrac{\partial U}{\partial v}2y\sigma_y^2 + \lambda P_y \leqslant 0, \qquad y \geqslant 0,$

$$y\left[\frac{\partial U}{\partial e}\bar\rho_y + \frac{\partial U}{\partial V}2y\sigma_y^2 + \lambda P_y\right] = 0$$

The equilibrium quantity of the financial asset held is

$$x = \max\left\{\frac{-\dfrac{\partial U}{\partial E}\bar\rho_x + \lambda P_x}{2\dfrac{\partial U}{\partial v}}\middle/ \sigma_x^2, 0\right\}$$

$$= \max\left\{\left(k\frac{\partial U}{\partial E}\bar\rho_x - k\lambda P_x\right)\middle/ \sigma_x^2, 0\right\} \qquad (3A\text{-}10)$$

where $k = -[1/2(\partial U/\partial V)]$ or a measure of risk aversion.

For the risk averter who associates risk with variance, $\partial U/\partial V$ will be negative and k positive; for the risk seeker, $\partial U/\partial V$ will be positive and k negative. We assume, of course, that $\partial U/\partial E > 0$.

For the issuance of a financial liability, the equilibrium quantity is

$$y = \max\left\{\frac{-\dfrac{\partial U}{\partial E}\bar\rho_y - \lambda P_y}{2\dfrac{\partial U}{\partial v}}\middle/ \sigma_y^2, 0\right\}$$

$$= \max\left\{\left(l\frac{\partial U}{\partial E}\bar\rho_y + l\lambda P_x\right)\middle/ \sigma_y^2, 0\right\} \qquad (3A\text{-}11)$$

where $l = -[1/2(\partial U/\partial v)]$, or a measure of risk aversion for the issuance of the financial liability. For the issuer, we assume $\partial U/\partial e < 0$.

Market Equilibrium: Two Economic Units

In a closed economy of two economic units, if unit b is to issue a financial liability, unit a must invest in it. In market equilibrium, $x_a = y_b$, the amount of the financial asset demanded by a must equal the amount that b desires to issue. Thus,

$$\max\left\{\frac{k\dfrac{\partial U}{\partial E}\bar{p}_{xa} - k\lambda_a P}{\sigma_{xa}^2}, 0\right\} = \max\left\{\frac{l\dfrac{\partial U}{\partial e}\bar{p}_{yb} + l\lambda_b P}{\sigma_{yb}^2}, 0\right\} \quad (3A\text{-}12)$$

If both x_a and y_b are greater than zero, the equilibrium price at time t of the financial asset is

$$P = \frac{k\left(\dfrac{\partial U}{\partial E}\right)\left(\dfrac{\bar{p}_{xa}}{\sigma_{xa}^2}\right) - \left(l\dfrac{\partial U}{\partial e}\right)\left\{\dfrac{\bar{p}_{yb}}{\sigma_{yb}^2}\right\}}{\dfrac{k\lambda_a}{\sigma_{xa}^2} + \dfrac{l\lambda_b}{\sigma_{yb}^2}} \quad (3A\text{-}13)$$

Equation (3A-13) suggests that the equilibrium price of the financial asset is a balancing of the expectations, net worths, and utility functions of the economic units involved. If both a and b are risk averters, an assumption we continue throughout this section, the price of the financial asset will vary directly, ceteris paribus, with the means of the probability distributions of prices that a and b expect at time t to prevail at time $t+1$.

The direction of the variation with the variances of the probability distributions will depend upon the relative marginal utilities of units a and b. When $(\partial U/\partial E)\bar{p}_{xa}/\lambda_a = (\partial U/\partial e)\bar{p}_{yb}/\lambda_b$, price does not vary with either the variance of a's probability distribution, σ_{xa}^2, or that of b's, σ_{yb}^2. When $(\partial U/\partial E)\bar{p}_{xa}/\lambda_a < (\partial U/\partial e)\bar{p}_{yb}/\lambda_b$, price varies directly with σ_{xa}^2 and inversely with σ_{yb}^2. Finally, when $(\partial U/\partial E)\bar{p}_{xa}/\lambda_a > (\partial U/\partial e)\bar{p}_{yb}/\lambda_b$, price varies inversely with σ_{xa}^2 and directly with σ_{yb}^2.

If expectations are homogeneous, so that the probability distributions of a and b are the same, Eq. (3A-13) becomes

$$P = \frac{\bar{p}\left(k\dfrac{\partial U}{\partial E} - l\dfrac{\partial U}{\partial e}\right)}{k\lambda_a + l\lambda_b} \quad (3A\text{-}14)$$

For the actual price at time t to equal the mean of the probability distribution of prices expected by a and b at time t to prevail at time $t+1$, $[k(\partial U/\partial E) - l(\partial U/\partial e)]$ must equal $(k\lambda_a + l\lambda_b)$. If $\partial U/\partial E$ and $-\partial U/\partial e$ are less than λ_a and λ_b, respectively, P, the actual price at time t, will be less than $\bar{p}$, the mean of the probability distribution.

Market Equilibrium: Multiple Financial Assets

Clearly, it is inappropriate to consider an economy of only one financial asset and two economic units. An individual economic unit may both invest in and issue a variety of financial assets and liabilities. Thus, Eq. (3A-1) must be expanded as follows:[4]

$$\max Z = U(M, X, R, Y) + \lambda \left(N - M - \sum_i P_i x_i - R + \sum_j P_j y_j \right) \quad (3A\text{-}15)$$

where X = a column vector of x_i, where x_i is the quantity of the ith financial asset

P_i = price of the ith financial asset at time t

Y = a column vector of y_j, where y_j is the quantity of the jth financial liability

P_j = price of the jth financial liability at time t

For the individual economic unit in equilibrium,

$$\frac{\partial U}{\partial x_i} - \lambda P_i \leqslant 0, \qquad x_i \geqslant 0,$$

$$x_i \left[\frac{\partial U}{\partial x_i} - \lambda P_i \right] = 0 \quad (i = 11, \ldots, mn) \tag{3A-16}$$

$$\frac{\partial U}{\partial y_j} + \lambda P_j \leqslant 0, \qquad y_j \geqslant 0,$$

$$y_j \left[\frac{\partial U}{\partial y_j} + \lambda P_j \right] = 0 \quad (j = 1, \ldots, n) \tag{3A-17}$$

---

[4]Again, we assume that R for each economic unit in the economy is nonnegative. However, M for certain units now may be negative. The monetary authorities and commercial banks are assumed to be able to issue money, while all other economic units cannot.

where mn is security n issued by the mth economic unit in the economy. We assume that individual economic units do not issue financial liabilities to themselves. As before, the utilities of holding financial assets and issuing financial liabilities are assumed to be functions of the mean and variance of the probability distributions of prices expected by the economic unit at time t to prevail at time $t+1$. The value of an individual's entire portfolio of financial assets expected at time t to rule at time $t+1$ is a random variable with a mean of

$$E = \sum_{i=11}^{mn} \bar{p}_i x_i \tag{3A-18}$$

where $\bar{p}_i$ is the mean of the probability distribution of prices of the ith financial asset expected to prevail at time $t+1$. The variance of the random variable is

$$V = \sum_{i=11}^{mn} \sum_{q=11}^{mn} x_i x_q \sigma_{iq} \tag{3A-19}$$

where σ_{iq} is the covariance between the price of financial asset i expected at time t to prevail at time $t+1$ and the price of financial asset q expected at time t to prevail at time $t+1$.

In equilibrium, Equation (3A-17) becomes[5]

$$\left[\frac{\partial U}{\partial E} \bar{p}_i + \frac{\partial U}{\partial V} 2 \sum_{q=11}^{mn} x_q \sigma_{qi} - \lambda P_i \right] \leqslant 0, \qquad x_i \geqslant 0,$$

$$x_i \left[\frac{\partial U}{\partial E} \bar{p}_i + \frac{\partial U}{\partial V} 2 \sum_{q=11}^{mn} x_q \sigma_{qi} - \lambda P_i \right] = 0 \qquad (i = 11,\dots,mn) \tag{3A-20}$$

Assuming $\partial U / \partial V < 0$, this equation becomes

$$\left[\sum_{q=11}^{mn} x_q \sigma_{qi} - k \left(\frac{\partial U}{\partial E} \bar{p}_i - \lambda P_i \right) \right] \geqslant 0, \qquad x_i \geqslant 0,$$

$$x_i \left[\sum_{q=11}^{mn} x_q \sigma_{qi} - k \left(\frac{\partial U}{\partial E} \bar{p}_i - \lambda P_i \right) \right] = 0 \qquad (i = 11,\dots,mn) \tag{3A-21}$$

[5]The development of the following equations is similar to that of Bierwag and Grove, *op. cit.*, 93.

In matrix notation, condition (3A-21) becomes[6]

$$X \geqslant 0 \leqslant CX - k\left(\frac{\partial U}{\partial E}\theta - \lambda\Phi\right) \tag{3A-22}$$

where C is the matrix of variances and covariances, X is a column vector of the quantities of financial assets $(x_{11},\ldots,x_{mn})$, where x_{mn} is security n issued by the mth economic unit, θ is a column vector of the means of the probability distributions of prices expected at time t to prevail at time $t+1$ for these financial assets $(\bar{p}_{11},\ldots,\bar{p}_{mn})$, and Φ is a column vector of their actual prices at time, $t(P_{11},\ldots,P_{mn})$. The equilibrium X vector for the individual economic unit may be expressed as

$$X = C^{-1}k\left(\frac{\partial U}{\partial E}\theta - \lambda\Phi\right) + C^{-1}\epsilon \tag{3A-23}$$

where $X \geqslant 0 \leqslant \epsilon$, and where C^{-1} is an inverse matrix.

In addition to investing in financial assets, the individual economic unit may issue a number of different financial liabilities.[7] As with financial assets, the risk averter will issue less of a particular financial liability as its contribution to the total variance of his financial liabilities increases. Assuming $\partial U/\partial v < 0$, the equilibrium Y vector of financial liabilities for the economic unit is

$$Y = T^{-1}l\left(\frac{\partial U}{\partial e}\Psi + \lambda\Phi\right) + T^{-1}\delta \tag{3A-24}$$

where $Y \geqslant 0 \leqslant \delta$, and where T^{-1} is an inverse matrix of variances and covariances, Y is a column vector of the quantities of financial liabilities $(y_{1m},\ldots,y_{nm})$, where y_{nm} is the quantity of security n issued by economic unit m, Ψ is a column vector of the means of the probability distributions of prices expected at time t to prevail at time $t+1$ for the financial liabilities, and Φ is a column vector of their actual prices at time t.

Equilibrium in the market requires that the total quantity of a financial asset demanded equal the quantity of the financial liability an economic unit desires to issue. If X and Y are greater than or equal to zero,

$$\sum_{f=1}^{m} X_f = W \tag{3A-25}$$

[6]We shall follow the notational convention that triplets of the form $[a \geqslant 0, \; b \geqslant 0, \; ab=0]$ are represented as $[a \geqslant 0 \leqslant b]$.

[7]Again, we assume that individual economic units do not issue themselves financial liabilities.

where f is the economic unit investing in a financial asset and W is a column vector of financial liabilities for economic units 1 through m (ordered such that the Y column vector of financial liabilities for economic unit 1 is followed by the Y column for unit 2, and so on all the way through unit m). Substituting Eqs. (3A-23) and (3A-24) into (3A-25), we obtain[8]

$$\sum_{f=1}^{m} C_f^{-1} k_f \left(\frac{\partial U}{\partial E_f} \theta_f - \lambda_f \Phi \right) = T^{-1} l \left(\frac{\partial U}{\partial e} \Psi + \lambda \Phi \right) \qquad (3A\text{-}26)$$

The Φ vector of equilibrium prices of financial assets in the market is

$$\Phi = \frac{\sum_{f=1}^{m} C_f^{-1} k_f \frac{\partial U}{\partial E_f} \theta_f - T^{-1} l \frac{\partial U}{\partial e} \Psi}{\sum_{f=1}^{m} C_f^{-1} k_f \lambda_f + T^{-1} l \lambda} \qquad (3A\text{-}27)$$

According to this equation, the price of a financial asset in the market is an intricate blending of the expectations, net worths, and utility functions of all economic units in an economy. The relative influence of an investor on market price varies according to his net worth, his utility functions, his probability distributions of prices expected at time t to prevail at time $t+1$, the covariances for the financial asset under consideration, and his probability distributions and covariances for all other financial assets and for all financial liabilities he may issue. Because expectations, net worths, and utility functions of the different economic units in the economy differ, determination of the equilibrium price of a financial asset is an extremely complex process.

---

[8]For the right-hand side of the equation, we assume the ordering mentioned earlier, namely, that the Y column vector, or $T^{-1} l [\partial U / \partial e) \Psi + \lambda \Phi]$, for unit 1 is followed by the Y column vector for unit 2, and so on through unit m.

The Term Structure of
Interest Rates

4   In the previous chapter, our focus was on how equilibrium rates of interest were determined for financial instruments in the economy. We analyzed the desired quantities of financial assets held and liabilities issued in relation to the total utility of an economic unit. In this chapter and in the next four, we are concerned with why rates of interest differ for different financial instruments. We shall study the relationship among yields on fixed-income securities by examining the term structure of interest rates in this chapter and the next; the default risk structure in Chapter 6; callability in Chapter 7; and the effect of taxes in Chapter 8. These factors should allow us to explain most of the observed differences in yield for nonequity securities.

The relationship between yield and maturity on securities differing only in length of time to maturity is known as the *term structure of interest rates*. Factors other than maturity must be held constant if the relationship studied is to be meaningful. In practice, this usually means holding constant the degree of default risk. The term structure may be studied graphically by plotting yield and maturity for equivalent-grade securities at a moment in time. Maturity is plotted on the horizontal axis and yield on the vertical axis, and their relationship is described by a yield curve fitted to the observations.[1] An example of a yield curve for default-free Treasury securities is shown in Fig. 4-1. The yield curves in this figure slope upward.

---

[1] For a specification of the term structure of interest rates in terms of prices as opposed to yields, see G. O. Bierwag and M. A. Grove, "A Model of the Structure of Prices of Marketable U.S. Treasury Securities," *Journal of Money, Credit and Banking*, 3 (August, 1971), 605–629.

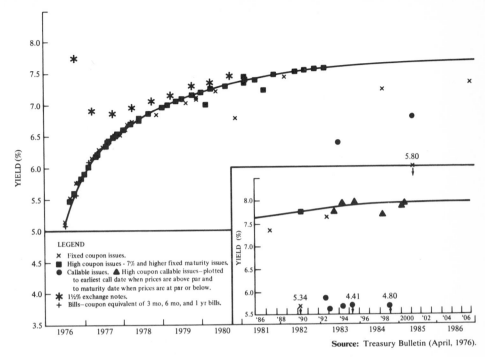

Figure 4-1. Yields on treasury securities, March 31, 1976.

However, yield curves may have other shapes; a more or less downward-sloping curve is illustrated in Fig. 4-2.[2]

Typically, yield curves tend to be upward-sloping during a recession or a period of moderate economic recovery, whereas they are downward-sloping in periods of vigorous economic expansion and inflation. For the period 1970–1976, the range of yields observed for U.S. Treasury securities of various maturities is shown in Fig. 4-3. As can be seen, the range is wide, going from roughly 3 per cent to 10 per cent for short-term securities

[2]The Treasury yield curves shown in Fig. 4-1 and 4-2 are fitted by eye to the data, using high coupon issues. For various methods of mathematically fitting yield curves to data, see Michael E. Echols and Jan Walter Elliott, "A Quantitative Yield Curve Model for Estimating the Term Structure of Interest Rates," *Journal of Financial and Quantitative Analysis,* 11 (March, 1976), 87–114; Kalmon J. Cohen, Robert L. Kramer, and W. Howard Waugh, "Regression Yield Curves for U.S. Government Securities," *Management Science,* 13 (December, 1966), 168–175; J. Huston McCulloch, "Measuring the Term Structure of Interest Rates," *Journal of Business,* 44 (January, 1971), 19–31; and Willard T. Carleton and Ian A. Cooper, "Estimation and Uses of the Term Structure of Interest Rates," *Journal of Finance,* 31 (September, 1976), 1067–1084.

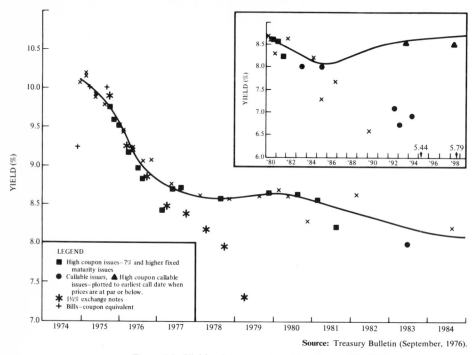

Source: Treasury Bulletin (September, 1976).

Figure 4-2. Yields of treasury securities, August 30, 1974.

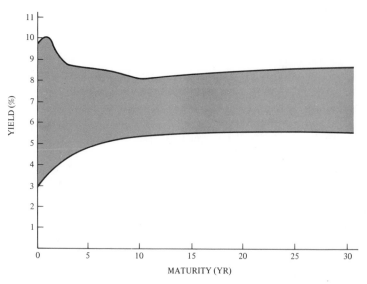

Figure 4-3. Range of yields on U.S. treasury securities by maturity, 1970-1976.

and $5\frac{1}{2}$ per cent to $8\frac{1}{2}$ per cent for long-term securities. Thus, short-term yields fluctuate within a wider band than do long-term yields.

In this chapter, we investigate why the term structure of interest rates has different shapes and different overall levels over time. It generally is agreed that expectations of the future course of interest rates are an important influence; controversy arises, however, as to whether there are other important factors. We begin by considering the unbiased expectations theory, where the term structure is explained entirely by interest-rate expectations. Using this theory as a building block, we then consider rival theories for explaining the yield-maturity relationship on securities differing only in the length of time to maturity.

The Unbiased Expectations Theory

In its basic form, the unbiased expectations theory states that the long-term rate of interest is an unbiased average of the current short-term rate and future short-term rates expected to prevail during the long-term obligation. This theory was first expressed by Irving Fisher and was developed further by Friedrich Lutz.[3] When considering the theory, we find it helpful to transform actual interest rates into forward rates of interest. J. R. Hicks analyzes the term structure as a market for funds similar to the futures market in commodities.[4] For example, a borrower obtains funds from a current spot transaction. At the same time, he executes a forward contract in which he promises to pay back the money at some future date or at a series of future dates. Implied in the term structure at any moment is a set of forward rates:[5]

$$(1 + {}_tR_n)^n = (1 + {}_tR_1)(1 + {}_{t+1}r_{1t})(1 + {}_{t+2}r_{1t}) \cdots (1 + {}_{t+n-1}r_{1t}) \quad (4\text{-}1)$$

where ${}_tR_n$ represents the actual rate of interest at time t on an N-period loan, ${}_tR_1$ is the actual rate on a one-period loan at time t, and ${}_{t+1}r_{1t}$, ${}_{t+2}r_{1t}$, and ${}_{t+n-1}r_{1t}$ are forward rates for one-period loans beginning at times $t+1$, $t+2$, and $t+n-1$, implied in the term structure at time t. Thus, a loan for four years is equivalent to a one-year loan plus a series of forward

---

[3]Irving Fisher, "Appreciation and Interest," *Publications of the American Economic Association*, XI (August, 1896), 23–29, 91–92; and F. A. Lutz, "The Structure of Interest Rates," *Quarterly Journal of Economics*, LV (November, 1940), 36–63.

[4]J. R. Hicks, *Value and Capital*, 2nd ed. (London: Oxford University Press, 1946), pp. 141–145.

[5]This formula assumes implicitly that coupon payments are reinvested, the lender receiving the principal and reinvested interest at maturity. The formula constrasts with one in which all payments are discounted back to present value in accordance with the times when they are to be paid.

contracts, each renewing the loan for a successive year. The formula for deriving the one-period forward rate beginning at time $t+n$, implied in the term structure at time t, is

$$1+_{t+n}r_{1t}=\frac{(1+_tR_{1t})(1+_{t+1}r_{1t})\cdots(1+_{t+n-1}r_{1t})(1+_{t+n}r_{1t})}{(1+_tR_{1t})(1+_{t+1}r_{1t})\cdots(1+_{t+n-1}r_{1t})}$$

$$=\frac{(1+_tR_{n+1})^{n+1}}{(1+_tR_n)^n}$$

$$_{t+n}r_{1t}=\frac{(1+_tR_{n+1})^{n+1}}{(1+_tR_n)^n}-1 \tag{4-2}$$

This formula permits calculation of the implied one-period forward rate for any future period based upon actual rates of interest prevailing in the market at a specific time. The forward rate computed need not be a one-period rate but may span any useful length of time. The calculation of the J-period forward rate beginning at time $t+n$ implied in the term structure at time t is

$$_{t+n}r_{jt}=\sqrt[j]{\frac{(1+_tR_{n+jt})^{n+j}}{(1+_tR_{nt})^n}}-1 \tag{4-3}$$

The forward rate defined in this way is merely a mathematical calculation which has no behavioral meaning. The unbiased expectations theory, however, adds behavioral content to the concept of the forward rate by implying that expected future interest rates are equivalent to the computed forward rates. According to this theory, $_{t+n}\rho_{1t}=_{t+n}r_{1t}$, where ρ_1 is the future one-period rate expected at time t to prevail at time $t+n$. To illustrate, suppose that the actual rates of interest prevailing in the market were 5 per cent for a two-year bond and $5\frac{1}{2}$ per cent for a three-year bond. The implied forward rate on a one-year loan two years hence would be

$$_{t+2}r_{1t}=\frac{(1+_tR_3)^3}{(1+_tR_2)^2}-1=\frac{(1.055)^3}{(1.050)^2}-1=6.50 \text{ per cent} \tag{4-4}$$

Because forward rates are equivalent to expected future rates, the unbiased expectations theory implies that the expected one-year rate two years hence is 6.50 per cent.

Perfect Substitutability

If we ignore transaction costs and assume for the moment that the unbiased expectations theory is valid, securities of different maturity would be perfect expected substitutes for one another. The prospective investor at any time has three choices: He may invest in an obligation having a maturity corresponding exactly to his anticipated holding period; he may invest in short-term securities, reinvesting in short terms at each maturity over his holding period; or he may invest in a security having a maturity longer than his anticipated holding period. In the last case, he would sell the security at the end of the given period, realizing either a capital gain or a loss. According to the unbiased expectations theory, the investor's expected return for any holding period would be the same, regardless of the alternative or combination of alternatives he chose. This return would be a weighted average of the current short-term interest rate plus future short rates expected to prevail over the holding period; this average is the same for each alternative. To illustrate, suppose that the following yields prevailed in the market for default-free treasury securities:

Maturity	Yield
One year	4.00 per cent
Two year	5.00
Three year	6.00
Four year	6.50

The one-year forward rates, implied in this term structure, may be derived with Eq. (4-2) and are found to be

Forward Rate	Per Cent
$_{t+1}r_{1t}$	6.01
$_{t+2}r_{1t}$	8.03
$_{t+3}r_{1t}$	8.02

If an investor has an anticipated holding period of three years, he may invest in the three-year security, from which he will obtain a 6.00 per cent yield to maturity. However, he may also invest in a one-year security and reinvest in one-year securities at maturity over his holding period. In this case, his expected return is

$$\sqrt[3]{(1.0400)(1.0601)(1.0803)} - 1 = 6.00 \text{ per cent} \tag{4-5}$$

or the same as that for investment in the three-year security. Finally, the investor can invest in a four-year security and sell it at the end of three years. If the security had a zero coupon rate, its price would have to be $77.73 (per $100 face value) for it to yield 6.5 per cent to maturity. Moreover, its expected market price at the end of the third year would have to be $92.58 for it to yield 8.02 per cent to maturity. The expected return to the investor can be found by solving the following equation for r:

$$77.73 = \frac{92.58}{(1+r)^3} \tag{4-6}$$

Solving for r, one finds it also to be 6.00 per cent. Thus, the investor could expect to do no better by investing in securities with maturities other than three years. Regardless of the maturity in which an investment is made, the expected return at the time of initial investment is the same. In other words, securities of different maturities are perfect substitutes for one another; one maturity strategy is as good as the next.

Arbitrage Support

Behaviorally, support for the unbiased expectations theory comes from the presence of market participants who are willing and able to exploit profit opportunities. Should forward rates differ from expected future rates, a large enough speculative element is said to exist in the market to drive the two sets of rates together.[6] With different rates, various market participants, sensing opportunity for expected gain, would exploit the opportunity until it was eliminated. As a result, forward rates would be unbiased estimates of expected future rates—i.e., the two would be the same. This does not imply that individual investors calculate expected future short rates mathematically for all maturities and then invest accordingly. As Joseph Conard points out,

> The thought process implied is not one of investors estimating future bill rates and then calculating the yield to be expected on other securities. Rather, it is one of estimating whether it will be more profitable to invest funds over a given period by purchasing shorts and reinvesting as they mature, or by buying a security whose term matches the time funds are to be invested, or by buying a still longer-term issue and considering the capital gain or loss as well as the yield for the period involved.[7]

[6]David Meiselman, *The Term Structure of Interest Rates* (Englewood Cliffs, N.J.: Prentice-Hall, Inc., 1962), p. 10.
[7]Joseph W. Conard, *An Introduction to the Theory of Interest* (Berkeley: University of California Press, 1959), p. 357.

Market participants seek to maximize their return based upon their expectations. By buying and selling securities of different maturities, the individual can, in effect, engage in forward transactions. Such a transaction may consist only of shifting from a six-year bond to a seven-year one, a shift that is marginally the same as making a forward contract for a one-year loan six years in the future.

The action of these market participants seeking profit results at any point in the term structure's being determined solely by expectations about future interest rates. According to the unbiased expectations theory, a horizontal yield curve implies that market participants expect future short rates to be the same as the current short rate. A downward-sloping yield curve signifies that future short rates are expected to fall. Investors are willing to buy long-term securities yielding less than short-term ones because they can expect to do no better by the continual reinvestment in short-term securities. On the other hand, a positively sloped yield curve implies that future short rates are expected to rise. Investors are then unwilling to invest in long-term securities unless the yield is in excess of that on short terms. They would be better off investing in short terms and reinvesting at maturity. With forward rates as unbiased estimates of expected future rates, different maturity securities must be perfect expected substitutes.

The previous discussion does not imply that long-term interest rates are caused by short rates. Instead, all rates depend upon the interaction of present and expected future supply and demand for funds over the span of the loan.[8] For purposes of analysis, expectations are reduced to the short rate. However, it is possible to build a system based upon long-rate expectations without disturbing the role of expectations. Although expectations can be reduced to a short rate, a long rate, or, for that matter, any rate, the important question is whether expectations are operative in determining the term structure. For simplicity, we shall use the one-year rate as the unit of measure; but this does not imply that market participants gear their individual expectations to this unit of measure.

Market Efficiency

The unbiased expectations theory implies that the bond markets are highly efficient. Efficient financial markets are said to exist when security prices reflect all available information which bears on the valuation of the instrument. Implied is that market prices of individual securities adjust very rapidly to new information. As a result, past security-price movements cannot be used to predict future market prices in

[8]Conard, *op. cit.*, p. 301.

such a way as to earn excess profits from these predictions. If excess profits were possible, a sufficient number of market participants with sufficient resources would recognize the opportunity and exploit it. In exploiting it, they would cause security prices to be valued in keeping with all available information. Thus, efficient markets imply an absence of market imperfections that impede the rapid diffusion of information and the rapid reaction to this information by market participants.

In the context of the expectations theory, it is suggested that all relevant information is incorporated in expectations about the future course of interest rates. To be sure, new information can develop, but when it does it is rapidly reflected in revised expectations. Consequently, there does *not* exist the opportunity for arbitrage profits to be earned on the basis of expectations about future interest rates. Once expectations adjust to new information, security prices for various maturities are said to fluctuate randomly about their intrinsic values. As a result, forward rates, which are calculated from these prices, would also fluctuate randomly. Only new information will cause prices to change in one direction or the other, and then the change is extremely rapid.[9] While a necessary condition for the unbiased expectations theory is the efficient markets notion, a combined theory of expectations and liquidity premiums is also consistent with this notion. To this topic we now turn.

Uncertainty and Liquidity Premiums

If complete certainty existed in the market, it is clear that forward rates would be exact forecasts of future short-term interest rates. Arbitrage would make all maturities consistent with expectations, so that the investor would receive the same return regardless of the maturity in which he invested. However, uncertainty raises the question of risk.

Here, Hicks and others argue, the unbiased expectations theory must be modified. The longer the maturity of the security, the greater the risk of fluctuation in value of principal to the investor. Because of this greater risk, investors are said to prefer to lend short. Borrowers, however, are said to prefer to borrow long in order to reduce the risk of inability to meet principal payments. Because of this "constitutional weakness" on the long side, a risk, or liquidity, premium must be offered to induce investors to purchase long-term securities. This premium is over and above the average

[9]For the development of the application of the efficient markets theory to the term structure of market rates, see Richard Roll, *The Behavior of Interest Rates: An Application of the Efficient Market Model to U.S. Treasury Bills* (New York: Basic Books, Inc., 1970); and Thomas J. Sargent, "Rational Expectations and the Term Structure of Interest Rates," *Journal of Money, Credit and Banking,* 4 (February, 1972), 74–97.

of the current short rate and expected future short rates. The premium structure itself is said to correspond to "normal backwardation" in the commodities futures market.[10]

The theory of normal backwardation supposes that the securities market is dominated by risk averters, who prefer to lend short unless offered a premium sufficient to offset the risk of lending long. Forward rates, therefore, would be biased estimates of future interest rates, exceeding them by the amount of the risk, or liquidity, premium. Thus,

$$_{t+n}r_{1t} = {}_{t+n}\rho_{1t} + {}_{t+n}L_{1t} \tag{4-7}$$

where $_{t+n}r_{1t}$, as before, is the forward one-period rate beginning at $t+n$ implied in the term structure at time t, $_{t+n}\rho_{1t}$ is the expected future rate for that period, and $_{t+n}L_{1t}$ is the Hicksian liquidity premium embodied in the forward rate. If risk increases with the remoteness of the future, liquidity premiums would be an increasing function of this distance.

$$0 < {}_{t+1}L_{1t} < {}_{t+2}L_{1t} < \cdots < {}_{t+n}L_{1t} \tag{4-8}$$

The presence of liquidity premiums implies a bias toward upward-sloping yield curves. Indeed, the yield curve could decrease monotonically only when expected future short rates were lower than the current short rate by amounts exceeding their respective liquidity premiums. To illustrate, suppose that market participants expected future short-term interest rates to be the same as the current short rate. On the basis of these expectatations alone, the yield curve would be horizontal. However, with liquidity premiums embodied in forward rates, it would be upward-sloping, as illustrated in Fig. 4-4. If a positive bias does exist in forward rates, securities of different maturities would not be perfect expected substitutes for one another. Investment in a long-term security would provide a higher expected return than would investment in a short-term security and reinvestment in short terms at each maturity. As we shall see, much of the empirical work on the term structure has been directed toward determining whether there is a systematic bias embodied in forward rates of interest.

Proponents of the unbiased expectations theory contend that speculators need not be offered a liquidity premium because they are risk seekers and will search for advantages in the term structure where forward rates exceed corresponding expected future rates. Speculators, together with investors who are indifferent as to maturity, are said to squeeze out any premium that might exist in the forward rate. All maturities then would have expected equal liquidity, according to the unbiased expectations theory.

[10]J. R. Hicks, op. cit., pp. 146–147.

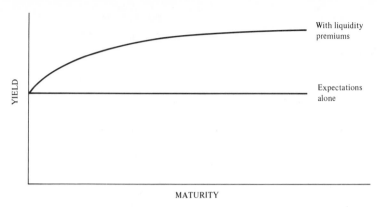

Figure 4-4. Combined expectations and liquidity premiums.

Level of Interest Rates

    If forward rates do contain liquidity premiums, these premiums are not necessarily constant over time. A widely held rationale for investor behavior suggests that risk in the market for loans varies with the overall level of interest rates.[11] If, on one hand, interest rates in general were believed to be high by "recent historical standards" and were not expected to go much higher, risk would seem to be relatively moderate. Risk averters would not be overly fearful about loss of principal. Additionally, those long-term investors primarily interested in certainty of income probably would be actively seeking investments, thereby exerting pressure analogous to a negative liquidity premium.

    If overall interest rates are believed to be low and susceptible to a rise, however, the balance is said to shift in the direction of a greater positive liquidity premium. Risk averters demand a higher liquidity premium in forward rates, anticipating a probable rise in interest rates and a corresponding drop in security prices. It also follows that those long-term investors interested in income certainty are less active in seeking investments at these lower prevailing rates of interest.

    Borrowers, on the other hand, would have an incentive to issue securities if interest rates were low and expected to rise because of the lower interest cost. By the same token, they would want to refrain from borrowing when interest rates were believed to be high and were expected to fall.

    The foregoing discussion implies that the level of interest rates has an influence apart from that of expectations in determining the term structure of interest rates. More specifically, liquidity premiums are said to vary

[11]See John Maynard Keynes, *The General Theory of Employment Interest and Money* (New York: Harcourt, Brace & World, Inc., 1936), pp. 201–202.

inversely with the level of interest rates relative to a level which is considered normal. This behavior would tend to accentuate the positive slope of the yield curve in cyclical troughs and to accentuate the downward-sloping portion of the yield curve at cyclical peaks. In other words, it is implied that interest rates tend to gravitate toward a "normal" level.

The idea of an inverse relationship between liquidity premiums and the level of interest rates contrasts with the view of Reuben A. Kessel, who claims that the relationship is direct.[12] His position stems from the belief that securities serve as money substitutes. Kessel reasons that because a rise in interest rates increases the cost of holding money, this rise also increases the cost of holding money sutstitutes. Because short-term securities are better money substitutes than longer-term securities, an increase in interest rates implies that the opportunity cost of holding short-term securities rises relative to the opportunity cost for holding longer-term, less liquid securities. With the greater relative opportunity cost for holding short-term securities, Kessel holds that yields on longer-term securities increase relative to those on short-term securities. As a result, liquidity premiums embodied in forward rates must rise. On the other hand, when interest rates fall, opportunity costs decline, and as a result liquidity premiums embodied in forward rates fall. Thus, Kessel maintains that liquidity premiums vary directly with the level of interest rates. More will be said about the effect of the level of interest rates on the term structure when we take up empirical testing later in this chapter.

Market Segmentation

A third theory of the term structure suggests that "hedging" or institutional pressures in the market basically determine the shape of the yield curve.[13] Hedging consists of offsetting a liability with an asset of equal maturity, and vice versa. In order to hedge against uncertain fluctuations in prices and yields, financial institutions are said to manage their investments so that the maturity composition of the portfolio matches to some extent the maturity composition of liabilities or prospective commitments.[14] For example, commercial banks typically prefer short- to medium-term maturities because of the nature of their deposit liability and

[12]Reuben A. Kessel, *The Cyclical Behavior of the Term Structure of Interest Rates* (New York: National Bureau of Economic Research, 1965), pp. 25–26.

[13]Some of the first proponents of this theory were J. M. Culbertson, "The Term Structure of Interest Rates," *Quarterly Journal of Economics*, LXXI (November, 1957), 489–504; and Charles E. Walker, "Federal Reserve Policy and the Structure of Interest Rates on Government Securities," *Quarterly Journal of Economics*, LXVIII (February, 1954), 22–23.

[14]For a study of how the maturity desires of different institutional investors differ, see William T. Terrell and William J. Frazer, Jr., "Interest Rates, Portfolio Behavior, and Marketable Government Securities," *Journal of Finance*, 27 (March, 1972), 1–35.

a traditional emphasis upon liquidity. Insurance companies and other lenders with long-term liabilities prefer longer maturities. On the other hand, borrowers are described as relating the maturity of their debt to their need for funds. Thus, a corporation constructing a plant often takes steps to assure that the maturity of the debt it undertakes in financing the plant corresponds to the expected cash flow to be generated from the plant.

The market is characterized as having participants who have preferred maturity ranges in which they operate. Maturities on either side of this range involve risk. Suppose that a long-term investor wishes to remain invested for 15 years. If he invests in a 25-year bond, he is assured of a steady flow of income over his holding period but is uncertain of the value of his investment at the end of the period. Thus, he incurs risk of loss of principal. If he invests in short-term securities, he is assured of receiving his capital in a short period of time but is uncertain of the return he will be able to obtain upon reinvestment. This risk is known as *income risk*. Because the Hicksian liquidity premium model only takes into account the risk associated with a loss of principal, it thereby implies a positive premium that rises with maturity. Income risk, on the other hand, implies a negative risk premium. In the total market for loans, the direction and magnitude of the net risk are what matter. The market segmentation theory suggests that both the principal risk and the income risk are important to market participants and that this double risk causes them to hedge. Thus, market participants are characterized as having definite maturity preferences and as not being likely to move from their preferred maturity ranges.

In its extreme form, the market segmentation theory implies that the rate of interest for a particular maturity is determined solely by demand and supply conditions for that maturity, with no reference to conditions for other maturities. In other words, borrowers and lenders have rigid maturity preferences and do not deviate from these preferences no matter how attractive the yields for other maturities. Thus, the markets for loans would be entirely segmented according to maturity. A more moderate version of the segmentation theory suggests that while investors have preferred maturity "habitats," they will leave these "habitats" if significant premiums or yield inducements are offered on one side or the other.[15] In the absence of sizable inducements, however, investors will stay in their preferred maturity areas, causing the market for loans to be partially segmented.

Overall, then, a market segmentation theory suggests that while forward rates may not equal expected future short rates, the direction and magnitude of the deviations are not known in advance. More specifically,

---

[15]Franco Modigliani and Richard Sutch, "Innovations in Interest Rate Policy," *American Economic Review*, LVI (May, 1966), 178–197.

the deviations are not systematic in the sense of increasing at a decreasing rate with maturity as suggested by the Hicksian liquidity premium theory. In fact, the forward rate minus the expected rate could even be negative for a particular maturity area if strong segmentation existed. Thus, whatever bias exists in forward rates as estimates of future interest rates is largely determined by demand and supply conditions in the particular maturity area involved.

A market segmentation theory on the demand side implies that changes in the relative supplies of various maturity securities affects the term structure of interest rates. For example, if a large relative quantity of long-term debt is offered, long-term rates presumably would rise relative to short-term rates. The opposite presumably would occur if the amount of short-term offerings were large relative to the amount of long-term offerings. Thus, the debt management policies of the Treasury, of municipalities, and of corporations in particular would have an influence on the term structure, assuming market segmentation. This would not occur if the expectations hypothesis entirely governed.

Transaction Costs

In addition to the factors already considered, transaction costs also may have an influence upon the shape of the yield curve.[16] On the basis of number of transactions alone, the long-term investor would find holding long terms more attractive than holding short terms and reinvesting in short terms at maturity. If he had a ten-year holding period, investment in a ten-year bond would involve only one transaction. If he were to invest in one-year securities, there would be ten transactions. In contrast, if the investor had a holding period of only one year, the purchase of a one-year security would involve only one transaction, whereas the purchase of a ten-year security would involve two—the *purchase* and the *sale*.

All other things being the same, each investor would have an incentive to invest in a security with a maturity corresponding to his holding period. If the distribution of holding periods for all investors were shorter in maturity than that of securities outstanding, and if transaction costs per transaction for all maturities were equal, a bias toward a positively sloped yield curve would exist. All other things being the same, longer-term securities would have to yield more than securities which corresponded in maturity to investors' holding periods, to offset the higher total transaction costs for investment in them. The opposite is implied if the distribution of

---

[16]This section draws on Burton G. Malkiel, *The Term Structure of Interest Rates* (Princeton, N.J.: Princeton University Press, 1966), Chapter 5.

holding periods is longer in maturity than the distribution of securities outstanding. The net impact of transaction costs on the term structure depends upon the distribution of holding periods for all investors relative to the maturity distribution of securities outstanding.

Another factor that must be considered, however, is that transaction costs in the secondary market for fixed-income securities tend to increase with the length of time to maturity. One reason for this occurrence is the greater risk of long-term securities to dealers who make the market. The increase in transaction costs with maturity offsets in whole or in part the previously described disadvantage to the long-term investor of investing in short-term securities and reinvesting in short terms upon maturity. On the other hand, the short-term investor must pay substantially higher transaction costs to purchase a long-term security and to sell it at the end of his holding period than he does to purchase a security which corresponds to his holding period.

Malkiel contends that the extremely low transaction costs for very short-term securities make it possible for a long-term investor to buy short terms, as total transaction costs would be very similar to the cost of a single long-term purchase. If this were true, there would be a bias toward an upward-sloping yield curve, all other things being the same. Long-term investors would be roughly indifferent to transaction costs, while short-term investors would prefer short-term securities. Accordingly, there would be buying pressure in favor of short-term securities relative to long-term ones, resulting in a decline of interest rates on short terms relative to long terms and a tendency toward a positively sloped yield curve.

From the standpoint of the borrower, transaction costs (comprised of underwriting and selling costs, legal fees, and inconvenience) make the relative cost per unit of time higher for short-term securities than for long-term securities.[17] Available evidence on corporate and municipal offerings suggests that the percentage cost of flotation varies inversely with the absolute amount of the issue being offered.[18] As a result of these factors, debt financing tends to be "lumpy." Thus, issuers are not inclined to sell bonds with maturities shorter than the time for which they will need the funds.

To the extent that the maturity distribution of debt outstanding is longer than the distribution of desired holding periods of investors, there is a bias toward a positively sloped yield curve. However, if the distribution of debt outstanding is shorter than the distribution of desired holding periods, the effect of transaction costs on the term structure will be neutral, according to Malkiel's analysis. The longer the holding periods of investors, the less the effect of transaction costs on the term structure, all other things remaining the same.

[17]See Lutz, *op. cit.*, pp. 41–46.

[18]See James C. Van Horne, "Implied Fixed Costs of Long-Term Debt Issues," *Journal of Financial and Quantitative Analysis*, 8 (December, 1973), 821–834.

Cyclical Behavior of the Term Structure

In the preceding sections several factors were considered that may influence the term structure of interest rates: expectations, liquidity preference, the level of interest rates, institutional pressures, and finally transaction costs. The support of these various theories must be based upon empirical testing, a subject we shall consider shortly. However, a certain amount of insight can be gained by examining the shape of the yield curve over various interest-rate cycles.[19]

Since World War II, the term structure for Treasury securities has shown the greatest positive slope at cyclical troughs and usually has evidenced a hump and downward slope during the peaks. In Figs. 4-1 and 4-2, early in the chapter, yield curves appearing at a cyclical trough and at a peak were illustrated. If the term structure were determined solely by interest-rate expectations, we might expect the negative yield differential between long- and short-term securities at cyclical peaks to approximate the positive differential at cyclical troughs. Since World War II, however, the positive yield differential between long- and short-term Treasury securities has been quite pronounced at cyclical troughs, the negative differential at cyclical peaks being relatively small in comparison.

This evidence is consistent with an expectations theory modified for liquidity preference. Hicksian liquidity premiums would tend to cushion any downward slope in the yield curve at cyclical peaks and to accentuate the upward slope at the troughs. Thus, the bias would be toward a positively sloped yield curve, holding expectations constant. To illustrate this notion, consider the yield curves in Fig. 4-5. In the upper panel of the figure, a yield curve based upon expectations alone is assumed to be downward-sloping.[20] However, when liquidity premiums are added, the yield curve becomes humped in the early maturities and downward-sloping thereafter. Thus, liquidity premiums cushion the downward slope. The lower panel of the figure depicts a positively sloped yield curve based upon expectations alone. Here, liquidity premiums result in the slope becoming more accentuated. A theory of expectations, modified for liquidity premiums, then is consistent with the observed predominance of yield differentials in favor of long-term over short-term yields.

The cyclical behavior of interest rates has corresponded closely to cyclical fluctuations in business: The troughs appear during recessions and the peaks during periods of prosperity. Over the 1900 to 1960 period, Phillip Cagan found that long-term interest rates tended to lag significantly behind the business cycle prior to World War I.[21] However, this lag

---

[19]For a more detailed analysis of interest-rate cycles, see Kessel, *op. cit.*, Chapters 3 and 4; and Phillip Cagan, *Changes in the Cyclical Behavior of Interest Rates* (New York: National Bureau of Economic Research, 1966).

[20]See Kessel, *op. cit.*, 84–92.

[21]See Cagan, *op. cit.*

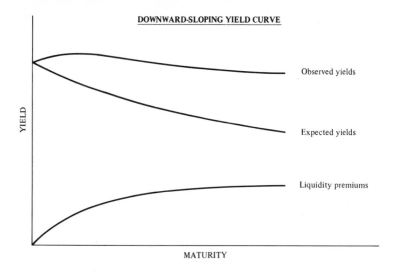

DOWNWARD-SLOPING YIELD CURVE

Observed yields

Expected yields

Liquidity premiums

YIELD

MATURITY

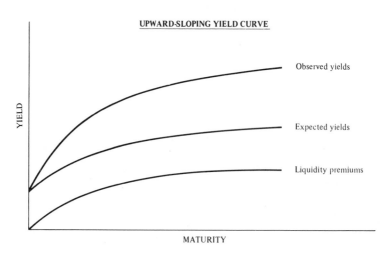

UPWARD-SLOPING YIELD CURVE

Observed yields

Expected yields

Liquidity premiums

YIELD

MATURITY

Figure 4-5. Expectations and liquidity premiums.

became quite small by the fifties. For short-term interest rates, Cagan found a mixture of leads and lags. During cyclical troughs, the short rates examined (Treasury bills, call money, commercial paper, bankers' acceptances, and bank loans) tended to lag the business cycle. In contrast, Treasury bills and call loans tended to lead the business cycle at cyclical peaks. Whereas in the past short-term rates led long-term rates by a significant margin, the turning points have clustered close together in recent years, according to Cagan. In summary, there currently is a strong degree of correspondence between interest-rate cycles and business cycles despite certain small leads and lags.

Empirical Studies of the Various Theories

In recent years there have been numerous empirical tests of the term structure of interest rates. Basically, there are two ways for testing for the effect of expectations: (1) surveying market participants, and (2) deriving expectations from past and present interest-rate data. As an example of the former, Edward J. Kane and Burton G. Malkiel surveyed a large sample of commercial banks, life insurance companies, and non-financial corporations which invest in government securities.[22] The authors found that while many investors formulate specific interest-rate expectations, others do not. Moreover, expectations of future interest rates were found to diverge among respondents. Also, the greater the futurity of the prediction, the greater the divergence. In other words, homogeneous expectations were not the case. A number of other interesting findings were made in this direct inquiry into interest-rate expectations. While the specific theories discussed earlier were not confirmed or denied by this inquiry, it is one of the few direct studies of interest-rate expectations.[23]

Many of the empirical studies dealing with the term structure of interest rates have been concerned either directly or indirectly with whether forward rates are accurate forecasts of future rates of interest. If it can be shown that forward rates correspond exactly to expected future rates, the unbiased expectations theory is supported. However, if the forward rates are found to be systematically biased in a particular direction, the evidence casts light on other theories of the term structure. The difficulty in testing is that expectations by market participants are not directly observable. Consequently, only indirect estimates can be made.

Probably the first empirical contribution of significance on the effect of interest-rate expectations was that of Frederick R. Macaulay.[24] Before the establishment of the Federal Reserve system, both call-money and 90-day loan rates displayed definite seasonal fluctuations. By comparing the movements for the two series of rates, Macaulay found that the time-money seasonal showed clear signs of attempted forecasting of the call-money seasonal. It tended to move ahead of the call-money seasonal, thus anticipating known seasonal movements in the latter. Macaulay concluded that this constituted evidence of relatively successful forecasting. However, when the seasonal factor was removed from both series, the evidence showed no attempted forecasting.

[22]Edward J. Kane and Burton G. Malkiel, "The Term Structure of Interest Rates: An Analysis of a Survey of Interest-Rate Expectations," *Review of Economics and Statistics*, LXIX (August, 1967), 343–355.

[23]A quarterly survey of interest rate expectations of various market participants is reported in the Goldsmith-Nagan, *Bond and Money Market Letter*. Only the consensus forecasts are shown in the *Letter*.

[24]Frederick R. Macaulay, *Some Theoretical Problems Suggested by The Movement of Interest Rates, Bond Yields, and Stock Prices in the United States since 1856* (New York: National Bureau of Economic Research, 1938).

More recent attempts to analyze coincidence in the movement of rates for various maturity securities have used cross-spectral analysis, in which pairs of interest-rate time series are analyzed to estimate the covariance between the two series. Thomas J. Sargent studied these relationships for 1951–1960 Treasury securities.[25] He found in general that longer-term rates led three-month Treasury bill rates and that, in several cases, the lead tended to increase with increases in maturity. This evidence is consistent with an expectations hypothesis which implies that long rates should lead short rates.[26]

One way in which various investigators have tested the unbiased expectations theory is through the use of a perfect-foresight model. Such a model assumes that not only are expectations held by market participants but also, on the average, they are realized. As expectations cannot be determined directly, the *actual* short rate for a given period of time is substituted for the rate predicted at some earlier time to prevail during the given period. If the long rate at the earlier point in time agrees closely with the average of actual short rates, substituted for expected short rates, the unbiased expectations theory is supported. Although this model provides meaningful information, it is not a truly valid test of the unbiased expectations theory. Actual short rates (*ex post*) cannot be substituted for expected short rates (*ex ante*) and then be used to determine long rates.

Another variation of a perfect-foresight model is to compare forward rates, as implied in the term structure at one point in time, with the actual short rates that they attempt to forecast. Regardless of which variation is used, it is not possible to refute the unbiased expectations theory simply by showing that implied forward rates at one point in time were poor forecasts of actual short rates. In essence, a perfect-foresight model tests whether predictions in the market, as evidenced by various forward rates, are accurate. Culbertson employed a variation of the perfect-foresight model in his analysis of holding-period yields in order to determine whether holding-period yields for securities of different maturity were equal for all holding periods. For his analysis, he used Treasury bills and long-term Treasury bonds for one-week and three-month holding periods during 1953. He concluded that the wide differences in holding-period yields that he found rendered the unbiased expectations theory inadequate

[25]Thomas J. Sargent, "Interest Rates in the Nineteen Fifties," *Review of Economics and Statistics*, L (May, 1968), 164–172.

[26]In contrast, C. W. J. Granger and H. J. B. Rees, "Spectral Analysis of the Term Structure of Interest Rates," *Review of Economic Studies*, XXXV (January, 1968), 67–76, found for British government securities that the one-year rate tended to lead longer-term rates for long-run frequencies. This lead pattern was not evident for shorter frequencies. The data employed were computed by J. A. G. Grant using varying maturities for the 1924–1962 period. As these data are subject to question (see footnotes 35 and 36 of this chapter), so may be the results of the cross-spectral analysis.

as a means of explaining the term structure of interest rates.[27] Like Culbertson, W. Braddock Hickman also used a perfect-foresight model. He compared actual rates with previously predicted rates, implied in the term structure, and concluded that forward rates did not forecast actual rates successfully.[28]

While it is reasonable to have errors in prediction, we would not expect these errors to take on any pattern or bias. Over a sufficient period of time, errors should be distributed randomly about the actual rate, with forward-rate forecasts being above actual rates about as often as below them. However, if a bias in one direction were evident, it would suggest that factors other than pure expectations were at work in the determination of the term structure. In computing the average forecasting error, one should try to eliminate any secular trend. Otherwise, the bias in forecasting error may be attributable to this trend.

Error-Learning Models

Until the work of David Meiselman, comprehensive empirical testing of interest-rate expectations was lacking.[29] Previous work had been hampered by an absence of direct evidence concerning expectations. Meiselman, however, maintained that since expectations were reflected already in the term structure, they could be analyzed. He asserted that interest-rate expectations are revised whenever previously held expectations prove to be in error. An error-learning model was introduced, which implied that expectations are a function of past and present learning experiences. As new information is received, expectations are adjusted in keeping with the learning process. In his model, changes in one-year forward rates are related to errors in forecasting the actual one-year rate of interest:

$$_{t+n}r_{1t} - _{t+n}r_{1t-1} = a + b(Et_1) + u \qquad (4\text{-}9)$$

where u is the error term, and Et_1 is the one-year forecasting error, defined as

$$Et_1 = {}_tR_{1t} - {}_tr_{1t-1} \qquad (4\text{-}10)$$

[27]John M. Culbertson, "The Term Structure of Interest Rates," *Quarterly Journal of Economics* LXXI (November, 1957), 499–502, 507–509.

[28]W. Braddock Hickman, "The Term Structure of Interest Rates: An Explanatory Analysis," Mimeographed Manuscript (New York: National Bureau of Economic Research, 1942).

[29]See Meiselman, *op. cit.*

Thus, the forecasting error is the actual one-year rate in period t minus the forward-rate forecast of a one-year loan beginning at time t embodied in the term structure one year earlier.

Market participants are assumed to adjust their expectations in keeping with unanticipated changes in the actual one-year rate of interest. Using the Durand basic corporate bond yield data, Meiselman computed the degree of correlation between forecasting errors and changes in various forward rates for the period 1900–1954.[30] He assumed a linear function and found that correlation coefficients ranged from 0.95 for changes in forward rates one year from t to 0.59 for changes eight years from t. In addition to high positive association, Meiselman found that the regression coefficients reflecting the responsiveness of dependent-variable changes to forecasting errors decreased with the remoteness in the future of the dependent variable.

Moreover, the constant terms were not found to differ significantly from zero. Meiselman argued that constant-term values were measures of liquidity premiums; and since these values did not differ significantly from zero, liquidity premiums were not present in the term structure. From this evidence, it was inferred that a significant portion of the variation in expectations could be explained by the one-year forecasting error.[31] Meiselman contended that the evidence was consistent with the unbiased expectations theory, in which forward rates are equivalent to expected future short rates.[32]

It is important to recognize that the error-learning model by itself does not corroborate the equality of forward rates and expected future short rates. Although Meiselman maintained that forward rates were unbiased estimates of expected future short rates, he was unable to substantiate this equality adequately in attempting to refute the Hicksian liquidity-premium theory. This logical weakness was brought out by John H. Wood in his review of Meiselman's book. Wood demonstrated that

[30]In the Durand annual basic yield data, estimates are made of the yield on the highest-grade corporate bonds. David Durand, *Basic Yields on Corporate Bonds, 1900–1942* (New York: National Bureau of Economic Research, 1942); and David Durand and Willis J. Winn, *Basic Yields of Bonds, 1926–1947: Their Measurement and Pattern* (New York: National Bureau of Economic Research, 1947).

[31]Stanley Diller, "The Expectations Component of the Term Structure," in Jack M. Guttentag, ed., *Essays on Interest Rates,* Vol. 2 (New York: National Bureau of Economic Research, 1971), 411–433, tested the error-learning model, together with an extrapolation model and a return-to-normality model to see which provided the most accurate forecast. Using the 1900–1954 Durand basic corporate yield curve data, he concluded that the three models were actually all variants of a general extrapolative formula because the results for the three models were statistically indistinguishable.

[32]Meiselman, *op. cit.,* pp. 21–22, 45–47, 60.

constant terms not significantly different from zero are consistent theoretically with forward rates as biased estimates of expected future rates.[33] Moreover, the 1900–1954 Durand yield-curve data do not entirely substantiate the equality of forward rates with expected future short rates. If we use a perfect-foresight model and subtract the actual rate obtained from the forward-rate forecast, we find that the average forecasting error over the 1900–1954 period was positive and increased from 0.14 for $_{t+1}r_{1t}$ to 0.83 for $_{t+9}r_{1t}$.[34] Thus, the evidence suggests that forward rates were biased and high estimates of actual rates, consistent with the Hicksian liquidity-premium theory. This finding, however, must be qualified for a moderate downward trend in interest rates over the period. If this trend were unanticipated, expected short rates would exceed the actual rates that they attempted to forecast.

The error-learning model has been applied to other sets of data. Using data on British government securities, J. A. G. Grant concluded that the error-learning model could not be used to predict successfully changes in expectations.[35] However, his data consisted of observations connected by straight lines, resulting in a jagged rather than a fitted yield curve. In light of these data, the lack of results is not surprising. A. Buse also used data on British government securities but worked with yield curves that were fitted. He found that the error-learning model was of value in explaining changes in expectations. Moreover, he discovered that the constant terms

---

[33]John H. Wood, "Expectations, Errors, and the Term Structure of Interest Rates," *The Journal of Political Economy*, LXXI (April, 1963), 165–166. If liquidity premiums are embodied in the forward rate, Meiselman's error-learning model, Eq. (4-9), becomes

$$(_{t+n}\rho_{1t}+_{t+n}L_{1t})-(_{t+n}\rho_{1t-1}+_{t+n}L_{1t-1})=a+b[_tR_{1t}-(_t\rho_{1t-1}+_tL_{1t-1})]$$

Rearranging them gives

$$(_{t+n}\rho_{1t}-_{t+n}\rho_{1t-1})+(_{t+n}L_{1t}-_{t+n}L_{1t-1})=a+b[_tR_{1t}-(_t\rho_{1t-1}+_tL_{1t-1})]$$

where, as before, ρ is the expected future rate, and L is the liquidity premium. We can see readily that when the expectations are realized and the constant term is zero, the first term above equals $b[_tR_{1t}-_t\rho_{1t-1}]$, and we are left with

$$(_{t+n}L_{1t}-_{t+n}L_{1t-1})=b(_tL_{1t-1})$$

Thus, a constant term of zero can be consistent with the presence of liquidity premiums embodied in forward rates.

[34]See James Van Horne, "The Expectations Hypothesis, the Yield Curve, and Monetary Policy: Comment," *Quarterly Journal of Economics*, LXXIX (November, 1965), 666–668.

[35]J. A. G. Grant, "Meiselman on the Structure of Interest Rates: A British Test," *Economica*, XXXI (February, 1964), 36–38.

differed significantly from zero, supporting the notion of liquidity preference.[36]

Using U.S. Treasury yield-curve data for the 1954–1963 period, I
tested certain variations of the error-learning model.[37] A high degree of
positive correlation was discovered between changes in forward rates and
errors in forecasting the one-year actual rate. For all of the forward rates
tested, the Treasury data resulted in a higher degree of correlation than
that which Meiselman had found using the Durand basic corporate yield
data. The results supported the notion that interest-rate expectations are
important in explaining the term structure of interest rates and that they
are revised systematically when actual rates of interest differ from those
that had been anticipated.

Furthermore, all of the constant-term values were significantly different from zero, a finding that supports the hypothesis that forward rates of
interest contain both expectations and a liquidity premium. Moreover, the
pattern of intercepts on the horizontal axis for the various regression
studies was consistent with liquidity premiums increasing at a diminishing
rate with the remoteness of the future period.[38]

---

[36] A. Buse, "Interest Rates, the Meiselman Model and Random Numbers," *Journal of Political Economy*, 75 (February, 1967), 49–62.

[37] James Van Horne, "Interest-Rate Risk and the Term Structure of Interest Rates," *Journal of Political Economy*, 73 (August, 1965), 344–351.

[38] If liquidity premiums are embodied in forward rates and no other factors exist that would cause the regression line not to pass through the origin, we have from footnote 33 in this chapter:

$$(_{t+n}\rho_{1t} - _{t+n}\rho_{1t-1}) + (_{t+n}L_{1t} - _{t+n}L_{1t-1}) = b[_tR_{1t} - (_t\rho_{1t-1} + _tL_{1t-1})]$$

We assume that $(_{t+n}\rho_{1t} - _{t+n}\rho_{1t-1})$ is revised relative to $_tR_{1t} - _t\rho_{1t-1}$. If $_{t+n}L_{1t}$ equaled $_{t+n}L_{1t-1}$, then the constant term would be $b(_tL_{1t-1})$. The intercept on the horizontal axis would be $-_tL_{1t-1}$ and would be the same for all regression studies.

Now, if $_{t+n}L_{1t-1}$ exceeds $_{t+n}L_{1t}$, the regression line and the constant term would be lower than if the two liquidity premiums were equal. If liquidity premiums increase with the remoteness of the future period, $_{t+n}L_{1t-1}$ would exceed $_{t+n}L_{1t}$. Thus, the intercept on the X, or horizontal, axis would be

$$X \text{ intercept} = -_tL_{1t} - \frac{_{t+n}L_{1t} - _{t+n}L_{1t-1}}{b}$$

If the negative X intercepts increased in magnitude with successive regression studies, this occurrence would be consistent with liquidity premiums increasing at a diminishing rate with the remoteness of the future period. The X intercepts in the results for the Treasury securities followed this pattern through $n=8$ for the dependent variable, after which point ($n=9$ through 11) they leveled off and fluctuated. Thus, the evidence on Treasury securities for the 1958–1963 period was consistent with liquidity premiums, increasing at a diminishing rate.

Additional Tests for Liquidity Premiums

Kessel, in his investigation of the term structure, also tested for the presence of liquidity premiums in forward rates of interest. Using error-learning models similar to those discussed, he analyzed the residuals in the regression results when the models were applied to the Durand yield-curve data and to certain Treasury bill data. In both cases, he found systematic positive bias in forward rates as estimates of expected future interest rates—i.e., they were high estimates.[39] In addition to this evidence and his theoretical argument for liquidity preference, Kessel pointed out that on the average, long-term yields on government securities exceeded short-term yields over the period 1921–1961. This finding also might be considered to be consistent with liquidity preference, if one isolated the effect of trend.

Joseph W. Conard and Jonathan Freudenthal conducted tests similar to those of Kessel and some additional ones.[40] While their results supported the idea that liquidity premiums are embodied in forward rates, they found that these premiums diminish rapidly beyond intermediate-term maturities. Moreover, they observed that if the depression of the 1930s and World War II and the post-war period of the 1940s were treated as abnormal, average yields on short-term securities over the period 1900–1961 exceeded those on long-term securities. Clearly, yield curves observed through the 1920s were not consistent with liquidity preference in the market for loans. Only since 1930 has there been a predominance of positively sloped yield curves.

In an extensive study of liquidity premiums in the post-accord period (after 1952), J. Huston McCulloch also found evidence of positive premiums.[41] However, liquidity premium estimates for long-term forward loans were very inaccurate. For very short forward loans, however, the estimates increased at a decreasing rate and eventually leveled off. Also, McCulloch found no evidence of liquidity premiums varying over the sample period.

Tests Concerning the Level of Rates

If liquidity premiums are embodied in forward rates and affect the term structure it is important to know whether they vary with the level of interest rates over time. Recall from our earlier discussion that one

[39]See Kessel, *op. cit.*, pp. 12–25; Chapter 3.

[40]See Joseph W. Conard, *The Behavior of Interest Rates* (New York: National Bureau of Economic Research, 1966), Chapter 7.

[41]J. Huston McCulloch, "An Estimate of the Liquidity Premium," *Journal of Political Economy*, 83 (January–February, 1975), 95–119.

rationale for investor behavior suggests that risk premiums vary inversely with the level of interest rates, relative to an accustomed (normal) interest-rate range. If interest rates were low and were expected to rise, investors would be expected to demand a relatively high risk premium; the opposite would hold if interest rates were high and were expected to fall.

Malkiel tested the hypothesis that the spread between long-term and short-term interest rates varied inversely with the deviation of the long rate from the midpoint of a "normal" range.[42] After transforming the variables to eliminate certain statistical problems, he tested this hypothesis on the Durand basic corporate yield data for the period 1900–1942. The results were found to support the hypothesis of an inverse relationship, thereby supporting indirectly the idea of an inverse relation between liquidity premiums and the level of interest rates relative to a normal level. He also tested for the combined periods 1900–1942 and 1951–1965, and again the results were found to be consistent with an inverse relationship between the yield spread and the level of interest rates.

Charles R. Nelson also found an inverse relationship between estimated liquidity premiums and the level of interest rates.[43] Using the 1901–1958 Durand yield data, Nelson computed liquidity premiums as the difference between forward rates and corresponding conditional expectations implied by a linear process model. Regressing these liquidity premium estimates against the level of interest rates and also against an index of business confidence, he found the regression coefficients for both to be negative and significant. He holds that this is consistent with the level of interest rates being a measure of risk since downward movements are bounded at zero.

Finally, certain empirical studies I undertook supported in some measure the notion that liquidity premiums vary inversely with the level of interest rates. In these studies, changes in forward rates were made a function of the one-year forecasting error and of the deviation of the level of forward rates from an accustomed level.[44] The results of regression studies using Treasury yield-curve data over the period 1958–1963 indicated alteration of forward rates depending upon whether interest rates were believed to be high or low with respect to an accustomed interest-rate range. These results, like the other two, were consistent with the idea of an inverse relationship between liquidity premiums and the relative level of interest rates.

[42]Malkiel, *op. cit.*, Chapter 3.

[43]Charles R. Nelson, *The Term Structure of Interest Rates* (New York: Basic Books, Inc., 1972), Chapter 6.

[44]Van Horne, "Interest-Rate Risk and the Term Structure of Interest Rates"; Richard Roll, "Comment," *Journal of Political Economy*, 74 (December, 1966), 629–632; and Van Horne, "Reply," *Journal of Political Economy* 74 (December, 1966), 633–635.

Others, however, have found evidence of a positive relationship between estimated liquidity premiums and the level of interest rates. These results are consistent with Kessel's theory that short-term securities are close substitutes for money. When interest rates rise, people incur a higher opportunity cost in holding money and seek short-term securities instead. This causes short-term rates to decline relative to long-term rates—all other things the same—which, in turn, increases the slope of the yield curve and forward rates. On the basis of tests of Treasury bills, Kessel discovered a positive relationship between estimated liquidity premiums and the level of interest rates.[45]

Conard and Freudenthal also tested the effect of the level of interest rates on the behavior of 28-day Treasury bills, three-month bills, one-year government securities, and five-year government securities.[46] They regressed "last year's forward rate minus today's actual rate" against both the change in interest rates and the level of interest rates for various periods during 1958–1963. They found that when changes in interest rates were held constant, the influence of level of interest rates on the dependent variable was positive for 28-day and three-month Treasury bills, but negative for one-year and five-year government securities. Their findings confirmed Kessel's results of a positive relationship between the level of interest rates and liquidity premiums for Treasury bills.

In somewhat the same vein, Phillip Cagan tested for the effect of the level of interest rates using Treasury bills over the 1951–1965 period.[47] These results also were consistent with a significant positive relationship between estimated liquidity premiums and the level of interest rates. When Cagan tested for the effect with Treasury bonds ranging in maturity from $2\frac{1}{2}$ to 10 years, however, the relationship was not found to be statistically significant, although it was positive.

Tests Concerning the Market Segmentation Theory

If the term structure is compartmentalized into separate markets according to maturity, a change in the relative supply or demand in one of these markets should change the shape of the yield curve. For example, an increase in the relative supply of long-term securities should result in an increase in long rates relative to short rates, if all other things remain the same. The reason is that because of institutional specialization

[45]Kessel, *op. cit.*, pp. 22–26.
[46]Joseph W. Conard, *op. cit.*, pp. 83–85, 100–105.
[47]"Liquidity Premiums on Government Securities," in Jack M. Guttentag and Phillip Cagan, *Essays on Interest Rates*, Vol. 1 (New York: National Bureau of Economic Research, 1969), pp. 223–242.

investors in other markets can be induced into long-term bonds only with the offer of higher interest rates.

One of the most interesting studies regarding market segmentation is that by Franco Modigliani and Richard Sutch, who employed a variant of an expectations model.[48] They labeled their theory "preferred habitat"; supposedly it blended the theories of expectations, liquidity preference, and market segmentation. The authors suggested that expectations of future interest rates are formed on the basis of past interest rates. However, there are two distinct influences in this history: the recent trend in interest rates and the "normal" level of interest rates based upon long-run experience. These influences were first used by Frank deLeeuw[49] to explain the term structure, and his work inspired the Modigliani-Sutch study. The first influence suggests that over the short run market participants expect current trends in interest rates to continue. The second influence is that interest rates are expected to regress toward a normal level.

Modigliani and Sutch combine both of these expectational influences into a single expectations variable, using an Almon lag structure, which resembles an inverted U. The yield differential between long and short rates is made a function of a moving average of past short rates, weighted according to the lag structure. Their model is

$$R_{Lt} - R_{st} = a - b_0 R_{st} + \sum_{i=1}^{16} B_i R_{st-i} + u \qquad (4\text{-}11)$$

where R_{Lt} is the long rate at time t, R_{st} is the short rate, the third term on the right represents the lag structure, and u is the error term. Through various tests, the most suitable lag was found to be 16 quarters. It should be noted that there is no explicit use of future rates; Modigliani and Sutch relate current spot rates to current and past spot rates. The data used to test the model was based on three-month Treasury bills and the average yield on long-term government securities, both on a quarterly basis over the 1952–1961 period. Overall, the model was successful in explaining the ex post differential between the long and short rates; the regression coefficients had the right sign and size. Because the lag structure had the predicted shape, the authors concluded that interest-rate expectations are based upon both of the influences discussed above.

In their first paper (*American Economic Review*, 1966), Modigliani and Sutch added various supply variables to their model and found that these

---

[48]Modigliani and Sutch, op. cit., 178–197; and Modigliani and Sutch, "Debt Management and the Term Structure of Interest Rates: An Empirical Analysis of Recent Experience," *Journal of Political Economy*, 75 (Supplement: August, 1967), 569–589.

[49]Frank deLeeuw, "A Model of Financial Behavior," in *Brookings Quarterly Econometric Model of the United States Economy* (Chicago: Rand McNally & Company, 1965), pp. 465–530.

variables exerted no significant influence upon the spread between the long and the short rate. Also, the authors tested for the effectiveness of "Operation Twist." This operation involved efforts by the Federal Reserve and Treasury in the early sixties to affect the shape of the yield curve. The idea was to keep short-term interest rates fairly high for balance-of-payments purposes while keeping intermediate and long rates at moderate levels to stimulate domestic growth. In essence, "Operation Twist" affected the maturity composition of the marketable government debt held by the public. Modigliani and Sutch used parameter estimates for the period 1952–1961 to extrapolate for the period 1962–1965. Because these predictions were accurate, they concluded that "Operation Twist" had little effect upon the term structure.

Elsewhere (*Journal of Political Economy*, 1967), they tested in more depth the influence of maturity composition of the debt upon the spread between the long and short rates. Their approach consisted of adding various maturity-composition variables to their expectations model and seeing if the effect of these additions was significant. Using their original data for the 1952–1965 period, they failed to uncover any significant relationships between the yield spread and the various measures of maturity composition. However, when the authors used average yield-to-maturity data prepared by Morgan Guaranty Trust Company, they discovered significant and positive relationships between the yield spread of intermediate and very short rates and variations in the supply of debt in the intermediate range. However, these relationships were not evident for yield spreads involving longer-term securities. Even from the evidence for intermediate-term securities, the term structure could not be considered very responsive to changes in the maturity composition of the debt.

In another related study, Steven W. Dobson, Richard C. Sutch, and David E. Vanderford undertook an extensive analysis of those predictive models of the term structure which were based on past interest-rate observations.[50] In all, eight distinct models were analyzed: (1) inertial, where the best estimate of the next period's rate is the present period's rate; (2) a linear regressive model where interest rates are expected to return to some "normal" rate over time; (3) a weighted regressive model where the "normal" rate is taken to be a weighted average of past rates with the most recent past rates being weighted more heavily; (4) a simple extrapolative model where the change in next period's rate is a constant fraction of recent changes in rates; (5) a weighted extrapolative model where the extrapolation is based on a weighted average of recent past rates; (6) an extrapolative-regressive model which combines both elements

[50]Steven W. Dobson, Richard C. Sutch, and David E. Vanderford, "An Evaluation of Alternative Empirical Models of the Term Structure of Interest Rates," *Journal of Finance*, 31 (September, 1976), 1035–1065.

as in the Modigliani-Sutch version described above; (7) an adaptive model, such as the error-learning models examined earlier, based on an exponential weighting of past rate observations; and (8) a convex model where expectations are taken to be a weighted average of multiple adaptive expectation processes.

All of the models examined endeavor to predict future interest rates based on a linear combination of past yield observations. The general form of the models was

$$R(m)_t = \sum_{t=0}^{\infty} \beta(m)_i r_{t-i} + Y(m)_t \qquad (4\text{-}12)$$

where $R(m)_t$ = the yield on an m-period loan at time t
$\beta(m)_i$ = a distributed lag function for past rates
r_{t-i} = the one-period rate at time $t - i$
$Y(m)_t$ = the liquidity premium for a m-period loan.

The summation of the $\beta(m)_i$ should equal 1. Thus, Eq. (4-12) is a general expression which states that the term structure is determined primarily by expectations of future short-term interest rates which, in turn, are determined by a distributed lag on past short rates, plus a liquidity premium which is assumed to be constant.

Dobson, Sutch, and Vanderford go on to test the various models using monthly U.S. Treasury security data for the period 1954–1968. The authors evaluate the results both in terms of the internal consistency of the models and in terms of their explanatory power. Of the eight models, only the linear, the simple extrapolative, and the extrapolative-regressive models were found to be internally consistent, with the latter having the most explanatory power. When unconstrained, the estimated distributed lag exhibits a humped shape. The authors contend that this shape is consistent with the pattern predicted by the Modigliani and Sutch version of the extrapolative-regressive model. As this model performs better than the various other models of expectations formation for the data examined, the authors contend that there is little advantage to using a more restrictive model.

In contrast, Michael J. Hamburger and Cynthia A. Latta tested the performance of the preferred habitat model relative to the performance of a simpler model in which the best estimate of next period's short-term rate is the current rate.[51] (The former model uses a weighted average of past interest rates in relation to the current rate as an estimate of the future rate.) Using Treasury bill and long-term government security data for the

[51] Michael J. Hamburger and Cynthia A. Latta, "The Term Structure of Interest Rates: Some Additional Evidence," *Journal of Money, Credit and Banking*, 1 (February, 1969), 71–83.

period 1951–1965, the authors found that the simpler model performed better. They concluded that past interest rates, as used in the preferred habitat model, are not very useful in predicting future interest rates.[52]

Another means for investigating the effect of maturity composition on the term structure, as well as on interest-rate expectations, is the use of term structure models to predict future rates. If investors base expectations of future rates on a weighted average of current and past rates in the manner suggested by Modigliani and Sutch, one might expect such a weighted average to have predictive value. Using this argument, Alan Kraus compared the ability of four basic models to forecast rates for Treasury bonds of different maturity for varying lengths of time into the future.[53] One model employed a simple "inertia" hypothesis; it used the current spot rate as a prediction of the future rate. A second model was based on fitting a relation between the *ex post* "forecast error" (forward rate less the subsequently observed actual rate) and the current spot rate. The third model, based on the Modigliani and Sutch research, used a fitted relation between the subsequently observed actual rate and a series of current and past spot rates. The fourth model incorporated the maturity composition of the debt as well as relative holdings of Treasury securities by various investor groups as variables for explaining the *ex post* forecast error.[54]

The statistical estimation of parameters for the models was made using monthly data for the period 1960–1964. For each model, the parameter values obtained were used in conjunction with monthly data for the 1965–1967 period to generate a series of predicted rates. The predictions were then compared with the actual 1965–1967 rates. The results Kraus obtained indicated that the model which incorporated the maturity composition and holdings of Treasury securities had more predictive value than the other three models. Although the model based on the Modigliani and Sutch research produced high multiple correlation coefficients during its fitting to the 1960–1964 data, it gave the least accurate predictions of rates during the 1965–1967 period. Kraus interpreted these results as evidence for the effect of maturity composition on the term structure.

John S. McCallum tested the unbiased expectations theory, the combined expectations and liquidity premium theory, and the preferred habitat

[52]For a similar test in which the same conclusion is reached, see Llad Phillips and John Pippenger, "Preferred Habitat vs. Efficient Market: A Test of Alternative Hypotheses," *Review of the Federal Reserve Bank of St. Louis*, (May, 1976), 11–19.

[53]Alan Kraus, "The Forecasting Accuracy of Models of the Term Structure of Interest Rates" (Ph.D. dissertation, Cornell University, 1969).

[54]In attempting to avoid the difficulties in using either broad maturity categories or average length of time to maturity as measures of maturity composition, Kraus employed a large number of very narrow maturity categories, with coefficients estimated by using a variation of the Almon distributed-lag procedure.

model using Canadian Government securities over the 1948–1968 period.[55] He analyzed the risk-return pattern for a three-month holding period for various maturity securities ranging from 3 to 240 months. While risk, as measured by the standard deviation and the beta, increased with maturity of the instrument held, the expected return did not. (The latter was "corrected" for unanticipated interest rate movements.) Expected returns were found to rise with maturity up to three years, but to level off thereafter. McCallum interprets this evidence as consistent with the preferred habitat theory. He reasons that investors were not able to acquire premiums commensurate with risk across the spectrum of maturities available. Only in the early maturities were they able to obtain such premiums. While this interpretation may follow from the evidence, there is some problem in adjusting for unanticipated changes in interest rates. As a result, the return data employed may not reflect true expected returns.

In another study bearing on the market segmentation theory, William T. Terrell and William J. Frazer, Jr., examine the maturity profiles of Treasury securities held by various institutional investors.[56] Over the 1960–1969 period, they found the maturity distributions of holdings by the various groups to be quite stable. Moreover, each institution was found to have a somewhat unique maturity structure. As the level of interest rates changed markedly over the sample period, the authors interpreted their findings as consistent with liquidity, as well as hedging motives being major determinants of the maturity distribution of portfolios held by institutional investors. Such stable maturity preferences are a necessary condition for market segmentation on the demand side. However, the real question is whether such preferences have a significant influence on the term structure of interest rates or whether the effect of these preferences can be offset by the overlap and speculative behavior in the market. On this issue, the study is silent.

In contrast, J. W. Elliott and M. E. Echols analyze Treasury yield data for direct signs of discontinuities which might support the notion of market segmentation.[57] Using piecewise linear regression, the method detects the presence of statistically significant discontinuities in the yield curve. For the 1964–1972 period, approximately half the months showed some evidence of significant yield curve discontinuities. In turn, this is said to be evidence of market segmentation. Moreover, a high percentage of the discontinuities appeared in maturities of eight years or more. The results

[55]John S. McCallum, "The Expected Holding Period Return, Uncertainty and the Term Structure of Interest Rates," *Journal of Finance*, 30 (May, 1975), 307–323.

[56]Terrell and Frazer, *op. cit.*

[57]J. W. Elliott and M. E. Echols, "Market Segmentation, Speculative Behavior, and the Term Structure of Interest Rates," *Review of Economics and Statistics*, LVIII (February, 1976), 40–49.

for the under eight year range, where banks are heavily involved as investors, by and large were consistent with a fully arbitraged structure of yields. Where speculative activity in the early maturities appears sufficient to ensure a continuity of yields, the authors consider market segmentation to be a factor in the later maturities.

Tests Involving the Efficient Markets Theory

There has been a handful of tests of the expectations theory within the context of the efficient markets notion. While most of these tests bear on topics that we have already discussed, it is useful to consider all the tests at once. In one interesting study, Thomas J. Sargent tests whether the Durand basic corporate yield curve data are consistent with the notion of an efficient market.[58] Using spectral analysis, he finds forward rates calculated from the data to have serial dependence. This, of course, is not consistent with the efficient markets theory. He then turns to examine the Meiselman model results in light of this finding. Sargent suggests that the regression coefficients for the error-learning model tests are biased downward.

In testing Treasury bills over the 1949–1964 period, Richard Roll found that while their price behavior was serially dependent, the dependence was due primarily to changes in expected returns.[59] As a result, he concluded that the bill market conforms closely to the efficient markets theory. With respect to the various term structure theories, Roll found that the unbiased expectations hypothesis performed poorly; most of the tests rejected it. The empirical results were consistent with positive liquidity premiums being embodied in forward rates of interest. However, the estimated premiums were not found to increase monotonically with maturity. The evidence also was consistent with a stationary market segmentation hypothesis. In interpreting these results, it is important to note that the data consisted only of Treasury bills of up to 12 weeks maturity for the 1949–1964 sample period and for up to 25 weeks for the 1959–1964 subperiod.

Michael J. Hamburger and Elliott N. Platt also used Treasury bill data (1961–1971) to test the efficient markets theory.[60] They tried to determine if the market employs all publicly available information in forming interest-rate expectations. Past bill rate movements were not

[58]Sargent, *op. cit.*
[59]Roll, *op. cit.*
[60]Michael J. Hamburger and Elliott N. Platt, "The Expectations Hypothesis and the Efficiency of the Treasury Bill Market," *Review of Economics and Statistics*, LVII (May, 1975), 190–199.

found to be significant in explaining interest-rate expectations. As with the Roll evidence, the Treasury bill market would appear to be efficient. Hamburger and Platt went on to test income and various monetary variables. The evidence again was found to be consistent with the efficient markets theory. Moreover, forward rates appeared to bear little relationship to the actual rates they were supposed to forecast. Again this is consistent with market efficiency.

Michael E. Echols and Jan Walter Elliott also tested the premise that interest-rate expectations are largely based on economic variables.[61] Using a loanable funds framework, the authors suggested that nominal interest rates are composed of a real component, a component for inflationary expectations, and a component related to the efficiency of the market equilibrium adjustments. More specifically, the nominal rate of interest is said to be a function of aggregate output, the government deficit or surplus, net exports, past inflation, the money supply, the level of interest rates, the price of bonds, the ratio of investment by banks to investment by insurance companies, and to the relative supplies of various maturity government securities. The use of yield curve data for U.S. Treasury securities for up to 20 years maturity over the 1964–1972 period demonstrated that a high degree of forward rate explanation was evident. Most of the variables behaved as expected, which together with the high explanatory power was said to support a rational expectations model of interest-rate expectations. However, forward rates were related positively to the level of interest rates, which is consistent with the Kessel thesis. The institutional demand variable was significant for maturities up to ten years, whereas the bond supply variable was not significant. The former finding supports the notion of a degree of market segmentation existing in the market for government securities. Thus, factors other than rational expected future rates were said to affect forward rates.

All of the empirical tests reviewed in this section involve an efficient markets framework. With the exception of tests involving use of the Durand basic corporate yield data, they suggest that interest-rate expectations are largely in accord with the notion of efficient markets and embody available information. However, there still is some indication of market segmentation effects, although these effects may not be large.

Empirical Studies: Summary

In summary, the evidence cited, plus additional empirical studies, attests to the importance of interest-rate expectations in the term structure of interest rates. The market appears to forecast the future course

[61]Michael E. Echols and Jan Walter Elliott, "Rational Expectations in a Disequilibrium Model of the Term Structure," *American Economic Review*, LXVI (March, 1976), 28–44.

of interest rates, and these forecasts are important in determining the yield on securities. In addition, empirical studies dealing with post-World War II data suggest that forward rates are biased and high estimates of expected future rates. Market participants during this period appear to have gauged their activities on expected future interest rates, plus a liquidity premium.

However, the evidence is mixed as to the shape of the liquidity premium profile. Most of the studies examined suggest that premiums increase at a decreasing rate with maturity, for the early maturities. However, the evidence for later maturities differs as to whether liquidity premiums increase monitonically with maturity. Moreover, the evidence is mixed as to whether liquidity premiums vary inversely or directly with the level of interest rates. Some studies show an inverse relationship; others show a direct relationship, whereas still other studies show no relationship at all.

The market-segmentation theory has been tested by studying the effect of shifts in the relative supply of various maturity securities and shifts in maturity demand by institutional investors. While certain studies suggest that market segmentation has some influence on the term structure, other studies point out no effect at all. On balance, the empirical evidence on market segmentation would have to be regarded as largely inconclusive. If there is an effect, the effect is of only moderate importance. That is, the term structure is largely determined by factors other than market segmentation. However, the impact of market segmentation could vary over time, being more important at some times than at others. We simply need to learn more about market imperfections.

Finally, we reviewed various studies which tested the efficient markets theory as applied to interest-rate expectations. This theory suggests that all available information is embodied in market prices for debt instruments and that prices adjust very rapidly to new information. Most of the studies examined suggested that debt markets are efficient.

It must be pointed out that the empirical evidence examined in this section is by no means all inclusive. Constraints of space have kept us from reviewing many other studies that have been undertaken. It should also be mentioned that the generalizations presented in this summary are not universally accepted. The question of what theory best explains the term structure of interest rates remains a subject of heated controversy.

Summary

The term structure of interest rates portrays the yield-maturity relationship on securities differing only in length of time to maturity. A number of theories attempt to explain the term structure. The unbiased expectations theory states that expectations of the future course of interest rates are the sole determinant. When the yield curve is upward-sloping, this theory implies that market participants expect interest rates to rise in the future; a downward-sloping curve implies that interest rates are expected to fall; while a horizontal yield curve suggests that interest rates are not expected to change. The theory also implies that securities of different maturity are perfect expected substitutes in the sense that the expected return is the same. Most analyses have used the unbiased expectations theory as a point of departure.

A combined theory of expectations and liquidity preference suggests that market participants generally prefer to lend short unless offered a premium sufficient to offset the risk of lending long. Thus, the term structure would be affected not only by expectations but also by Hicksian liquidity premiums. If risk increases with the remoteness of the future, these premiums would be an increasing function of remoteness. The presence of liquidity premiums in the term structure implies a bias toward upward-sloping yield curves. These premiums may vary with the level of interest rates; the theory that interest rates return to some normal level suggests an inverse relationship between liquidity premiums and the level of interest rates whereas a money-substitute theory implies a direct relationship.

A market segmentation theory implies that maturity preferences of lenders and borrowers are so strong that they usually will not leave their preferred maturity range to take advantage of yield differentials. As a result, there are a number of different markets, and interest rates are said to be determined by the interaction of supply and demand in each. Because these markets are separate, interest rates for various maturities would be largely independent of one another. In addition to the theories considered, transaction costs may also influence the yield curve. We examined the role of these costs and their effect on the term structure. We also analyzed cyclical changes in the term structure over time.

The empirical studies examined give considerable insight into the factors that best explain the term structure. Most of the studies show the important role of expectations of the future course of interest rates. In recent years, there has been evidence of a bias toward positively sloped yield curves, all other things being the same. This evidence is consistent with an expectations theory modified for liquidity preference. Whether or not liquidity premiums vary with the level of interest rates is an inconclusive topic, as some evidence is consistent with an inverse relationship whereas other evidence is consistent with a direct relationship. In addition, tests of the market segmentation theory have been mixed. If there is an effect here, it would appear to be modest. Finally, tests of the efficient markets notion suggest that the Treasury securities market is efficient.

SELECTED REFERENCES

Cagan, Phillip, *Changes in the Cyclical Behavior of Interest Rates*. New York: National Bureau of Economic Research, 1966.

Conard, Joseph W., *Introduction to the Theory of Interest*. Berkeley: University of California Press, 1959.

_____, *The Behavior of Interest Rates*. New York: National Bureau of Economic Research, 1966.

Culbertson, John M., "The Term Structure of Interest Rates," *Quarterly Journal of Economics*, LXXI (November, 1957), 485–517.

Dobson, Steven W., Richard C. Sutch, and David E. Vanderford, "An Evaluation of Alternative Empirical Models of the Term Structure of Interest Rates," *Journal of Finance*, 31 (September, 1976), 1035–1065.

Elliott, J. W., and M. E. Echols, "Market Segmentation, Speculative Behavior, and the Term Structure of Interest Rates," *Review of Economics and Statistics*, LVIII (February, 1976), 40–49.

_____, "Rational Expectations in a Disequilibrium Model of the Term Structure," *American Economic Review*, LXVI (March, 1976), 28–44.

Guttentag, Jack M., ed., *Essays on Interest Rates*, Vol. 2. New York: National Bureau of Economic Research, 1971.

_____, and Phillip Cagan, eds., *Essays on Interest Rates*, Vol. 1. New York: National Bureau of Economic Research, 1969.

Hicks, J. R., *Value and Capital*, 2nd ed. London: Oxford University Press, 1946.

Kessel, Reuben H., *The Cyclical Behavior of the Term Structure of Interest Rates*. New York: National Bureau of Economic Research, 1965.

Lintner, John, "Interest Rate Expectations and Optimal Forward Commitments for Institutional Investors," *Explorations in Economic Research*, 3 (Fall, 1976), 445–520.

Lutz, Friedrich A., "The Structure of Interest Rates," *Quarterly Journal of Economics*, LV (November, 1940), 36–63.

Malkiel, Burton G., "Expectations, Bond Prices, and the Term Structure of Interest Rates," *Quarterly Journal of Economics*, LXXVI (May, 1962), 197–218.

_____, *The Term Structure of Interest Rates*. Princeton, N.J.: Princeton University Press, 1966.

McCulloch, J. Huston, "An Estimate of the Liquidity Premium," *Journal of Political Economy*, 83 (January–February, 1975), 95–119.

Meiselman, David, *The Term Structure of Interest Rates*. Englewood Cliffs, N.J.: Prentice-Hall, Inc., 1962.

Michaelsen, Jacob B., *The Term Structure of Interest Rates*. New York: Intext Educational Publishers, 1973.

Modigliani, Franco, and Richard Sutch, "Innovations in Interest Rate Policy," *American Economic Review*, LVI (May, 1966), 178–197.

_____, "Debt Management and the Term Structure of Interest Rates: An Empirical Analysis of Recent Experience," *Journal of Political Economy*, 75 (Supplement: August, 1967), 569–589.

Nelson, Charles R., *The Term Structure of Interest Rates*. New York: Basic Books, Inc., 1972.

Roll, Richard, *The Behavior of Interest Rates: An Application of the Efficient Market Model to U.S. Treasury Bills*. New York: Basic Books, Inc., 1970.

Sargent, Thomas J., "Rational Expectations and the Term Structure of Interest Rates," *Journal of Money, Credit and Banking*, 4 (February, 1972), 74–97.

Telser, L. G., "A Critique of Some Recent Empirical Research on the Explanation of the Term Structure of Interest Rates," *Journal of Political Economy*, 75 (Supplement: August, 1967), 546–561.

Terrell, William T., and William J. Frazer, Jr., "Interest Rates, Portfolio Behavior, and Marketable Government Securities," *Journal of Finance*, 27 (March, 1972), 1–35.

Van Horne, James, "Interest-Rate Expectations, the Shape of the Yield Curve, and Monetary Policy," *Review of Economics and Statistics*, XLVIII (May, 1966), 211–215.

_____, "Interest-Rate Risk and the Term Structure of Interest Rates," *Journal of Political Economy*, 73 (August, 1965), 344–351.

_____, "The Expectations Hypothesis, the Yield Curve, and Monetary Policy: Comment," *Quarterly Journal of Economics*, LXXIX (November, 1965), 664–668.

_____, and David A. Bowers, "The Liquidity Impact of Debt Management," *The Southern Economic Journal*, XXXIV (April, 1968), 526–537.

Wood, John H., "Expectations, Error, and the Term Structure of Interest Rates," *Journal of Political Economy*, 71 (April, 1963), 160–171.

The Term Structure and
Interest Rate Expectations:
Some Extensions

5 In the previous chapter we explored the basic theories of the term structure of interest rates as well as empirical studies related to these theories. In this chapter we extend our examination to two topics that exert an important influence on the term structure and interest-rate expectations. The first is the effect of the coupon rate on the "true" maturity of a debt instrument and on fluctuations in its price. In this regard, we investigate the use of a duration measure as a substitute for maturity. The second topic is the impact of inflation on interest-rate expectations. In particular, this topic has received wide attention in recent years. While we are unable to explore the complete spectrum of work that has been done, we hope to impart an understanding of the major issues.

The Coupon Effect

We know in general that the longer the maturity of a debt instrument, the greater the change in price that accompanies a shift in interest rates.[1] However, price changes also are dependent on the level of coupon. This phenomenon is known as the *coupon effect*. It is important to distinguish the coupon effect that arises from the mathematics of interest rates, to be studied here, from that which arises from the call feature

[1] For a thorough examination of the mathematics of bond price movements, see Sidney Homer and Martin L. Leibowitz, *Inside the Yield Book* (Englewood Cliffs, N. J.: Prentice-Hall, Inc., 1972); and Burton G. Malkiel, "Expectations, Bond Prices, and the Term Structure of Interest Rates," *Quarterly Journal of Economics*, LXXVI (May, 1962), 197–218.

and/or the taxation of interest income and capital gains at different rates. Our concern in this chapter is solely with the former. The latter effects are explored in Chapters 7 and 8, when we deal with callability and taxability.

Sensitivity of Price Changes to Coupons

For a given bond, the lower the coupon the greater the price change for a given shift in interest rates. This is illustrated in Table 5-1 for 20- and 30-year bonds. In the upper part of the table, a yield increase is assumed, while in the lower part a yield decline is assumed to occur. We

Table 5-1. Change in Price Accompanying Shift in Yield for Various Coupons

	YIELD INCREASE FROM 7.11% TO 9.48% (BY 1/3)	
Coupon	Price Decline 20-Year Bond	Price Decline 30-Year Bond
8%	−20.64%	−23.09%
7	−21.14	−23.50
6	−21.76	−24.03
5	−22.54	−24.73
4	−23.58	−25.72
3	−25.00	−27.20
2	−27.07	−29.69
1	−30.40	−34.61
0	−36.57	−49.48

	YIELD DECREASE FROM 9.48% TO 7.11% (BY 1/4)	
Coupon	Price Increase 20-Year Bond	Price Increase 30-Year Bond
8%	26.01%	30.02%
7	26.80	30.71
6	27.81	31.62
5	29.10	32.86
4	30.85	34.62
3	33.33	37.36
2	37.13	42.19
1	43.67	52.93
0	57.64	97.92

Source: Sidney Homer and Martin L. Leibowitz, *Inside the Yield Book* (Englewood Cliffs, N. J.: Prentice-Hall, Inc., 1972), Chapter 3.

see that the lower the coupon the more sensitive market prices are to changes in yields. The reason for this is that with lower coupons more of the total return to the investor is reflected in the principal payment at maturity as opposed to interest payments which are discounted from nearer coupon dates. In effect, then, the "true" maturity is longer for a low coupon bond than it is for a high coupon one. Put another way, the investor realizes his return sooner with a high coupon bond than he does with a low coupon one.

In general, the further in the future an income stream, the more volatile its present value when changes in the discount rate occur.[2] To illustrate, suppose we had a contract to pay us $100, 15 years hence, and another contract to pay us $100, 30 years hence. If the present discount rate were 8 per cent and we wished to know the effect of changes in it to 10 per cent and to 6 per cent, the following present values would be relevant:

Discount Rate	Present Value 15-Year Contract	Present Value 30-Year Contract
10%	$23.94	$ 5.73
8	31.52	9.94
6	41.73	17.41

Percentagewise, the changes in the two contracts are as follows:

Change in Discount Rate	15-Year Contract	30-Year Contract
From 8% to 10%	−24.05%	−42.35%
From 8% to 6%	32.39	75.15

The point of these examples is to emphasize that one gets very different market price movements, depending on the coupon rate. With high coupons, the total income stream (interest and principal payments) is closer to realization than it is with low coupons. The nearer the income stream, the less the present value effect, given a change in yields. Thus, even if high and low coupon bonds have the same maturity, the low coupon bonds tend to be more volatile.

[2]For very long maturities, volatiltiy can decrease with further increases in maturity. We will investigate this situation shortly.

The Duration Measure and its Implications

The problems associated with different market price movements for different coupon rates has led many to question the usefulness of maturity as a measure of the length of a financial instrument. Instead they suggest the use of another measure—the duration of a security, which is simply a weighted average of the times in the future when interest and principal payments are to be received. This measure was first proposed in 1938 by Frederick R. Macaulay in his monumental study of yields.[3] Macaulay made it clear that the number of years to maturity is an inadequate measure of the time element of a loan because it tells only the date of final payment and omits essential information about the size and date of payments that occur before the final payment.

To remedy this problem, he proposed the following measure, which was called *duration*.

$$D = \frac{\displaystyle\sum_{t=1}^{n} \frac{C_t(t)}{(1+r)^t}}{\displaystyle\sum_{t=1}^{n} \frac{C_t}{(1+r)^t}} \tag{5-1}$$

where C_t = interest and/or principal payment at time t

(t) = length of time to the interest and/or principal payments

n = length of time to final maturity

r = yield to maturity

The denominator of the equation is simply the present value of the stream of interest and principal payments. The numerator is the present value, but the interest and principal payments are weighted by the length of the interval between the present time and the time that the payment is to be received.

To illustrate, suppose that we wished to determine the duration of a bond with 4 years to maturity which had an 8 per cent coupon rate and yielded 10 per cent to maturity. Assume also that interest payments are received at the end of each of the four years and that the principal payment is received at the end of the fourth year. The duration of the

[3]Frederick R. Macaulay, *Some Theoretical Problems Suggested by the Movements of Interest Rates, Bond Yields, and Stock Prices in the United States since 1856* (New York: National Bureau of Economic Research, 1938). For a historical review of the duration measure, see Roman L. Weil, "Macaulay's Duration: An Appreciation," *Journal of Business*, 46 (October, 1973), 589–592.

bond would be:

$$D = \cfrac{\dfrac{\$80(1)}{(1.10)} + \dfrac{\$80(2)}{(1.10)^2} + \dfrac{\$80(3)}{(1.10)^3} + \dfrac{\$1,080(4)}{(1.10)^4}}{\dfrac{\$80}{(1.10)} + \dfrac{\$80}{(1.10)^2} + \dfrac{\$80}{(1.10)^3} + \dfrac{\$1,080}{(1.10)^4}} = 3.56 \text{ years}$$

If the coupon rate were 4 per cent, its duration would be:

$$D = \cfrac{\dfrac{\$40(1)}{(1.10)} + \dfrac{\$40(2)}{(1.10)^2} + \dfrac{\$40(3)}{(1.10)^3} + \dfrac{\$1,040(4)}{(1.10)^4}}{\dfrac{\$40}{(1.10)} + \dfrac{\$40}{(1.10)^2} + \dfrac{\$40}{(1.10)^3} + \dfrac{\$1,040}{(1.10)^4}} = 3.75 \text{ years}$$

If the coupon rate were zero, however, duration would be:

$$D = \cfrac{\dfrac{\$1,000(4)}{(1.10)^4}}{\dfrac{\$1,000}{(1.10)^4}} = 4 \text{ years}$$

Thus, if there is but a single payment, duration equals maturity. For bonds with interim coupon payments, however, duration is always less than maturity.

In examining Eq. (5-1), one can visualize also that the higher the interest rate, as denoted by r, the shorter the duration. For the bond with an 8 per cent coupon, 4 years to maturity, and a 10 per cent yield, we determined earlier that its duration was 3.56 years. Suppose now that its yield to maturity were 6 per cent instead of 10 per cent. The duration of the bond then would be:

$$D = \cfrac{\dfrac{\$80(1)}{(1.06)} + \dfrac{\$80(2)}{(1.06)^2} + \dfrac{\$80(3)}{(1.06)^3} + \dfrac{\$1,080(4)}{(1.06)^4}}{\dfrac{\$80}{(1.06)} + \dfrac{\$80}{(1.06)^2} + \dfrac{\$80}{(1.06)^3} + \dfrac{\$1,080}{(1.06)^4}} = 3.59 \text{ years}$$

Thus, the lower the interest rate, the longer the duration of the instrument, all other things remaining the same.

In summary, duration can be considered a measure of the average life of a debt instrument on a present-value basis.[4] That is, it is a weighted average of the present values of coupon and principal payments.

The Relationship between Duration and Maturity

For bonds selling at their par value or above, duration increases at a decreasing rate with maturity. For bonds selling at a discount, duration increases at a decreasing rate up to some fairly long maturity and then declines. Lawrence Fisher and Roman L. Weil calculate duration measures for various discount bonds and their results for bonds yielding 8 per cent to maturity are shown in Table 5-2.[5] We see that for 2, 4, and 6 per cent coupon rates, duration declines with maturity after 50 years. For the 8 per cent coupon bond selling at par, duration increases with maturity at a decreasing rate throughout. Thus, for bonds selling at a discount, duration eventually declines with maturity. However, this occurs many years out. As most bond issues have original maturities of 30 years or less, duration increases with maturity for most of the bonds we observe. However, it is important to recognize that for discount bonds this need not be the case.

Table 5-2. Duration for Bonds Yielding 8 Per Cent (Semiannual Coupons)

Years to Maturity	COUPON RATE			
	2%	4%	6%	8%
1	0.995 year	0.990 year	0.985 year	0.981 year
5	4.742	5.533	4.361	4.218
10	8.762	7.986	7.454	7.067
20	14.026	11.966	10.922	10.292
50	14.832	13.466	12.987	12.743
100	13.097	13.029	13.006	12.995
Perpetual	13.000	13.000	13.000	13.000

Source: Lawrence Fisher and Roman L. Weil, "Coping with the Risk of Interest-Rate Fluctuations: Returns to Bondholders from Naive and Optimal Stratigies, " *Journal of Business*, 44 (October, 1971), 418.

[4]See Michael H. Hopewell and George G. Kaufman, "Bond Price Volatility and Term to Maturity: A Generalized Respecification," *American Economic Review*, LXIII (September, 1973), 749–753.
[5]Lawrence Fisher and Roman L. Weil, "Coping with the Risk of Interest-Rate Fluctuations: Returns to Bondholders from Naive and Optimal Strategies," *Journal of Business*, 44 (October, 1971), 418.

It has also been shown that bond prices vary proportionally with duration.[6] That is, the maximum variation in price occurs when duration is the greatest. In contrast, the relation between bond prices and maturity is more complicated. For example, volatility for a discount bond can actually decline as maturity increases, because duration is declining. Other times, volatility increases with maturity, but at a decreasing rate. The lack of a linear mathematical relation between bond prices and maturity has led many people to use duration instead.

Implications for Investment

One implication of the above involves investment strategy. When an investor has a specific holding period in mind, he can be assured that his realized return will equal the yield promised at the time of investment only if he invests in a bond with a duration equal to his holding period.[7] Two types of risk are germane: *price risk* and *coupon reinvestment risk*. The former is the risk that with changing interest rates the bond will need to be sold at a different price from what was expected. Of course, price risk could be reduced to zero if bonds were selected whose maturity equaled the intended holding period. However, there still would be *coupon reinvestment risk*. This is the risk associated with reinvesting the coupons received at yields that are different from the yield of the bond when it was purchased.

Together these two risks represent the total risk associated with a bond investment for an investor with an intended holding period. Moreover, these risks vary in opposite directions. An increase in interest rates reduces the price of a bond, but increases the yield possible from reinvestment of coupons. In contrast, a decline in interest rates results in a price increase, but lowers the yield possible from coupon reinvestment. Thus, the two types of risk are offsetting. To "immunize" a bond investment from subsequent interest-rate changes, these two risks must be balanced in such a way as to be completely offsetting. This occurs only when the duration of the bond(s) investment equals the desired holding period.[8] As the duration of a coupon bond is less than its maturity, this means that the bond's maturity will exceed one's holding period if an immunization strategy is followed.

[6]Hopewell and Kaufman, *op. cit.*, 751–752.

[7]See G. O. Bierwag and George C. Kaufman, "Coping with the Risk of Interest Rate Fluctuations: A Note," *Journal of Business*, forthcoming, on which the subsequent discussion is based.

[8]For proof of this statement, see Bierwag and Kaufman, *ibid*; and Paul A. Samuelson, "The Effect of Interest Rate Increases on the Banking System," *American Economic Review*, XXXV (March, 1945), Appendix B. For simulation of immunization strategies as well as proof of the proposition, see Fisher and Weil, *op. cit.*, 420–431.

If maturity equaled or were less than the intended holding period, price risk would be zero but coupon reinvestment risk would be positive.[9] On the other hand, if the duration of the bond exceeded one's holding period, reinvestment risk would be zero but price risk would be positive. Only when the duration of the investment equals the intended holding period is the investment immunized. At that point, a change in interest rates causes the return from price and the return from coupon reinvestment to change by equal amounts, but in opposite directions. As a result, price risk and coupon reinvestment risk cancel out, and the yield realized equals the yield promised at the time of initial investment. While frequent reference is made to reducing risk to zero by investing in maturities equal to one's intended holding period, it is clear that this strategy does *not* reduce total risk to zero; only price risk is reduced.[10] To reduce total risk to zero, one must take account of both price and coupon reinvestment risks and equate the duration of the investment with the desired holding period.

The Yield-Duration Relationship

In the analysis of the term structure of interest rates, the yield-maturity relationship is studied on securities differing only in the length of time to maturity. Now one might ask would not it be more appropriate to study the yield-duration relationship? When bonds used in the drawing of yield curves have significantly different coupons, the results may be distorted when yield–maturity alone is examined. To illustrate, consider the following bonds:

Coupon	Maturity (yr)	Yield	Coupon	Maturity (yr)	Yield
7%	1	$6\frac{1}{2}$%	4%	15	$8\frac{1}{4}$%
8%	2	8%	3%	20	8%
7%	3	9%	4%	25	8%
5%	5	$9\frac{1}{2}$%	3%	30	8%
9%	10	9%			

When these yields are plotted against maturity, we obtain the yield curve shown in the upper panel of Fig. 5-1. As seen, it is humped and

[9]When maturity is shorter than the intended holding period, the roll over is assumed to be made in such a way that the final maturity on the roll over occurs at the end of the holding period.

[10]The exception is a zero coupon bond.

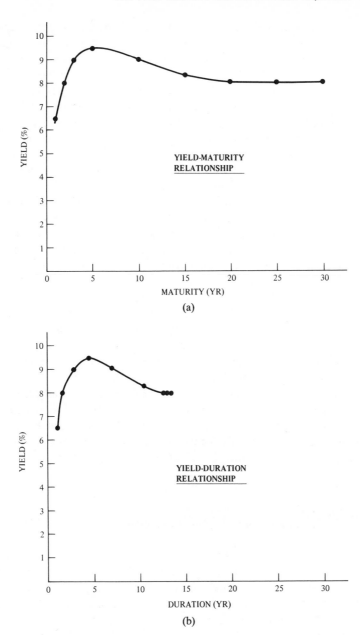

Figure 5-1. Yield-maturity and yield-duration relationships.

downward-sloping through year 20, after which it becomes level. Because of the differing coupon rates, we know the picture will change if duration instead of maturity is used. When we calculate duration for each of the bonds and plot the yield-duration relationship, we see in the lower portion of Fig. 5-1 that the results are changed. The yield curve is even more humped and downward-sloping. Moreover, the last three issues have essentially the same duration, and, overall, the yield curve is much shorter than in the upper panel. Recall that with discount bonds, duration does not necessarily increase with maturity.

While the coupon effect is of moderate importance in affecting the shape of the yield curve, it has pronounced implications for the calculation of forward rates. From the previous chapter we know that the calculated forward rate is extremely sensitive to the two yields used for the end points. If the two bonds used have widely different coupons, the forward rate computed is likely to have little economic meaning. Suppose, for example, a 20-year bond had a high coupon while a 19-year bond had a low coupon and we wished to compute the implied forward rate for a 1-year loan that will be made 19 years in the future. It could well be that the high coupon, 20-year bond had a shorter duration than the 19-year low coupon bond. As a result, its yield might be lower if investors geared their activities to duration instead of maturity.[11] The forward rate calculated under these circumstances has little economic meaning and should not be used in testing theories about the term structure of interest rates.

In summary, when bond issues outstanding have significantly different coupon rates, the yield-maturity relationship as well as the implied forward rates may be distorted. In these cases, it is important to consider the coupon effect. By computing the yield-duration relationship, one can gain more consistent and rational insight into the term structure of interest rates.

Inflation and Interest-Rate Expectations

The second extension to our consideration of the term structure of interest rates has to do with inflation. Because interest and principal payments are expressed in terms of money and because the monetary standard changes over time, the real rate of return on a security can differ from its money, or nominal, return. For example, if the nominal rate on a 10-year bond were 9 per cent and prices increased at a compound rate of 5 per cent over this time span, the real return on investment would

[11]See Hopewell and Kaufman, *op. cit.*, 752.

be approximately 4 per cent. The real and nominal rates are the same only if prices are stable over the length of the loan contract.

The Fisher Effect

Many years ago, Irving Fisher expressed the nominal rate of interest on a bond as the sum of the real rate, the rate of price change expected over the life of the instrument, and the cross product.[12] This relationship has become known as the *Fisher effect*, and it has dominated the theoretical and empirical consideration of the inflation-interest rate issue. To explore it in more detail, we define R' as the nominal rate of interest, R as the real rate, and α as the expected rate of inflation over the life of the bond. For simplicity, suppose further that the bond is only one period in length, and that there is no default risk. For each $1 in loans, the lender supposedly will require at the end of the period

$$1 + R' = (1 + R)(1 + \alpha) \tag{5-2}$$

This merely states that the lender requires a nominal rate of interest sufficiently high so that he can earn the real rate of interest. Put another way, the lender must be compensated for the anticipated increase in price level that will make the dollars received in repayment at the end of the period of less value than the dollars loaned. If we rearrange Eq. (5-2), R', the nominal rate of interest, must be

$$R' = R + \alpha + R\alpha \tag{5-2}$$

For moderate rates of anticipated inflation, it is customary to ignore the cross product term, as it is unimportant. Thus, the nominal rate of interest can be thought of as being comprised of the real rate of interest plus an inflation premium.

The expected rate of inflation has been estimated in various ways. Fisher himself obtained an estimate by regressing the nominal rate on a geometrical declining weighted average of past rates of price change. The distributed lag technique for estimating future inflation has been used by a number of subsequent investigators. These studies have shown that prior to the mid-1960s there were long lags in the formation of price expectations. That is, bond yields adjusted very slowly to past changes in prices, taking a

---

[12]Irving Fisher, "Appreciation and Interest," *Publications of the American Economic Association*, XI (August, 1896), 1–100.

number of years before a change in inflation was fully reflected.[13]

Studies using the distributed lag type of analysis with data obtained since the mid-1960s have shown a marked acceleration in the formulation of price expectations.[14] With the sharp increase in the rate of inflation since that time, bond yields have been found to adjust relatively quickly to these changes in prices. Price expectations, as reflected in bond yields, appear to adjust more rapidly to large observed changes in prices, such as those that have occurred since the mid- to late-1960s, than they do to small changes. Rather than use a distributed lag model of past price changes, other investigators have used inflation forecasts by a group of business economists. The investigators have found these estimates to be relatively accurate in depicting the inflation premium embodied in nominal yields.[15] All in all, then, the evidence, particularly in recent years, supports the notion of a Fisher effect, where nominal rates of interest embody an element attributable to expected future inflation. While the relationship usually is not found to be one for one, nonetheless it is found to be quite important.

Problems in Empirical Investigation

Nominal rates usually are not found to vary *exactly* with changes in inflation expectations. This may be attributable to difficulties in empirical testing as well as to some underlying theoretical considerations. From an empirical standpoint, there are a number of problems in testing for the Fisher effect. For one thing, the real rate of interest is not known; it must be estimated.[16] There have been several approaches to deriving proxies for the real rate of interest. In the capital-market equilibrium

[13]See, for example, William E. Gibson, "Price Expectations Effects on Interest Rates," *Journal of Finance*, 25 (March, 1970), 19–34; Roman L. Weil, "Realized Interest Rates and Bondholders' Returns," *American Economic Review*, LX (June, 1970), 502–511; and Martin Feldstein and Otto Eckstein, "The Fundamental Determinants of the Interest Rate," *Review of Economics and Statistics*, LII (November, 1970), 363–375.

[14]See Patric H. Hendershott and James C. Van Horne, "Expected Inflation Implied by Capital Market Rates," *Journal of Finance*, 28 (May, 1973), 301–314; William P. Yohe and Dennis P. Karnosky, "Interest Rates and Price Level Changes, 1952–1969," *Review of the Federal Reserve Bank of St. Louis*, 52 (December, 1969), 18–38; and Thomas F. Cargill and Robert A. Meyer, "Interest Rates and Prices since 1950," *International Economic Review*, 15 (June, 1974), 458–471.

[15]See William E. Gibson, "Interest Rates and Inflationary Expectations: New Evidence," *American Economic Review*, LXXII (December, 1972), 854–865; and David H. Pyle, "Observed Price Expectations and Interest Rates," *Review of Economics and Statistics*, 54 (August, 1972), 275–280. The survey consists of one by Joseph A. Livingston of the *Philadelphia Bulletin* of between 40 and 60 well-known business economists on a semiannual basis.

[16]The immediately subsequent discussion is based on Hendershott and Van Horne, *op. cit.*, 301–304.

approach, one attempts to infer rates of expected inflation from differences in the expected returns on two different types of assets; the asset whose return tends to be expressed in real terms and the asset whose return tends to be expressed in nominal terms. Fisher studied the difference in yield on bonds payable in gold and bonds payable in money.[17] Milton Friedman and Anna J. Schwartz, as well as a number of others, have used the difference in return on stocks and bonds.[18] The idea is that stocks and bonds are close substitutes and that equilibrium in the capital markets is based on expected real returns and not nominal returns.

A second approach to estimating the real rate of return is a loanable funds model, one used by Thomas J. Sargent and others.[19] In this approach, the real rate is broken down into two components: (1) *the equilibrium real rate*, which equates *ex ante* savings and investment; and (2) *the deviation of the current real rate from the equilibrium rate*. The equilibrium real bond rate is said to be a function of such variables as the change in real output, the Federal deficit, real income, tax rates, and real wealth. The deviation of the current real bond rate from the equilibrium real rate is said to depend on the variables that shift the demand for bonds, such as changes in the monetary aggregates. In yet another approach to estimating the real bond rate, a Keynesian liquidity-preference model is employed. Martin Feldstein and Otto Eckstein define the real bond rate as that rate which equates the demand for real liquidity with its supply.[20] The principal determinants of the real bond rate are the real stock of liquidity and the level of real income.

All of these approaches represent attempts to estimate the real expected rate of return on bonds. As the latter is not directly observable, these indirect estimates vary widely from study to study depending on the model used and the sample period studied. The concern, of course, is with the expected future real rate of interest, not the present or past real rates. Consequently, past levels of, and changes in, various series of data may not be a good proxy for the expected future real rate of interest.

Similarly, estimates of the inflation premium often are based on past levels of, and changes in, some price index. Here too the past may not be a good proxy for the future, particularly when inflation is rapidly changing as it was in the 1970s. It is not surprising then that when past inflation

[17]Irving Fisher, *The Theory of Interest* (New York: The Macmillan Co., 1930), pp. 401–407.

[18]Milton Friedman and Anna J. Schwartz, *A Monetary History of the United States, 1867–1960* (New York: National Bureau of Economic Research, 1963), pp. 583–584. For an excellent analysis of these studies and their shortcomings, see Richard Roll, "Interest Rates on Monetary Assets and Commodity Price Index Changes," *Journal of Finance*, 28 (May, 1972), 251–278.

[19]Thomas J. Sargent, "Commodity Price Expectations and the Interest Rate," *Quarterly Journal of Economics*, LXXXIII (February, 1969), 127–140.

[20]See Feldstein and Eckstein, *op. cit.*

rates are used the distributed lag estimates of future inflation vary widely. A possible solution is to use direct inflation estimates by various people. However, these estimates are not without their problems. The sample of people surveyed is usually small and specialized, so generalization to all market participants is difficult. Also, the survey technique often biases the results, and the method by which a "consensus" inflation estimate is derived is inconsistently applied over time.[21]

Another problem common to most studies involves the period over which inflation is estimated. Conceptually, we are interested in expected inflation over the life of the debt instrument. For a 15-year bond, it would be a weighted average of expected inflation rates for each of the next 15 years; for a five-year bond, the next five years. The anticipated rate of price change may vary with the length of the loan contract. For example, if the current rate of inflation were 6 per cent and this rate were expected to decline gradually to 3 per cent over the next five years and level off thereafter, the anticipated rate of price change for a one-year loan would be much higher than that for a ten-year loan. As a result, the nominal rate of interest on the one-year loan would be higher than that on a ten-year loan, all other things being the same.

Most of the studies of the impact of inflation on nominal yields use the same estimated future rate of inflation for all maturities being examined. Implied is that expected future inflation in all future periods is the same as that which is expected to occur in the next period. Thus, a change in short-term inflation estimates changes inflation estimates for all future periods as well. While this may be a reasonable approximation of reality, theoretically it certainly need not occur. In concept expected inflation in the next period can change without inflation estimates for subsequent periods changing at all. As a result, the inflation premium embodied in a long-term bond would change very little with a change in expected inflation for the next period. In practice, we might expect inflation estimates for all future periods to change roughly together. However, they need not change by the same magnitude. Unfortunately, there has been little testing involving differing inflation expectations for different future periods. Most tests have dealt with the impact of inflation expectations on a simple rate of interest, usually a long-term bond rate, rather than on the term structure of interest rates. The latter, of course, is the more interesting question from the standpoint of our focus. In summary, we have limited empirical knowledge of the impact of inflation on the full-term structure of interest rates.[22]

[21]For an analysis of the problems with the Livingston estimates described in footnote 13, see Hendershott and Van Horne, *op. cit.*, 311–312.

[22]The exception is the short end of the term structure where there have been some studies of the effect of inflation expectations on liquidity premiums. Robert A. Olsen, in "The Effect of Interest-Rate Risk on Liquidity Premiums: An Empirical Investigation," *Journal of Financial and Quantitative Analysis*, 9 (November, 1974), 901–910, tests for liquidity premiums varying

Money, Inflation, and Interest Rates

When changes in monetary policy are incorporated into the analysis, the effect of lags in adjustment becomes an important factor in determining the impact of inflation expectations on interest rates. The monetarist view, as espoused by Milton Friedman, suggests that the initial impact of an expansion of the money supply is to lower nominal interest rates.[23] This decline in interest rates is known as the *liquidity effect*. It occurs because a drop in interest rates is necessary to bring the demand for liquidity in balance with the supply. Over time, however, economic units will purchase additional assets with their excess cash balances. Also, the lower interest rate will stimulate capital expenditures on the part of business and others. This is known as the income effect.

It is argued then that the expansion of money has very little initial effect on income and prices. However, over time the increase in demand for assets will cause both income and prices to rise. Whereas initially real income may rise above its normal rate of growth, eventually its growth rate is said to return to that which is considered normal. At that point, the expansion of money is reflected entirely in a rise in prices.

With the increase in prices, the inflation premium rises, causing nominal interest rates to rise. In final equilibrium, it is argued that the nominal rate rises by exactly the amount of the increase in the inflation rate. In other words, the Fisher effect is entirely realized. Implied is that the increase in prices and income has no effect on the real rate of interest in final equilibrium.[24]

---

with uncertainty about expected future inflation. As estimates for future inflation he uses the Livingston survey of business economists and computes the variance of these estimates as a measure of the uncertainty of inflation expectations. (See footnotes 15 and 21 for more on the Livingston data.) Using three- and six-month Treasury bill rates over the 1959–1971 period, he regresses the three-month forward rate minus the actual three-month rate subsequently observed against the variance measure and a distributed lag of past changes in bill rates. The variance term was found to be positive and significant; Olsen interprets this finding as suggesting that liquidity premiums vary directly with uncertainty about future rates of inflation.

In another study of this sort, James E. Pesado, "Determinants of Term Premiums in the Market for United States Treasury Bills," *Journal of Finance*, 30 (December, 1975), 1317–1327, uses a distributed lag on past bill rates and a distributed lag on past inflation rates to estimate the expected future bill rate. Using data for the 1957–1971 period, the estimated liquidity premium is derived by subtracting the expected future rate from the forward rate. Various theories of the term structure then are tested.

[23]Milton Friedman, "Factors Affecting the Level of Interest Rates," in *Conference on Savings and Residential Financing* (Chicago: U.S. Savings and Loan League, 1968). See also William E. Gibson, "Interest Rates and Monetary Policy," *Journal of Political Economy*, 78 (May–June, 1970), 431–455; Phillip Cagan, *The Channels of Monetary Effects on Interest Rates* (New York: Columbia University Press, 1972); Frank G. Steindl, "Price Expectations and Interest Rates," *Journal of Money, Credit and Banking*, 5 (November, 1973), 939–949; and Michael R. Darby, "The Financial and Tax Effects of Monetary Policy on Interest Rates," *Economic Inquiry*, 13 (June, 1975), 266–276.

[24]This question will be examined shortly.

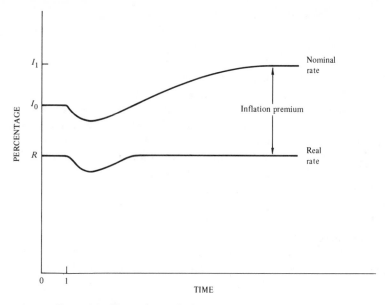

Figure 5-2. Change in nominal rate with monetary expansion.

If nominal rates behave in the manner described, the time sequence can be illustrated by the graph in Fig. 5-2.[25] The initial real rate of interest is R and the initial rate of inflation is $I_0 - R$. As a result, the initial nominal rate is $R + (I_0 - R) = I_0$. At time 1 on the horizontal axis, an expansion of money takes place. The initial liquidity effect of this money expansion is reflected in a decrease in the nominal rate of interest as well as in the real rate. As new inflation occurs with the increased spending by economic units, however, the nominal rate of interest rises. Moreover, the real rate is said to rise to where it was before. In final equilibrium, the nominal rate rises by the full amount of the increase in the rate of inflation. This inflation increase is represented by $I_1 - I_0$, and the new rate of inflation is $I_1 - R$. In other words, there is a one-for-one relationship between the change in inflation and the change in the nominal interest rate.

Leaving aside for now the question of whether this relationship holds, it is clear that a lagged effect may cause problems in empirical testing. Unless the nominal and real rates are measured at final equilibrium, there will be a bias in studying the effect of inflation on nominal interest rates. In a period marked by frequent changes in monetary policy, the measurement problems will pose great difficulty if this model of behavior holds.

[25]This figure is based on Darby, *op. cit.*, 270.

Less Than Full Conformity of Nominal Rate Changes
to Anticipated Inflation Changes

On a theoretical level, there are reasons why the nominal interest rate does not necessarily change in conformity with changes in inflation. Robert Mundell presents a theory where changes in the anticipated rate of inflation raise or lower the nominal rate of interest by less than the anticipated inflation-rate change.[26] In the case of an increase in anticipated inflation, this change is said to be reflected in both an increase in the nominal rate of interest and a decrease in the real rate. (The change in the differential between the two rates equals the increase in the anticipated rate of inflation.)

The crux of Mundell's contention that the real rate of interest declines under such circumstances is that inflation reduces real money balances. In other words, money assets depreciate in real terms. As a result, real wealth declines, and this stimulates increased savings. In turn, this brings downward pressure on the real rate of interest. Finally, the decline in the real rate of interest stimulates investment and an acceleration in growth, according to this theory.

In the case of a decrease in anticipated inflation or increased deflation, the opposite occurs. Here the real rate rises and, as a result, the nominal rate falls by less than the change in inflation. Accompanying this is a deceleration of growth. Mundell concludes that fluctuations in the rate of inflation affect real economic activity and not just nominal rates of interest.

Others have taken issue with this theory.[27] Frank G. Steindl suggests that Mundell's model is appropriate only if the reduced real demand for money balances that accompanies an increase in anticipated inflation is reflected in an increased real demand for bonds.[28] Under these circumstances, the nominal demand for bonds does not decline by the full amount that the increase in anticipated inflation would warrant. There is an excess of real demand for bonds, and this causes the real rate of interest to fall. In essence, there is a wealth transfer from real money balances to real bonds. On the other hand if the reduced real demand for money balances that accompanies an increase in anticipated inflation is reflected only in an increased real demand in the commodity market, Steindl demonstrates that the real rate rises. Here the increased demand for commodities, which follows from the reduced real demand for money

[26]Robert Mundell, "Inflation and Real Interest," *Journal of Political Economy*, 71 (June, 1963), 280–283.

[27]See, for example, Edmund S. Phelps, "Anticipated Inflation and Economic Welfare," *Journal of Political Economy*, 73 (February, 1965), 1–17.

[28]Steindl, *op. cit.*, 944–948.

balances, shifts the demand curve for commodities and brings upward pressure on the real rate. Steindl concludes that it is not clear a priori whether the decreased real demand for money will be felt primarily in the bond market or primarily in commodity markets. (If it were felt equally in both, the effect would be neutral and nominal rates of interest would change by the full amount of the change in inflation expectations.) Accordingly, Steindl concludes that it is not possible to predict the exact impact of changes in inflation on nominal rates of interest.

The relationship between changes in expected inflation and changes in nominal rates of interest may be affected also by the presence of taxes. With taxes, Michael R. Darby shows that a rise in expected inflation results in nominal rates rising by a greater per cent.[29] The after-tax real return to a lender whose loan is specified in nominal dollars is

$$R^* = i - it - \alpha \tag{5-3}$$

where i is the nominal rate of interest
t is the marginal tax rate
α is the expected rate of inflation

all of which are expressed in terms of the length of the loan.

Rearranging Eq. (5-3), the nominal rate of interest is

$$i = \frac{(R^* + \alpha)}{(1-t)} \tag{5-4}$$

Suppose now that expected inflation increases from α to α', but that the marginal tax rate remains unchanged as does the after-tax real return that is required. From Eq. (5-4) it is seen that the nominal rate must rise by

$$\Delta i = \frac{\alpha' - \alpha}{(1-t)} \tag{5-5}$$

If the tax rate were positive, the nominal rate would increase by more than the increase in anticipated inflation. This is needed simply to pay the additional taxes. The higher the tax rate, the greater the nominal rate increase that is required.

Overall, then, we know that inflation expectations have an important influence on interest-rate expectations and on the determination of interest rates. However, both theoretically and empirically we are unable to establish the precise relationship between changes in inflation expectations and changes in interest rates. We know that the relationship has been positive

[29]Darby, *op. cit.*

and significant in recent years, but that is about all that can be said with exactness. However, any theory of the term structure of interest rates must allow for the important role of inflation in shaping interest-rate expectations. With additional empirical testing in this important area we hope to come to a better understanding of the underlying relationship between inflation and interest rates.

Summary

Bond price changes that accompany a shift in interest depend in part on the coupon rate. The lower the coupon, the greater the price change for a given shift in interest rates. The reason for this is that more of the total return is realized at maturity when the principal is paid, as opposed to interim coupon payments. The problems associated with the coupon effect led to the development of the duration measure, which is a time-weighted average of interest and principal payments. Duration represents the average life of an investment on a present-value basis. For a coupon bond, duration is always less than maturity.

While duration increases with maturity for bonds trading at par or above, for discount bonds it eventually declines with maturity. Bond prices vary proportionately with duration but not with maturity. When an investor has a desired holding period, he should concern himself with both price risk and with coupon reinvestment risk. These risks vary in opposite directions. To assure that the realized return on an investment over one's holding period equals the promised yield at the time of initial investment, the duration of the investment must equal the intended holding period. In cases where coupon rates on outstanding bonds vary widely, the yield curve and the implied forward rates may be distorted. As a result, it may be more appropriate to study the yield-duration relationship as opposed to the yield-maturity relationship.

Inflation expectations have an important influence on interest-rate expectations and, hence, on the term structure of interest rates. The Fisher effect suggests that the nominal rate of interest changes exactly with changes in anticipated inflation. Empirical studies in recent years generally have supported the idea of a Fisher effect, although the relationship between inflation-rate changes and nominal yield changes usually is found to be other than one for one. There are a number of problems in empirically testing for this relationship, and these problems were reviewed.

When changes in monetary policy are integrated into the study of inflation and interest rates, nominal rates have been theorized to adjust only over time to changes in monetary policy. In the case of money expansion, nominal rates are said to decline first as a result of a liquidity effect and then to rise with the inflation that accompanies increased spending. Whether the real rate remains unaffected or whether it falls or rises in the process is a subject of much controversy, and this controversy was examined. Depending on the view taken, nominal rates will ultimately change to entirely or partially reflect the change in anticipated inflation. Finally, we analyzed the effect of taxes and saw that with taxes nominal rates must rise by more than an increase in anticipated inflation.

SELECTED REFERENCES

Bierwag, G. O., and George G. Kaufman, "Coping with the Risk of Interest-Rate Fluctuations: A Note," *Journal of Business*, forthcoming.

Caks, John, "The Coupon Effect on Yield to Maturity," *Journal of Finance*, 32 (March, 1977), 103–116.

Carr, J. L., P. J. Halpern, and J. S. McCallum, "Correcting the Yield Curve: A Re-interpretation of the Duration Problem," *Journal of Finance*, 29 (September, 1974), 1287–1294.

Darby, Michael R., "The Financial and Tax Effects of Monetary Policy on Interest Rates," *Economic Inquiry*, 13 (June, 1975), 266–276.

Feldstein, Martin, and Otto Eckstein, "The Fundamental Determinants of the Interest Rate," *Review of Economics and Statistics*, LII (November, 1970), 363–375.

Fisher, Irving, "Appreciation and Interest," *Publications of the American Economics Association*, XI (August, 1896), 1–100.

_____, *The Theory of Interest*, New York: The Macmillan Co., 1930.

Fisher, Lawrence, and Roman L. Weil, "Coping with the Risk of Interest-Rate Fluctuations: Returns to Bondholders from Naive and Optimal Strategies," *Journal of Business*, 44 (October, 1971), 408–431.

Friedman, Milton, and Anna J. Schwartz, *A Monetary History of the United States, 1867–1960*. New York: National Bureau of Economic Research, 1963.

Gibson, William E., "Interest Rates and Inflationary Expectations: New Evidence," *American Economic Review*, LXII (December, 1972), 854–865.

_____, "Price Expectations Effects on Interest Rates," *Journal of Finance*, 25 (March, 1970), 19–34.

_____, "Interest Rates and Monetary Policy," *Journal of Political Economy*, 78 (May–June, 1970), 431–455.

Hendershott, Patric H., and James C. Van Horne, "Expected Inflation Implied by Capital Market Rates," *Journal of Finance*, 28 (May, 1973), 301–314.

Homer, Sidney, and Martin L. Leibowitz, *Inside the Yield Book*. Englewood Cliffs, N.J.: Prentice-Hall, Inc., 1972.

Hopewell, Michael H., and George G. Kaufman, "Bond Price Volatility and Term to Maturity: A Generalized Respecification," *American Economic Review*, LXIII (September, 1973), 749–753.

Kaufman, George G., "Promised Yields, Realized Yields, and Bond Investment Strategy," Eugene, Oregon: Center for Capital Market Research, University of Oregon, June, 1975.

Macaulay, Frederick R., *Some Theoretical Problems Suggested by the Movements of Interest Rates, Bond Yields, and Stock Prices in the United States since 1856*. New York: National Bureau of Economic Research, 1938.

Mundell, Robert, "Inflation and Real Interest," *Journal of Political Economy*, 71 (June, 1963), 280–283.

Roll, Richard, "Interest Rates on Monetary Assets and Commodity Price Index Changes," *Journal of Finance*, 28 (May, 1972), 251–278.

Steindl, Frank G., "Price Expectations and Interest Rates," *Journal of Money, Credit and Banking*, 5 (November, 1973), 939–949.

The Default Risk Structure
of Interest Rates

6 In the preceding chapter we examined one reason for relative differences in market rates of interest—the term to maturity. In this chapter, an additional reason is examined—the default risk of the security involved. This is simply the risk that the borrower will default in the contractual payment of principal or interest. The default risk structure of interest rates depicts the relationship between the yield on securities and their risk of default, holding all other factors constant. In particular, maturity is held constant by studying different financial instruments of the same maturity. The relationship between yield and default risk may be similar to that shown in Fig. 6-1. In the figure, yield is plotted along the vertical axis and risk along the horizontal. The intercept on the vertical axis represents the yield on a default-free security; for all practical purposes, it represents the yield on Treasury securities. The figure shows that investors demand a higher yield, the greater the perceived risk of default.

Promised, Realized, and Expected Rates

In this chapter a *risk premium* is defined as the differential in yield between a security being studied and a default-free one, with all factors other than default risk being held constant. It is represented by the distance on the vertical axis in Fig. 6-1 between the intercept and the yield on the security being studied.

The *promised rate* on a security is the *ex ante* yield at a moment in time. If a corporation issues a bond with a $8\frac{1}{2}$ per cent coupon rate at a

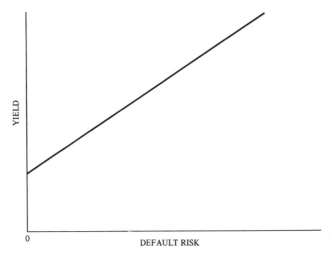

Figure 6-1. Yield-default risk relationship.

price of $1,000 to the public, the rate promised by the issuer is $8\frac{1}{2}$ per cent. However, if the bond rises in price so that one month later it yields $8\frac{1}{4}$ per cent to maturity, the promised rate at that time would be $8\frac{1}{4}$ per cent. It is important to recognize that the promised rate is not necessarily the rate actually realized if the bond is held to maturity.

The *realized rate* is the rate of discount that equates all payments actually received by investors with the market price of the security at the time the security was purchased. Any difference between the promised rate at the time the security was bought and the realized rate is known as the *loss rate* attributable to default.[1] It is clear that if the issuer does not default in the payment of principal and interest, the promised and the realized rates are the same.

At any moment in time, the risk structure of interest rates is determined by differences between promised rates and *expected* rates—the latter being the rate investors at the margin actually expect to receive. If there is a possibility of default, the expected yield on a security will be less than the promised one. To carry this reasoning one step further, if capital markets were perfect and investors' risk neutral, the rate expected by investors at the margin would equal the rate on a default-free security. In other words, the difference between the promised rate and the expected

[1]This assumes that we have held constant all other factors, in particular callability. See W. Braddock Hickman, *Corporate Bond Quality and Investor Experience* (New York: National Bureau of Economic Research, 1958), introductory chapter and pp. 64–66.

rate on a security would correspond to the risk premium defined earlier. The implication of this notion is that the differential between the promised and default-free rates is equal to the expected default loss for investors at the margin.

Distribution of Possible Returns

To better understand this notion, consider the behavior of a perspective investor. At some moment in time, he foresees a number of possible returns associated with owning a risky fixed-income security. We might picture him as forming a subjective probability distribution of these returns. This distribution is not symmetrical but highly skewed to the left. For the typical fixed-income security, there is a high probability that the issuer will meet all principal and interest payments. However, no probability exists for the realized yield to exceed the promised yield, assuming the security is held to maturity.[2] The promised rate, then, represents the highest return possible from holding the security to maturity. However, if the issuer defaults in any of the principal or interest payments, the realized rate will be less than this promised rate.

Legally, an issuer defaults anytime he is unable to meet the terms of the contract. However, degrees of default vary from a simple extension all the way to liquidation involving legal procedures. An extension is nothing more than creditors extending the maturity of the obligation voluntarily or allowing the postponement of interest payments. Because of the time value of money, however, the realized yield will be less than the promised yield even in the case of an extension. To illustrate, suppose that the promised yield on a 20-year security at the time of issuance were $8\frac{1}{2}$ per cent, the market price $1,000, and the coupon rate $8\frac{1}{2}$ per cent. Suppose, however, that the issuer was unable to meet the annual interest payment at the end of the third year and that this payment were postponed until the end of the fourth year, at which time it was paid. Suppose further that the regular interest payment at the end of the fourth year as well as all other payments were met by the borrower. With annual interest payments,[3] the realized yield on the security would be found by solving the following equation

---

[2] Again, maturity is held constant. Any selling of the security prior to maturity would be based upon considerations taken up in Chapters 4 and 5.

[3] For simplicity, we assume annual interest payments. The problem can be worked out for semiannual or quarterly payments with Eq. (3-3) in Chapter 3. All of the problems associated with the yield-to-maturity measure raised in Chapters 4 and 5 hold here. Because it is almost always employed, however, we use it to illustrate the general concepts about to be discussed.

for r:

$$1,000 = \frac{85}{(1+r)} + \frac{85}{(1+r)^2} + \frac{170}{(1+r)^4} + \frac{85}{(1+r)^5}$$
$$+ \cdots + \frac{85}{(1+r)^{20}} + \frac{1,000}{(1+r)^{20}} \tag{6-1}$$

The yield realized in this case would be 8.45 per cent—only slightly less than the promised rate.

With the liquidation of a corporate borrower, investors are likely to receive much less. To illustrate, suppose that the issuer of the security described above paid interest for the first three years but defaulted at the end of the fourth year because of inadequate liquidity. Suppose further that investors felt the borrower had no hope of turning the situation around and that liquidation was the only feasible alternative. Through bankruptcy proceedings, its assets are liquidated and investors receive an eventual settlement of 60¢ on the dollar at the end of the fifth year. In this case, the investors' cash outflow of $1,000 exceeds the total cash inflows they receive. As a result, the realized yield on the security will be negative. For negative yields, Eq. (6-1) is not appropriate; it computes smaller and smaller negative yields the further in the future that final settlement occurs. The implication is that it is more desirable to receive the $600 final settlement at the end of year 5 than it is at the end of year 4, when default actually occurs. Obviously, investors would like to receive final settlement as early as possible, all other things the same. To take account of the investor's opportunity cost, it is necessary to modify Eq. (6-1) when total cash inflows to the investor are less than his cash outflow.

To *approximate* the realized yield in an economic sense, we discount the final settlement amount back to the time of the actual default—the end of year 4. The discount rate used is the initial promised yield on the security. If this yield is significantly out of line with prevailing yields in the market for the time span considered, however, an opportunity rate more closely in line with market rates of interest should be used. Using the promised rate, the realized yield for our example can be found by solving the following equation for r:

$$1,000 = \frac{85}{(1+r)} + \frac{85}{(1+r)^2} + \frac{85}{(1+r)^3} + \frac{\dfrac{600}{(1.085)}}{(1+r)^4} \tag{6-2}$$

When we solve for r, we find it to be -4.47 per cent. In a manner similar to that in Eqs. (6-1) and (6-2), the realized yields for other possible default situations can be determined.

For each possibility, a probability should be attached and the possibilities ordered according to the magnitude of realized yield to form a probability distribution. An example of such a distribution is seen in Fig. 6-2. The figure illustrates that a relatively high probability exists for all interest and principal payments to be met by the borrower, resulting in the realized yield's equaling the promised one. However, the distribution is skewed to the left, indicating that a definite possibility exists for default. The further to the left in the figure, the higher the degree of default.

The *expected rate* for a security can be approximated by

$$ER = \sum_{x=1}^{n} Y_x P_x \qquad (6\text{-}3)$$

where Y_x is the xth possible yield, P_x is the probability of occurrence of that yield, and n is the total number of possibilities. Suppose that an individual formulated the probability distribution of possible yields for a municipal security shown in Table 6-1. The approximate expected yield for the security would be

$$ER = (7)0.80 + (6)0.04 + (5)0.03 + (4)0.02 + (3)0.015$$
$$+ (2)0.015 + (1)0.015 + (0)0.01 - (5)0.01$$
$$- (10)0.01 - (15)0.01 - (20)0.01 - (25)0.005$$
$$- (30)0.005 - (40)0.005$$
$$= 5.17 \text{ per cent} \qquad (6\text{-}4)$$

Thus at time t the prospective investor expects an approximate return of 5.17 per cent on the security.

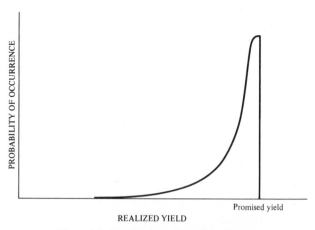

Figure 6-2. Distribution of possible returns.

Table 6-1. Probability Distribution of
Possible Yields

Possible Yield (%)	Probability
7 (promised yield)	0.80
6	0.04
5	0.03
4	0.02
3	0.015
2	0.015
1	0.015
0	0.01
−5	0.01
−10	0.01
−15	0.01
−20	0.01
−25	0.005
−30	0.005
−40	0.005

The *expected default loss* on the security is the difference between its promised and expected yields, or

$$7.00 - 5.17 = 1.83 \text{ per cent} \qquad (6\text{-}5)$$

This percentage may or may not correspond to the *market risk premium*, defined as the differential between the promised yield and the yield on a comparable risk-free security. If the risk premium in the market is more than the prospective investor's expected default loss, one rationale would suggest that he should invest in the security. He stands to benefit from an expected yield, adjusted for expected default loss, which is higher than that available on a risk-free security. By the same reasoning, if his subjectively formulated expected default loss exceeds the risk premium on the security, he should not invest. Here, the expected yield realized from the security would be less than that from a default-free one. If the expected default loss equaled the risk premium in the market, the investor should be willing simply to hold the security.

The action of all investors behaving in this manner would tend to raise or lower the differential between the promised and the default-free rates until it equals the default loss expected by investors at the margin.[4]

[4]In efficient markets, investors would be able to diversify in order to average out some default risk. However, a certain amount of risk of net default losses would remain. For example, in a depression, there are likely to be default losses. See Hickman, *op. cit.*, pp. 15–16. With diversification, the probability distributions in the above example would be formulated on the basis of nondiversifiable default losses. This is the systematic risk that remains after efficient diversification has been undertaken. See Chapter 3 for an additional discussion of this point.

Thus, the market risk premium would equal the expected default loss, and the expected rate would equal the default-free one, according to this school of thought. If the actual default-free rate in the example above were 5.17 per cent, the risk premium would be 1.83, and this premium would equal the default loss expected by investors at the margin.

The equilibrating process described above implies that market participants are neutral with respect to risk; only the expected value of the distribution of possible realized returns is important. However, the distribution not only displays dispersion, but it is highly skewed to the left. Such a distribution means that there is a possibility for very unfavorable returns. To the extent that investors at the margin demand a higher return for dispersion and skewness, the risk premium in the marketplace would exceed the default loss expected by these investors.[5] The more risky the security, of course, the greater the expected default loss. Thus, over a long period of time we would expect that the average promised rate for a large sample of bonds would exceed the average realized rate and that this differential would vary inversely with the quality of the security.

In summary, investors are assumed to form subjective probability distributions of possible realized returns for each security. Differences in these probability distributions will determine differences in risk premiums for the securities and, accordingly, will determine yield differentials between the securities. Figure 6-3 illustrates several of these distributions. The first probability distribution a represents the least risky security, while the last c is the most risky. On the basis of probability distributions of this sort, risk premiums are assumed to be determined in the market. However, these premiums may or may not conform to the expected default loss. We turn now to the empirical evidence.

Empirical Evidence on Default Losses

The most logical way to test the ideas discussed thus far is to compare actual realized yields on a large sample of securities with previous promised yields. The opportunity to test for default, however, depends upon a severe economic downturn. Only then are a significant number of issues likely to default. In other words, the probability of default on most securities is very small; it takes a sharp downturn to shake out those issuers possessing significant default risk. In this century, the depression of the 1930s provides the most valid test.

---

[5]Theoretically the required return would vary with the amount of undiversifiable dispersion and skewness—that is, the incremental variance and skewness of a security as part of an efficiently diversified portfolio. In theory, this portfolio would be the market portfolio which is comprised of all financial assets (see Chapter 3).

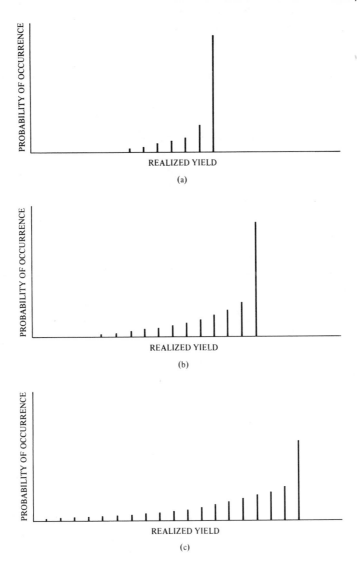

Figure 6-3. Illustration of different distributions of possible returns.

If risk premiums consistently equaled expected default losses by investors at the margin, we would expect that the average difference between the promised yield at time t and the realized yield at maturity would equal the average risk premium at time t for a large sample of bonds over a long period of time. The only comprehensive testing of this sort has been by Hickman, who investigated the default experience of fixed-income single-maturity corporate bonds over the period 1900–1943.[6] The sample consisted of all bonds over $5 million and a 10 per cent sample of smaller issues. For the sample, "life-span" default rates were computed depicting the proportion of bonds offered that defaulted between the offering date and extinguishment. In addition, loss rates representing the difference between promised and realized rates were computed.

Hickman's loss rate differed somewhat from the rate used earlier to measure default loss. For one thing, the call feature was not held constant. If a bond were called, there was usually a capital gain because the call price was in excess of the par value of the bond. As a result, realized rates tended to be higher than they would have been otherwise. Additionally, there were a number of bonds outstanding at the end of the sample period, January 1, 1944. The realized rates computed for these bonds were based upon the market prices of the bonds at that date. Because of wartime controls on interest rates, however, yields were low and bond prices were relatively high at that time. This occurrence caused the realized rates on bonds outstanding at the end of the sample period to be artificially high. Both of these factors tended to bias the results in the direction of high realized rates in relation to promised ones. For all bonds, Hickman found that the weighted averages of both promised and realized rates were 5.6 per cent. Thus, the loss rate, as defined, was zero—an unusual phenomenon, explained primarily by the biases described. Capital gains from calls and favorable conditions at the end of the sample period simply offset the capital losses attributable to default.[7]

When he analyzed realized rates according to the quality of the bond as described by its agency rating, Hickman found that these rates were higher for low-grade bonds than for high-grade ones. Over the sample period, the investor would have been better off on the average to have invested in low-grade bonds. To be sure, the loss rates were higher, but these rates were more than offset by the higher promised yields. Hickman conjectured that this phenomenon was the result of institutional investors' restricting their activity to higher-grade bonds. As these investors were the ones who were able to diversify adequately, he reasoned that promised yields on low-grade bonds must be relatively high to attract smaller investors unable to diversify adequately. However, the evidence also is consistent with the idea that the lower the grade of bond, the greater the skewness to the left, and the greater the risk premium required in relation

---

[6]*Ibid.*

[7]Over the sample period, different loss rates were experienced for the various subperiods. For bonds offered during 1900–1931 and extinguished during 1932–1943, the average promised yield was 5.4 per cent and the average realized yield 4.6 per cent, the average loss rate being 0.8 per cent. For securities both offered and extinguished during the 1932–1943 period, the loss rate was more than offset by capital gains. The average promised yield in this case was 4.9 per cent and the average realized yield 6.0 per cent.

to the expected value of default loss. As a result, the average realized rate would be greater, the lower the grade of the security.

While Hickman's study contains a wealth of information, his aggregate comparisons suffer from underlying movements in interest rates. As we have discussed, these movements biased the results in the direction of high realized rates in relation to promised rates.

Harold G. Fraine and Robert H. Mills attempted to correct for these biases by removing the effect of market influences on final liquidating values from the estimates of realized yields and loss rates.[8] The authors derived modified averages for large corporate bonds, using Hickman's data for the 1900–1943 period. For bonds which did not default and whose realized yield was in excess of the promised one, they substituted the contractual yield for the realized yield. (The implication of this modification is that bonds called at premiums are assumed to run until maturity, when they are redeemed at par. The same implication applies to undefaulted bonds outstanding at the end of the sample period.) After these substitutions were made, modified realized yields were computed; these yields are shown in Table 6-2. The results show that when realized yields are modified for gains attributable to changes in interest rates, the realized yield is less than the promised one. Still, the difference between the two yields was somewhat smaller than the typical yield spread between corporate and government securities (the risk premium as defined) from 1920 to 1943.[9] Therefore, the results still would appear to be biased.

*Table 6-2. Promised vs. Modified Realized
Yields, 1900–1943*

| | WEIGHTED MEAN ANNUAL RATE | |
Agency Rating	Promised Yield (%)	Modified Realized Yield (%)
I	4.5	4.3
II	4.5	4.3
III	4.9	4.3
IV	5.4	4.5
I–III	4.7	4.3
I–IV	4.8	4.3

Source: Harold G. Fraine and Robert H. Mills, "Effects of Defaults and Credit Deterioration on Yields of Corporate Bonds, *Journal of Finance*, 16 (September, 1961), 428.

[8]Harold G. Fraine and Robert H. Mills, "Effects of Defaults and Credit Deterioration on Yields of Corporate Bonds," *Journal of Finance*, 16 (September, 1961), 423–434.

[9]Prior to World War I, there were few U.S. Treasury securities outstanding. Because the market for government bonds was so thin, comparisons are not possible.

Table 6-3. Corporate Bond Average Annual
Default Rates, 1900–1965

Period	Default Rate (%)
1900–1943	1.70
1944–1965	0.10
1900–1909	0.90
1910–1919	2.00
1920–1929	1.00
1930–1939	3.20
1940–1949	0.40
1950–1959	0.04
1960–1965	0.03

Source: Thomas R. Atkinson, *Trends in Corporate Bond Quality* (New York: National Bureau of Economic Research, 1967), p. 43.

In a follow-up study, Thomas R. Atkinson extends the analysis of corporate bond quality through 1965.[10] Average annual default rates for the 1900–1965 period are shown in Table 6-3. These rates represent the ratio of the amounts of bonds that went into default during a year to the amount of bonds *not* in default at the beginning of the year. Both the numerator and the denominator are based on par values as opposed to market values. (If market values were used, default rates undoubtedly would have been less.) As seen in the table, the incidence of default in the post-World War II era was very small. The defaults that did occur were concentrated in the railroad industry. From this as well as previous evidence, we can conclude that default experience is highly correlated with the economic cycle. Put another way, it takes a severe economic downturn before the *ex ante* possibility of default becomes a significant reality and realized yields differ from those originally promised. If the evidence were extended into the 1970s, however, I am sure that the incidence of corporate bond default would have increased—with the bankruptcies of the Penn Central, W.T. Grant & Co., and other lesser known corporations. Recall that this period was marked by two recessions, 1970 and 1974–1975, and the latter was the most severe recession of the post-World War II period.

Similar in many ways to the Atkinson study, George H. Hempel studied the default experience for municipal securities over the 1839–1965 period.[11] The results are reported in terms of number of defaults as

[10]Thomas R. Atkinson, *Trends in Corporate Bond Quality* (New York: National Bureau of Economic Research, 1967).

[11]George H. Hempel, *The Postwar Quality of State and Local Debt* (New York: National Bureau of Economic Research, 1971).

opposed to ratio of default or the relative amount of defaults in dollar terms. As the total number of state and local governments has increased dramatically over the period studied, there is a bias toward exaggerating the default experience in the later years relative to the earlier ones. These problems notwithstanding, the numbers are still revealing. They suggest that defaults increase significantly in periods of major depressions. Studying these depressions in more detail, Hempel found:

Depression	Percent of Debt Outstanding Defaulting
1837–1843	51.0
1873–1879	24.5
1893–1899	10.0
1929–1937	15.4

Furthermore, he found that most payment problems occurred in the latter stages of a depression. For milder economic reversals, significant debt payment problems did not seem to occur although some municipalities failed even in good times.

As with corporate bonds, then, only a severe economic downturn will cause significant default losses and differences between promised and realized returns for municipal bonds (see Table 6-4). This phenomenon also is confirmed when one looks at loss rates on consumer installment credit, mortgages, bank loans, and other types of lending arrangements.[12]

Table 6-4. Number of Defaults of State and Local Government Bonds, 1839–1965

Period	Number of Defaults	Period	Number of Defaults
1839–1849	13	1910–1919	36
1850–1859	17	1920–1929	186
1860–1869	38	1930–1939	4,770
1870–1879	168	1940–1949	79
1880–1889	97	1950–1959	112
1890–1899	258	1960–1965	192
1900–1909	149		

Source: George H. Hempel, *The Postwar Quality of State and Local Debt* (New York: National Bureau of Economic Research, 1971), p. 30

[12]For a comprehensive compilation of data on credit losses and on loan and borrower characteristics that are used as indicators of credit risk, see Edgar R. Fiedler, *Measures of Credit Experience and Risk* (New York: National Bureau of Economic Research, 1971). The book also contains extensive references to other sources of data.

Default Prediction with Financial Ratios

In recent years there has been considerable empirical testing of the use of financial ratios and other accounting information as predictors of various future events. One of the events of principal concern is that of *corporate bankruptcy*. By studying the past behavior of significant financial ratios, one hopes to determine the relative probability of future default. This suggests that the causes for failure evolve gradually and that these causes emit certain signals which can be detected in advance of actual failure. If this is true, the lender may be able to take corrective action before actual failure occurs.

In an extensive research study, William H. Beaver used financial ratios to predict failure.[13] The study encompassed a sample of 79 relatively large firms which failed during the 1954–1964 period.[14] For each of these companies, another firm was selected that did not fail but was in the same industry and was of approximately the same size as the firm that failed. The data collected for the nonfailed companies were for the same years as those for the failed firms. These samples were used to test the predictive ability of thirty financial ratios. The mean values of the ratios for the two samples were compared over the five-year period prior to failure. An example of such a comparison, using the cash-flow/total-debt ratio, is shown in Fig. 6-4. We see that the mean ratio for the failed firms differs significantly from that for the nonfailed firms. Not only is it lower, but it deteriorates markedly as failure approaches.

In a similar type of study, Edward I. Altman employed multiple discriminant analysis to predict bankruptcy, using various financial ratios.[15] Altman worked with a sample of 33 corporations that filed for bankruptcy during the period 1946–1965. Like Beaver, he collected a paired sample of 33 nonbankrupt firms on a stratified random basis. Starting with 22 financial ratios, he selected the five that did the best combined job of predicting bankruptcy. These ratios were used to discriminate between bankrupt and nonbankrupt firms, using data from one to five years prior to bankruptcy. As expected, the predictive accuracy of the multiple discriminant model declined with the number of years prior to

[13]William H. Beaver, "Financial Ratios as Predictors of Failure," *Empirical Research in Accounting: Selected Studies* in *Journal of Accounting Research* (1966), pp. 71–111. For further testing in this regard where capitalized lease data is included, see Rick Elam, "The Effect of Lease Data on the Predictive Ability of Financial Ratios," *Accounting Review*, 50 (January, 1975), 25–43. Elam found that the inclusion of this data did not increase the power of financial ratios to predict bankruptcy. For an excellent overall discussion of this type of research, see Baruch Lev, *Financial Statement Analysis: A New Approach* (Englewood Cliffs, N.J.: Prentice-Hall, Inc., 1974), Part Two.

[14]*Failure* was defined as the inability of a firm to meet its financial obligations.

[15]Edward I. Altman, "Financial Ratios, Discriminant Analysis and the Prediction of Corporate Bankruptcy," *Journal of Finance*. 23 (September, 1968), 589–609.

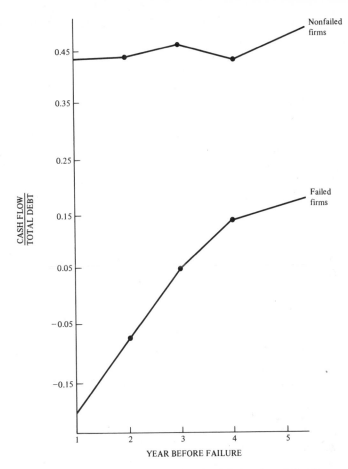

Figure 6-4. Comparison of mean values for failed and nonfailed firms.

bankruptcy. However, the model was able to forecast failure quite well up to two years before bankruptcy. Altman also tested the model with secondary samples of bankrupt and nonbankrupt firms. Using the parameter estimates obtained in the original sample, he found the model to have considerable predictive accuracy when used in conjunction with the secondary samples.

In his investigation, Altman, like Beaver, found that the financial ratios of bankrupt firms deteriorated as bankruptcy approached, the greatest deterioration occurring between the third and the second year. Altman concluded that through discriminant analysis a creditor can predict potential bankruptcy successfully. In yet another study, Altman studied the railroad industry and found that certain liquidity, profitability, and leverage ratios were significantly worse for failing railroads than for the industry as a whole.[16] Moreover, the ratios for the former group deteriorated as bankruptcy approached.

Robert O. Edmister tested the usefulness of financial ratio analysis for predicting the failure of small businesses.[17] Similar to the others, he employed multiple discriminant analysis and found it to be an accurate predictor of failure if ratios were averaged over a three-year span. Unlike the results of Beaver and Altman, however, an analysis based upon one year's financial statements was not sufficient to descriminate failing from nonfailing firms. Consecutive financial statements were necessary for the successful analysis of small business failures.

On the basis of the empirical studies described above, it would appear that signs of potential failure are evident before actual failure occurs. For the creditor, the lag may allow time to take corrective actions. However, it is important to recognize that the parameters of a model change over time. Indeed, most investigators have found them to be unstable. In order for the models to have predictive power, then, they must be constantly updated with new empirical testing.

Quality Ratings and Risk Premiums

For the typical investor, risk is judged not by a subjectively formulated probability distribution of possible returns but in terms of the quality rating assigned to the bond by investment agencies. The principal rating agencies are Moody's Investors Service and Standard & Poor's. These agencies evaluate the quality of bonds and give their opinion in the form of letter grades, which are published for use by investors. In their ratings, the agencies attempt to rank issues according to the probability of default. The highest grade bonds, whose risk of default is felt to be negligible, are rated triple A. The ratings used by the two agencies, as well as brief descriptions, are shown in Table 6-5. The first four grades in either case are considered to represent investment quality issues, whereas other rated bonds are considered speculative. The ratings by these two agencies

---

[16]Edward I. Altman, "Railroad Bankruptcy Propensity," *Journal of Finance*, 26 (May, 1971), 333–345. In a specific analysis of Penn Central, Roger F. Murray contends that evidence of deterioration was clearly evident prior to the actual collapse of Penn Central. "The Penn Central Debacle: Lessons for Financial Analysis," *Journal of Finance*, 26 (May, 1971), 327–332.

[17]Robert O. Edmister, "An Empirical Test of Financial Ratio Analysis for Small Business Failure Prediction," *Journal of Financial and Quantitative Analysis*, 7 (March, 1972), 1477–1493. Other studies dealing with failure prediction include E. B. Deakin, "A Discriminant Analysis of Predictors of Business Failure," *Journal of Accounting Research*, 10 (Spring, 1972), 167–179; and Paul A. Meyer and Howard W. Pifer, "Prediction of Bank Failures," *Journal of Finance*, 25 (September, 1970), 853–868.

Table 6-5. Ratings by Investment Agencies

Moody's	Explanation
Aaa	Best quality
Aa	High quality
A	Higher medium grade
Baa	Medium grade
Ba	Possess speculative elements
B	Generally lack characteristics of desirable investment
Caa	Poor standing; may be in default
Ca	Speculative in a high degree; often in default
C	Lowest grade

Standard & Poor's	Explanation
AAA	Highest grade
AA	High grade
A	Upper medium grade
BBB	Medium grade
BB	Lower medium grade
B	Speculative
CCC-CC	Outright speculation
C	Reserved for income bonds
DDD-D	In default, with rating indicating relative salvage value

are widely respected and are recognized by various government regulatory agencies as measures of default risk. In fact, many investors accept them without further investigation of the risk of default.

Hickman investigated the reliability of these ratings for corporate bonds over the period 1900–1943 and found a close correspondence between the rating category and the subsequent default experience.[18] The results of his investigation and the correspondence described are shown in Table 6-6. Hickman concluded that the record of the rating agencies over the sample period was remarkably good. Issues that were rated as high-grade at the time of the offering generally had a much lower default rate than issues rated in lower categories.[19] On the basis of this study, confidence would seem to be justified in the ability of the rating agencies to discriminate among issues of bonds as to the probability of default. However, it is important to understand that the rating categories portray *relative risk* among issuers of securities, not *absolute risk*. As evident in the depression of the 1930s, the possibility of default for all classes of risky

[18]Hickman, *op. cit.*, p. 176.
[19]*Ibid.*, p. 141.

Table 6-6. Default Experience, 1900–1943 (Per Cent)

Size of Issues	RATING					
	I	II	III	IV	V–IX	No Rating
Large issues (over $1 million)	5.9	6.0	13.4	19.1	42.4	28.6
Small issues (under $5 million)	10.2	15.5	9.9	25.2	32.6	27.0

Source: W. Braddock Hickman, *Corporate Bond Quality and Investor Experience* (New York: National Bureau of Economic Research, 1958), p. 176.

bonds can increase. As a result, the yield differential between bonds subject to default and Treasury securities can increase. More will be said about this when we examine the cyclical behavior of risk premiums.

A number of scholars have investigated the reasons for the assignment of a rating by a rating agency. Using the rating as the dependent variable, they have searched for statistically significant relationships between this variable and measures of past performance.[20] For corporate debt, higher ratings generally are associated with: (1) lower debt ratios; (2) higher return-on-asset ratios; (3) lower relative variation in earnings over time; (4) larger companies; (5) higher interest coverage ratios; and (6) the lack of subordination. The studies varied somewhat in explanatory variables employed and in the sample periods tested. Over all, these studies were able to predict correctly anywhere from 56 per cent to 80 per cent of the ratings assigned by the rating agencies.

The Fisher Study and Other Studies

In an extensive and classic study of risk premiums, Lawrence Fisher undertook a multiple regression analysis of five cross-sectional samples of corporate bonds for 1927, 1932, 1937, 1949, and 1953.[21] Using

[20]See Thomas F. Pogue and Robert M. Soldofsky, "What Is in a Bond Rating?" *Journal of Financial and Quantitative Analysis*, 4 (June, 1969), 201–228; James O. Horrigan, "The Determination of Long-Term Credit Standing with Financial Ratios," *Empirical Research in Accounting: Selected Studies in the Journal of Accounting Research* (1966), 44–62; George E. Pinches and Kent A. Mingo, "A Multivariate Analysis of Industrial Bond Ratings," *Journal of Finance*, 28 (March, 1973), 1–18; and Richard R. West, "An Alternative Approach for Predicting Corporate Bond Ratings," *Journal of Accounting Research*, 8 (Spring, 1970), 118–127. James S. Ang and Kiritkumar A. Patel, in "Bond Rating Methods: Comparison and Validation," *Journal of Finance*, 30 (May, 1975), 631–640, test the usefulness of these various models in predicting financial distress. Using the same corporate data that Hickman used for 1928–1938, they found that the Pogue and Soldofsky model performed best with respect to predictive accuracy, although all models performed poorly for longer lead times.

[21]Lawrence Fisher, "Determinants of Risk Premiums on Corporate Bonds," *Journal of Political Economy*, 67 (June, 1959), 217–237.

the risk premium (market yield less the corresponding default-free rate) as the dependent variable, he regressed this variable against four explanatory variables: the earnings variability of the company, the length of time the company has been solvent and creditors have not taken a loss, the equity/debt ratio, and the market value of all publicly traded bonds of the company. The first three variables relate to the risk of default, while the last attempts to depict the marketability of the bond. The last measure was justified on the basis of the market value of publicly traded bonds being a proxy for transaction frequency. Supposedly, the fewer bonds that change hands, the thinner the market and the more uncertain the market price.

Fisher found that the four variables explained approximately 75 per cent of the variance in the logarithm of the risk premium. Moreover, the elasticity of the dependent variable with respect to these four variables was relatively stable over time. The regression coefficients for the explanatory variables all had the proper sign, and practically all were significant over the five dates. The sign for the first variable was positive, indicating that the greater the variability of earnings of the firm, the greater the default risk and the greater the risk premium embodied in the bond yield. The signs of the remaining three variables were negative. The second and third suggest that the greater the period of solvency and the greater the equity/debt ratio, the less the default risk and the lower the risk premium required. The sign for the last variable suggests that the greater the market value of total bonds outstanding, the greater the marketability of the issue to investors and the lower the risk premium. Over all, Fisher's study represents the first thorough and direct study of factors responsible for risk premiums. As such, it offers much insight into the bases for these premiums as well as the applicability of regression analysis as a tool for investigating them.

Richard R. West reexamines the Fisher model in relation to bond ratings.[22] In addition, he gives a historical perspective on the origination and development of ratings and on the use of ratings as tools for the regulation of investments by financial institutions. This use began in the late 1930s and was in the form of a constraint on investment behavior of financial institutions to "investment grade" issues (Baa or better.) Using Fisher's data, West analyzes the residuals according to their Moody's rating. For the 1927, 1932, and 1937 results, the residuals were mixed as to sign and showed no significant relationship to the bond ratings. For 1949 and 1953, however, the residuals for the speculative grade ratings (Ba or lower) were mostly positive and significant, while those for the investment grades (Baa or higher) showed a lesser tendency toward negative residuals. West interprets this finding as consistent with the argument that ratings

[22]Richard R. West, "Bond Ratings, Bond Yields and Financial Regulation: Some Findings," *Journal of Law and Economics*, 16 (April, 1973), 159–168.

have an independent impact on yields because of their use as tools for financial regulation. In other words, speculative grade issues show higher yields than predicted by the Fisher model, whereas investment grade issues show lower yields. Put yet another way, this finding is consistent with institutional restrictions on investment leading to a segmented market for bonds. The implication of a segmentation effect will be examined later in this chapter.

In another study, which is similar in many respects to that of Fisher's, Avery B. Cohan investigates the behavior of yields on a sample of direct placements for the 1951–1961 period.[23] A direct placement is a corporate debt or equity instrument which is sold directly to one or more institutional investors, such as to a life insurance company. In other words, it is not a public offering but is sold privately to a limited number of investors. Cohan regresses the logarithm of yield against certain variables said to depict the quality of the promise to pay. Of the 20 variables tested, 10 proved to be significant for industrial and utility debt issues. They were the size of issue, the total capitalization of the company, the debt ratio, the amount of earnings before interest and taxes (EBIT), the maturity of the instrument, the average length of time the principal was expected to be outstanding, the length of time to the first call date, the type of security (senior or junior debentures, or mortgage bonds), the classification of the borrower as to line of business, the the total interest paid by the borrower on all debt outstanding. As hypothesized, all but the last variable had a negative sign. For finance company direct placements, five risk variables proved to be significant: the size of issue, the debt ratio, EBIT, the variation of EBIT, and the type of security. Like Fisher's study, Cohan's study assesses the relationship between various risk variables and promised yields. For both public debt issues and direct placements, then, there is a significant and positive relationship between the yield required by investors and the degree of risk as depicted by various risk measures.

It should be noted that the causal relationship between interest rates paid by a borrower and its default risk works both ways. The higher the interest rate, the larger is the amount of debt charge and the lower is the cash flow ability of the borrower to service these charges, all other things the same. Hence, higher interest rates raise the probability of default and hence the default risk of the security.[24] Thus, the causal relationship between interest rates and default risk runs both ways, and a case can be made for their simultaneous determination.

[23] Avery B. Cohan, *Yields on Corporate Debt Directly Placed* (New York: National Bureau of Economic Research, 1967).

[24] Harold Bierman, Jr., and Jerome E. Hass, in "An Analytic Model of Bond Yield Differentials," *Journal of Financial and Quantitative Analysis*, 10 (December, 1975), 757–773, relate the required rate of return to the probability of survival.

Cyclical Behavior of Risk Premiums

Another aspect of risk premiums is their cyclical behavior over time. A priori, we might expect risk premiums in the market for bonds to fluctuate in a systematic manner with the business cycle. During periods of economic downturn the risk premium might be expected to widen, while during periods of economic prosperity it might be expected to narrow. This pattern of behavior is attributable to investors' utility preferences for bonds changing with different states of nature. In a recession, their prime concern may be with safety. To invest in more risky bonds, the investor would have to be offered a substantial risk premium. On the other hand, during a period of prosperity, investors may be less concerned with safety and may be willing to bear more risk of default. During such a time, there may be a tendency for them to seek out the highest yielding investments. A sufficient number of investors behaving in this manner would narrow risk premiums in periods of prosperity and widen them in times of recession.

It is important to differentiate this effect from the effect of underlying changes in the default risk of borrowers over the business cycle. In a recession, the default risk for some borrowers increases as their cash flow ability to service debt charges deteriorates. The opposite tends to occur in an economic expansion. While the rating services tend to downgrade issues in the contraction phase of a business cycle and upgrade them in the expansion phase, the number of changes is small.[25] Therefore, it is likely that changes in underlying default risk occur without commensurate adjustments in ratings. This is understandable inasmuch as the rating services desire to maintain a degree of stability in their ratings over time. The import of all of this is that changes in yield differentials between various-grade securities may reflect more than changes in the way that investors view risk. They may also reflect underlying changes in default risk.

Yield Differentials over Time

Recognizing this limitation, let us examine the cyclical behavior of yield differentials. In Fig. 6-5, yield differentials between long-term Treasury bonds and Aaa corporates and between Treasury bonds and Baa corporates are shown for the 1946–1976 period. We note first that both sets of yield differentials widened considerably after 1965 and remained wide. It must be borne in mind, however, that interest rates in

[25]For a study of the adjustment of bond prices to changes in ratings, see Steven Katz, "The Price Adjustment Process of Bonds to Rating Reclassifications: A Test of Bond Market Efficiency," *Journal of Finance*, 29 (May, 1974), 551–559.

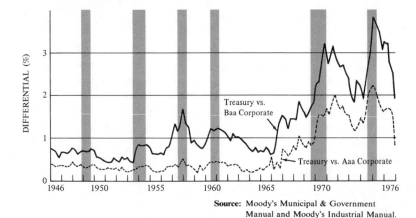

Source: Moody's Municipal & Government
Manual and Moody's Industrial Manual.

Figure 6-5. Yield differentials between Treasury bonds, Aaa corporate
bonds, and Baa corporate bonds.

general rose dramatically during this period of time, in keeping with the
increased level of inflation and uncertainty. Whereas, the average yield for
Aaa corporate bonds in 1965 was 4.49 per cent, it was 8.83 per cent in
1975.

In the figure, we see that the yield differential between Treasury
bonds and Baa corporates widened during the recessionary periods of
1949, 1953–1954, 1957–1958, 1960, 1970, and 1974–1975. This widening
was particularly evident in the recessions of 1957–1958, 1970, and
1974–1975. In recessions other than those, however, the widening was not
nearly so distinctive. Moreover, during the 1950–1952 and 1955–1956
periods of economic expansion, the differential narrowed only slightly.
However, the narrowing was much more pronounced during other periods
of economic expansion. While the pattern for the 1961–1969 period
showed a significant narrowing in yield differential through 1965, there
was a sharp widening during 1966. Subsequently, the Baa–Treasury yield
differential varied over time until the 1970 recession, when further and
significant widening occurred. The 1966 widening in yield differential in
some measure might be attributable to the perceived credit crunch and to
the great uncertainty in financial markets which occurred at that time.

With the rapid rise in interest rates in general from the relative low
and stable levels of 1961–1965, it is not surprising that the differential
widened during the 1966–1970 period. Also during this period Treasury
financing was confined mainly to short- and intermediate-term maturities,
owing to the $4\frac{1}{4}$ per cent coupon-rate ceiling on Treasury bonds imposed
by Congress. With interest rates above this ceiling, the Treasury was

unable to finance in the long-term area. In 1971, Congress gave the Treasury authority to issue a limited amount of bonds with coupon rates above $4\frac{1}{4}$ per cent. This limit subsequently was increased several times, which permitted the Treasury flexibility in tapping the long-term market. From 1966 to 1971, however, the Treasury was effectively precluded from long-term financing whereas corporations, of course, were not. To the extent that there are institutional restrictions on investment such that a market segmentation effect exists, one might expect the differential between long-term corporate bonds and Treasury bonds to increase. More will be said about this effect in the next section. However, part of the rapid widening of the yield differential in the 1966–1971 period may be attributable to this factor. It is important to note also that of the post-World War II recessions, the 1974–1975 recession was the most severe. The differential also was the largest during this recession.

The pattern for the yield differential between Treasuries and Aaa corporates is not as distinct as that for the differential between Treasuries and Baa corporates. The former differential widened somewhat during the 1953–1954, 1957–1958, and 1960 recessions. The patterns during periods of economic expansion were much the same as that for the Baa corporate–Treasury yield differential described previously, but less pronounced. Because of the relatively low default risk of Aaa corporates, the less pronounced fluctuation of this differential is to be expected. In Fig. 6-6, the yield differential between Aaa corporate bonds and Baa corporate

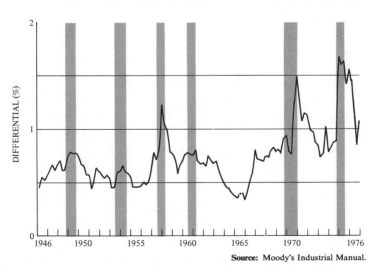

Source: Moody's Industrial Manual.

Figure 6-6. Yield differentials between Aaa corporate bonds and Baa corporate bonds.

bonds is shown. While this can be deduced from Fig. 6-5, it is useful to show it separately. As seen in the figure, the widening of yield differentials during the 1949, 1957–1958, 1970, and 1974–1975 recessions is more pronounced than that shown in Fig. 6-5, as is the subsequent narrowing of the differential in periods of economic expansion. Again this is attributable to the lesser variation of Aaa corporate yields over the business cycle.

When we examine the yield differential for different grades of municipal bonds, the pattern is less clear. Figure 6-7 shows the differential between Aaa municipal bonds and Baa municipals during the period 1946–1976. As seen in the figure, there is a tendency for the differential to widen during the 1949, 1953–1954, 1957–1958, and 1960 recessions. There also is a pronounced narrowing of the differential during the 1950–1952 period of economic expansion and again during the 1961–1965 period of prosperity. However, there is no widening of the differential during the 1970 recession, in sharp contrast to the evidence on corporate bonds. As is also seen in the figure, the most pronounced widening in yield differential occurred from mid-1974 to mid-1976. This spans the 1974–1975 recession, and such a widening during a recession is consistent with the evidence for corporates. However, in contrast to corporates, the differential continued to widen well after the recession was over.

The main explanation of this occurence is that during this time the financial condition of New York City triggered great concern over default risk for municipal securities in general. In 1975, the city was on the verge of default and such default was prevented only by the Federal government

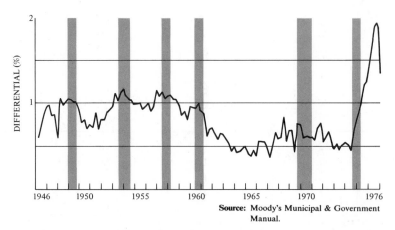

Source: Moody's Municipal & Government Manual.

Figure 6-7. Yield differential between Aaa municipal bonds and Baa municipal bonds.

eventually providing a $2.3 billion three-year revolving credit. During 1975, there were also potential default problems for the state of Massachusetts, for the New York Port Authority, and for various housing agencies of the state of New York. These problems caused great uncertainty in the market for municipal securities and a general reassessment of the default risk of municipal securities in general—and the securities of large urban cities in particular. The "flight to quality" at this time is said to be the reason for the widening of the yield differential between Aaa municipals and Baa municipals.

Over all, however, the evidence on municipals gives only moderate support to the notion that risk premiums widen during recessions and narrow during periods of economic expansion. This contrasts with the evidence on corporates which was much stronger.

Other Studies of Cyclical Behavior

For the earlier 1900–1943 period, Hickman found that when low-grade corporate bonds were purchased near the troughs of an investment cycle and sold during the peaks, the investor fared better than he did with similar purchases and sales of high-grade corporates. On the other hand, investors fared better with high-grade corporates bought near peaks and sold near troughs. He concluded that the market usually overpriced low-grade issues (and underestimated default risks) near the peaks of major investment cycles.[26] This behavior is consistent with risk premiums narrowing during periods of prosperity and widening during recessions.

In another study, Michael D. Joehnk and James F. Nielsen examined promised yields and the volatility of such yields for speculative-grade corporate bonds in relation to investment-grade bonds.[27] The speculative-grade bonds consisted of samples of industrial and railroad issues rated Ba and B by Moody's. The investment-grade bonds consisted of a sample of Aa rated industrial and public utility bonds. Two four-year time periods were studied: 1961–1964, which was characterized as a period of interest-rate stability; and 1969–1971, which was more volatile in comparison. However, 1968 and 1969 were still years of economic expansion, while 1970 was marked by a recession. For our purposes it is useful to look at the

---

[26]Hickman, *op. cit.*, p. 15.

[27]Michael D. Joehnk and James F. Nielsen, "Return and Risk Characteristics of Speculative Grade Bonds," *Quarterly Review of Economics and Business*, 15 (Spring, 1975), 27–46. The authors also examine realized returns and their volatility, but we do not review this part of their article.

results for 1961–1964, 1968–1969, and 1970–1971. The average yield and (standard deviation) for these time periods were:

Rating	1961–1964		1968–1969		1970–1971	
Investment grade	4.41%	(0.11%)	6.80%	(0.29%)	7.94%	(0.38%)
Ba industrial	5.84	(0.44)	8.02	(1.22)	10.18	(1.76)
B industrial	7.18	(0.53)	8.65	(0.90)	11.40	(2.02)
Ba railroad	6.46	(0.76)	8.16	(1.36)	10.76	(2.34)
B railroad	8.98	(1.20)	9.14	(1.52)	12.20	(5.59)

Thus, average yields were higher, the lower the grade of security. (The relevant comparisons are Ba and B industrials with the investment grade, and Ba and B railroads with the investment grade.) Moreover, the standard deviation, which is a relative measure of the variability of yields, tended to be higher, the lower the grade of the security.[28] Finally, for the 1970–1971 period, in which there was a recession, yield differentials tended to be wider and variability larger relative to the other two periods. This evidence is roughly consistent with evidence on corporate bonds rated Baa or better which we examined earlier. Yield differentials tend to widen during recessions and narrow during periods of economic expansion. However, the fact that the differentials here were lower in 1968–1969 than they were in 1961–1964, despite higher interest rates in general, is unexplainable.

In an extensive study of the causes of the cyclical behavior of risk premiums, Dwight M. Jaffee regressed corporate yield differentials against certain business cycle variables.[29] These variables included a measure of consumer sentiment, the unemployment rate, the growth of corporate retained earnings, the growth of capital expenditures, and an inflation variable. The dependent variable involved yield differentials for Baa grade bonds and high-grade issues (Aaa, Aa, and A). These differentials were for overall corporates and for the various components—industrial, utilities, and railroads. Tests for the 1954–1969 period showed that yield differentials were negatively related to consumer sentiment, to growth in retained earnings, and to growth in investment, while they were positively related for the most part to unemployment and inflation. The first three variables were said to portray the degree of optimism with respect to economic activity. Yield differentials would be expected to narrow as optimism increased. In contrast, unemployment and the growth in prices are

[28]The average yield and variability of speculative-grade bonds differed significantly statistically from those for the investment-grade bonds.

[29]Dwight M. Jaffee, "Cyclical Vartiations in the Risk Structure of Interest Rates," *Journal of Monetary Economics*, 1 (July, 1975), 309–325.

associated with uncertainty and economic contraction. Therefore, yield differentials would be expected to widen as these variables increased.[30]

Of the explanatory variables examined, consumer sentiment was by far the most significant. Other variables tended to be significant for the overall corporate and industrial categories. For the utility category, however, the results were mixed both with respect to sign and significance. For railroads, they were mixed with respect to significance. Over all, however, the Jaffee study supports the notion that people's utility toward investing varies with the phase of the economic cycle. In turn, this variation causes changes in yield differentials between various grades of corporate bonds.

In summary, for yield differentials between corporate bonds and Treasuries, for yield differentials between different grades of corporate bonds, and, to a lesser extent, for yield differentials between different grades of municipals, there appears to be a tendency for risk premiums to vary with the business cycle. Certain evidence gives support to the notion that risk premiums narrow during periods of economic expansion and widen during periods of economic downturn. One explanation for this phenomenon is that the utility of investors changes with the changes in the state of the economy. Put another way, investors are said to be more safety conscious in a recession than they are in a period of economic prosperity.

The Market Segmentation Effect

Other investigators say that the cause of the cyclical behavior of yield differentials is more complex. More specifically, it is argued that the pattern of behavior is affected by institutional restrictions on investing in and on issuing securities. In turn, these restrictions are said to lead to segmented financial markets in the same sense as we discussed for the term structure of interest rates. In this case, segmentation refers to the type and grade of security in which one can invest or which one can issue. We have already discussed one type of institutional restriction and that was the $4\frac{1}{4}$ per cent coupon-rate ceiling on Treasury bond offerings. This restriction effectively precluded long-term Treasury borrowings from 1966 to 1971 and may explain in part the widening in yield differentials between corporates and Treasuries observed during this time.

Other institutional restrictions on the supply side include voter constraints on borrowing by municipalities. In many state and local governments, voter approval is required before a bond issue can be floated.

---

[30]The results were the most pronounced for the Baa–Aaa yield spread with respect to such things as the goodness of fit and the size and significance of the coefficients; the results lessened as one moved to the Baa–A yield spread.

Moreover, some municipalities have a legal ceiling on what they can pay in interest, similar to the $4\frac{1}{4}$ per cent Treasury bond ceiling already discussed. If interest rates in general move up, these municipalities may be precluded from borrowing unless voter approval to remove the ceiling can be obtained. When inflation occurs, it typically brings with it not only higher interest rates but increased costs to the municipality and higher property taxes. Since few people like higher taxes, there tends to be a correspondence between the percentage of bond issues turned down by the electorate and inflation. As lower-grade municipalities pay higher interest rates and typically have more funded indebtedness outstanding, it is not unreasonable to expect them to feel restrictions on borrowing to a greater extent than do prime-grade municipalities.

On occasion, corporations also face restrictions on the issuing of bonds. If a company has existing debt outstanding which is covered by a loan agreement or bond indenture, there frequently exists a restriction on the company with respect to future debt. This constraint is likely to be more binding for the lower-grade company that it is for the prime-grade company. For both municipalities and corporations, then, it is not unreasonable to expect lower-grade borrowers to feel institutional restrictions to a greater extent than do higher-grade borrowers in times of inflation and economic contraction or stagnation. As a result, the supply of various-grade securities may be affected differently by institutional restrictions over the business cycle.

On the demand side there are institutional restrictions as well. For example, a common restriction is the limiting of the types and grades of securities in which certain institutions can invest. In turn, these restrictions on institutions may cause them to select different securities than they would if they were free to invest in any security. In other words, institutional restrictions may cause greater relative demand for restricted securities vis à vis unrestricted securities, if all other conditions are the same. This notion is illustrated in Fig. 6-8, where it is seen that restricted investors can invest only in restricted securities, while unrestricted investors can invest in all securities.

The restrictions placed on investment take many forms. For all practical purposes commercial banks cannot invest in corporate bonds, being restricted to Treasury securities and municipals. Public deposits in commercial banks must be secured by collateral, principally U.S. Treasury or government agency securities. This restriction affects their investment behavior. For commercial banks not members of the Federal Reserve System, part of their reserve requirement can be satisfied by holding Treasury securities. Obviously this may influence their investment behavior. Life insurance companies and certain other institutions are restricted in their investment by the states in which they operate. They are

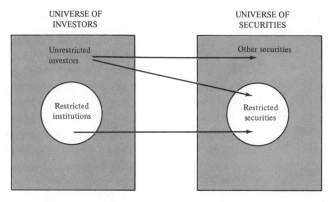

Figure 6-8. Effect of institutional restrictions on demand.

allowed to invest only in securities on the "legal list." With respect to bonds, this restriction frequently takes the form of investment-grade bonds —those rated Baa or better. Bonds rated Ba and below would not qualify, and the institution involved would be precluded from buying them. Similarly, commercial banks tend to be restricted to investment-grade bonds. These are only examples of some of the more important restrictions on the type and grade of security in which an institution may invest.

The combination of restrictions on the supply of and the demand for different types and grades of securities may lead to a market segmentation effect. If significant, this effect would have an influence on the cyclical behavior of yield differentials and risk premiums apart from the influences already discussed.

Unfortunately, empirical studies of the effect of market segmentation on the risk structure of interest rates are lacking. Still there is some evidence which bears on the matter. We already have described the West study,[31] in which he concluded that whether or not a corporate bond was rated investment grade had an effect on yield differentials apart from underlying factors accounting for risk. An investment-grade rating (Baa or above) was said to give a bond additional demand owing to restrictions on the investment behavior of financial institutions.

Ray C. Fair and Burton G. Malkiel tested the hypothesis that government bonds, high-grade utility bonds, and high-grade industrial bonds are not perfect substitutes.[32] Because of legal requirements and other market imperfections affecting the demand for bonds, these markets may be segmented to a degree. As a result, changes in relative supply would affect

[31]West, *op. cit.*

[32]Ray C. Fair and Burton G. Malkiel, "The Determination of Yield Differentials between Debt Instruments of the Same Maturity," *Journal of Money, Credit and Banking*, 3 (November, 1971), 733–749.

yield differentials between the various types of bonds mentioned above. Fair and Malkiel regressed yield differentials against differences in the amounts of bonds outstanding. In the case of utility bonds, the "visible supply" of bonds during the next six months was added as an explanatory variable. Testing for the 1961–1969 period, the supply and anticipated new financial variables were found to have a significant effect on yield differentials. While the methodology leaves something to be desired in that supplies of bonds are assumed to be exogenous as opposed to simultaneously determined with yields, the study nonetheless supports the idea of a market segmentation effect on yield differentials.

In addition to the aspect discussed previously, Jaffee's study tests for market segmentation.[33] He contends that if perfect market segmentation exists, yields will depend only on those exogenous forces which influence the supply and demand for bonds. On the other hand, if a perfect substitutes hypothesis holds, the risk structure will be fixed over time and the yield on a bond would be a function only of the risk-free rate. Jaffee suggests that a mix of these two results would be consistent with the preferred habitat theory, where partial segmentation exists. Using the corporate data previously described, Jaffee could find no evidence of market segmentation. For municipal bonds, however, certain variables pertaining to the ability of commercial banks to invest were found to be significant, supporting the notion of a segmentation effect. However, the tests were not well suited to pick up this effect; the primary contribution of the study was the analysis of other factors which explain the cyclical behavior of yield differentials.

Over all, the empirical results are mixed on whether or not there is a market segmentation effect on the behavior of yield differentials over time. While conceptually there are reasons to believe that there may be an effect, there have been few empirical studies of this issue. Until further studies are undertaken which either support or refute this effect, it will not be possible to make generalizations on the importance of this effect on the default risk structure of interest rates.

Risk Structure and the Term Structure

With differences in both default risk and the length of time to maturity, yield curves may differ for different grades of securities. In other words, the default risk premium is not necessarily a constant function of the length of time to maturity. If the default risk premium were 2 per cent on a long-term bond, it does not follow that the premium on a

---

[33] Jaffee, *op. cit.*, 316–320.

short-term security of the same grade also would be 2 per cent. A priori, it might seem that the risk of default as perceived by investors for a particular grade of bond would vary directly with maturity. As the length of time to maturity grows shorter and the issuer does not default, a degree of uncertainty is resolved. With this resolution, investors may require a risk premium different from before, all other things the same.

However, it is questionable whether all other things are the same. The problem is the grading category. For default-free securities, the yield-maturity relationship is internally consistent over various maturity points. However, for securities subject to default risk it is not necessarily consistent. For example, at 25 years to maturity, the observations used to determine the yield curve for a particular grade of corporate bond consist of a sample of bonds with that maturity. Ten years later, at time $t + 10$, these bonds will have 15 years until final maturity. However, the universe from which the sample observations are drawn is not the same. Only those bonds which have not defaulted, have not been called, or have not been upgraded or downgraded during the intervening period will remain in the universe. The point is that the bonds used to construct the yield curve for 15 years to maturity at time $t + 10$ will not be the same bonds as those used to construct the yield curve for 25 years to maturity at time t. Some bonds will have been dropped for the reasons cited, while others will have been added because they have been upgraded or downgraded from a previous rating category or because they are newly issued.

The rating agencies may apply the same quality standards as before. However, with the passage of time the probability of default as perceived by investors for a particular rating category may lessen for the higher-grade categories. Accordingly, bonds of companies whose financial condition remained unchanged would need to be upgraded as the final maturity approached. This upgrading is not done; they are upgraded only if their financial condition improves. The problem is that we would like to study the yield-maturity relationship on bonds that have the same probability of default throughout all maturities. However, most investigations are limited to a particular rating category of bonds. For the higher-grade rating categories, the probability of default as perceived by investors would seem to lessen as maturity decreases and uncertainty is resolved.[34] Implied then is a bias toward an upward-sloping yield curve.

However, the direction of the bias may differ for different rating categories. For those where the financial condition of the typical company

[34]Roland I. Robinson, in comparing the yield spread between Aaa and Baa municipal securities with the length of time to maturity, found that in most cases yield differentials were greater for long-term securities than they were for short-term ones. He concluded that default risk was an increasing function of maturity. *Postwar Market for State and Local Government Securities* (New York: National Bureau of Economic Research, 1960), pp. 184–188.

is sufficient to service debt, the probability of default perceived by investors would seem to lessen as maturity approaches. However, for rating categories where the financial condition of the typical company is insufficient or marginal with respect to servicing debt and meeting the final redemption, the perceived probability of default may increase as maturity decreases.[35] Consequently, for lower-grade categories of bonds, the risk of default is unlikely to be an increasing function of maturity. For these grades, the probability of default may increase as the final redemption date grows nearer and the company is unable to improve its financial condition. Implied is a bias toward a downward-sloping yield curve.

Ramon E. Johnson defines the latter problem as "crisis-at-maturity."[36] This viewpoint, which arose during the depression, suggests that because of the difficulty of refinancing and meeting the final redemption payment during crisis periods, short maturities are more risky than long maturities. During periods of economic prosperity, crisis-at-maturity would be a factor only for lower quality bonds. The two types of bias are illustrated in Fig. 6-9. In both cases, the yield curve for default-free securities is assumed to be horizontal. The upper panel shows the pattern for high-grade securities, and the lower one the pattern for low-grade securities.

The most interesting part of Johnson's study was the construction of yield curves based upon empirical data for five grades of corporate securities and the comparison of these yield curves with Durand's basic corporate yield curves. Recall from the previous chapter that Durand's yield curves depict the yield-maturity relationship for corporate bonds of the lowest default risk. Johnson plotted yield curves for 1910 through 1944, although only 14 of them were shown in the article. Of particular interest were the yield curves which occurred during the depression. From 1933 on, the highest-grade issues tended to be upward-sloping, as was Durand's basic yield curve, while lower-grade issues were downward-sloping. Examples of yield curves for 1934 and 1938 are shown in Fig. 6-10. The line with the *B*s refers to the basic yield curve, while the numbers 1 to 5 refer to different grading categories, from high to low.

Johnson postulated that the downward-sloping yield curves for lower quality issues, seen particularly during the depression, were primarily the result of crisis-at-maturity considerations.[37] Upward-sloping yield curves for low-grade bonds occurred only when the prospect for crisis-at-maturity was slight. Moreover, Johnson contended that upward-sloping yield curves

[35]In many cases, the redemption of a bond issue comes through refinancing with a new bond issue. As the ability to go to market with a new bond issue depends upon the financial condition of the company, the above argument holds regardless of the intended means for redemption.

[36]Ramon E. Johnson, "Term Structures of Corporate Bond Yields as a Function of Risk of Default," *Journal of Finance*, 22 (May, 1967), 318–321.

[37]Johnson, *op. cit.*, 340–345.

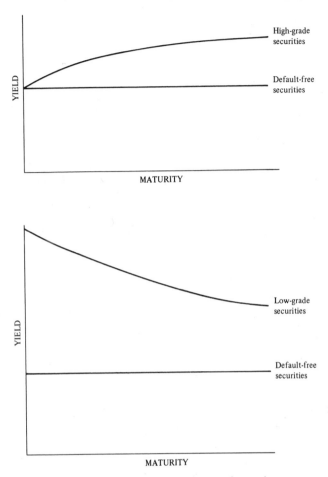

Figure 6-9. Default risk premiums and maturity.

for high-grade securities were the result of risk premiums increasing with maturity. On the other hand, U-shaped curves were said to result from a combination of crisis-at-maturity considerations and expectations that default risk premiums would increase in the future. Similarly, other shaped yield curves were explained in terms of risk premiums increasing with maturity, crisis-at-maturity, and expectations of changing risk premiums.

While one may quarrel with Johnson's interpretations of the causes of various shaped yield curves, he provided much needed evidence on default risk and maturity. To be sure, the construction of his yield curves is subject to a number of technical and measurement problems.[38] Consequently, it is

[38]See David Durand, "Comment," *Journal of Finance*, 22 (May, 1967), 348–350, for a discussion of these problems.

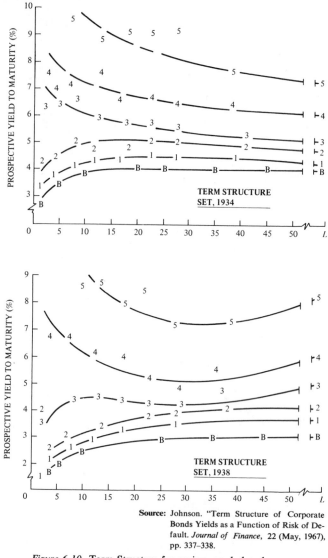

Source: Johnson. "Term Structure of Corporate Bonds Yields as a Function of Risk of Default. *Journal of Finance,* 22 (May, 1967), pp. 337–338.

Figure 6-10. Term Structure for various grade bonds.

inappropriate to make precise distinctions among various shaped yield curves over time. Nevertheless, the curves give general indication of yield-maturity relationships for various grades of bonds. The evidence tends to support the notion that measured risk premiums are an increasing function of maturity for high-grade securities and a decreasing function for low-grade ones. This finding is consistent with the idea that uncertainty is resolved for a particular grade of security as maturity grows shorter.

Rather than compare yield differentials with maturity, J. B. Silvers investigates the behavior of derived certainty equivalent coefficients.[39] This approach can be expressed as

$$P_0 = \frac{\alpha_1 C_1}{(1+i_1)} + \frac{\alpha_2 C_2}{(1+i_2)^2} + \cdots + \frac{\alpha_n C_n}{(1+i_n)^n} \qquad (6\text{-}6)$$

where P_0 is the market price of the bond at time 0
$\quad \alpha_t$ is the certainty equivalent coefficient for period t
$\quad C_t$ is the payment of interest and/or principal in period t
$\quad n$ is the number of years until the final payment
$\quad i_t$ is the risk-free rate in period t

The coefficient α_t is a value between 0 and 1.00 and it varies inversely with the degree of risk. It supposedly represents the ratio of what market participants would regard as a certain cash flow in period t to the promised amount of cash flow.

Silvers studies the pattern of the α_t with respect to maturity, i.e., when t is varied. Recall from our discussion of Fig. 6-10 that "normal" risk adjustment for high-grade securities implies that risk premiums increase with maturity as uncertainty increases. For lower-grade securities, however, the "crisis-at-maturity" argument implies that risk premiums decrease with maturity. These two situations are illustrated in Fig. 6-11 for certainty equivalent coefficients. On the left-hand side, the relationship between yield and maturity is illustrated, similar to the relationship shown in Fig. 6-9. On the right-hand side, these relationships are transformed into patterns of relationship between certainty equivalent coefficients and maturity. In the case of "crisis-at-maturity," certainty equivalent coefficients drop very rapidly at first and then decrease at a decreasing rate. For the risk adjustment of high-grade securities, certainty equivalent coefficients decline much more gradually at first. Thus, the shape of the certainty equivalent curve gives evidence of the pattern of risk premium variation with maturity.

Silvers estimates certainty equivalent coefficients for 5- , 15- , and 30-year maturities, attempting to hold constant the effects of marketability, callability, and capital gains. The sample period was 1952 to 1964, and Aaa through Baa grade corporate bonds were studied. On the basis of the three observations, certainty equivalent curves were drawn. The results for Aaa and A ratings are shown in Fig. 6-12. Among other things, Silvers found that the certainty equivalent coefficients tended to be lower, the lower the grade of the bond. Also, the coefficients tended to be lower in a period of

[39] J. B. Silvers, "An Alternative to the Yield Spread as a Measure of Risk," *Journal of Finance*, 28 (September, 1973), 933–955.

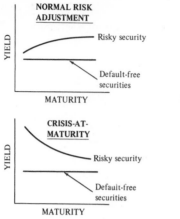

Source: Silvers. "An Alternative to the Yield Spread as a Measure of Risk." *Journal of Finance*, 28 (September, 1973), 938.

Figure 6-11. Patterns of certainty equivalent coefficients.

economic contraction than they were in a period of expansion. (In the figure, recessions are denoted by the shaded areas.) Together these findings are consistent with previous evidence on the cyclical behavior of risk premiums. Additionally, the findings give indication that the "crisis-at-maturity" argument is more important during recessions and for lower-grade securities.

In another study of default risk premiums for different maturities, I analyzed commercial paper and long-term bond rates for a sample of individual companies over the 1972–1974 period.[40] Risk premiums for short- and long-term debt instruments were found to behave differently over time. In the latter part of the sample period, the average commercial paper risk premium was above the average long-term bond risk premium, whereas it was below in the earlier part. In the 1974 recession, there was an alleged "flight to quality" in the capital markets where investors were said to seek high-grade securities, in particular Treasury securities. The late 1973–1974 evidence for commercial paper risk premiums, relative to long-term bond risk premiums, was consistent with "crisis-at-maturity." However, when default risk premiums were analyzed company by company, the notion that short-term default risk premiums should be higher in relation to long-term risk premiums for lower-grade companies than they are for higher-grade companies was not supported. In this regard, a number of risk measures were used to depict the grade of company. Moreover, factor

[40]James C. Van Horne, "Behavior of Default-Risk Premiums for Corporate Bonds and Commercial Paper," *Journal of Business Research*, forthcoming.

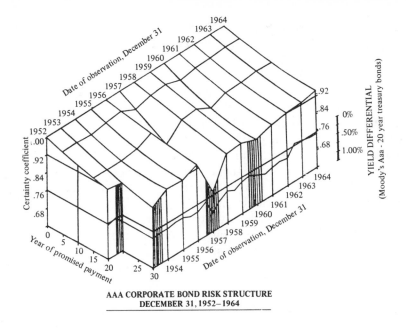

AAA CORPORATE BOND RISK STRUCTURE
DECEMBER 31, 1952–1964

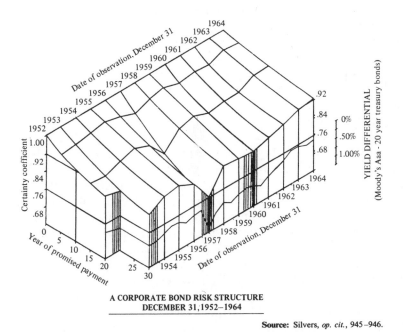

A CORPORATE BOND RISK STRUCTURE
DECEMBER 31, 1952–1964

Source: Silvers, *op. cit.*, 945–946.

Figure 6-12. Certainty equivalent coefficients and maturity over time.

analysis was employed and it did not reveal any underlying pattern of relationship for the company-by-company behavior of short- and long-term default risk premiums over time.

In summary, the Johnson, Silvers, and Van Horne studies give us insight into the relationship between risk premiums and maturity, as well as insight into changes in this relationship depending on the phase of the economy. There is some indication in the first two studies that the lower the grade of the bond, the greater the risk premium tends to be in the early maturities, while all three studies support the notion that the lower the state of economic activity, the greater the short-term risk premium tends to be on a relative basis. In studying the risk structure of interest rates, we have been concerned with differences in yield for different types and grades of securities, holding maturity constant. However, one must be mindful that the risk structure is different for different maturities and that the relationship between the risk structure and maturity can change over time.

Summary

The relationship between yield and the risk of default, with other factors constant, is known as the *risk structure* of interest rates. This relationship usually is studied through the analysis of risk premiums, the difference between the yield on a security and the yield on a corresponding security which is free of default risk. The promised yield on a security is its *ex ante* yield at a moment in time. The expected yield, on the other hand, is the expected value of the probability distribution of possible realized yields. The distribution itself is highly skewed to the left. In perfect markets and with risk neutrality, the expected yield for investors at the margin should equal the risk-free rate. If this relationship held, the expected default loss on a security would equal the market-determined risk premium. However, to the extent that the market as a whole is adverse to dispersion and skewness to the left of the probability distribution, the risk premium will exceed the default loss expected by investors at the margin.

Empirical studies of default losses show that default experience is highly correlated with the economic cycle. It is only with a severe economic downturn, such as a depression, that widespread default occurs and there are differences between promised and realized returns for a significant number of securities. Various investment agencies rate securities as to their probability of default. Available evidence suggests that these ratings are consistent with respect to default risk. They also suggest consistency with respect to certain financial ratios involving earnings, earnings stability, and debt coverage. Another method for analyzing yield differentials is through regression analysis, and various studies concerning its use were examined. For both public debt issues and private placements, there is a significant and positive relationship between promised yields and various variables which depict the risk of a corporation. In recent years, considerable attention has been directed toward predicting corporate bankruptcy on the basis of the pattern of past financial ratios. The empirical studies examined suggest that signs of potential failure are evident before actual failure occurs.

An important facet of the default risk structure of interest rates is the cyclical behavior of risk premiums. Various evidence indicates a tendency for risk premiums to widen during a period of economic contraction and to narrow during a period of expansion. This is consistent with investors' utility preferences changing with the state of the economy—investors being more concerned with safety in an economic downturn than they are in a period of prosperity. In addition to this effect, there may be a market segmentation effect that influences the behavior of yield differentials over time. Various institutional restrictions on the demand for and the supply of bonds of various types and grades were discussed. Limited empirical testing is largely inconclusive regarding whether or not these restrictions have a meaningful impact on the behavior of risk premiums over time. Finally, the default risk structure and the term structure of interest rates were examined jointly in an effort to explain differing shapes of yield curves for different risk categories of securities. The idea that uncertainty is resolved as maturity grows shorter implies a bias toward an upward-sloping yield curve for high-grade securities and a downward-sloping yield curve for low-grade securities. Empirical studies have shown this tendency to be evident during economic downturns.

SELECTED REFERENCES

Atkinson, Thomas R., *Trends in Corporate Bond Quality*. New York: National Bureau of Economic Research, 1967.

Cohan, Avery B., *The Risk Structure of Interest Rates*. Morristown, N.J.: General Learning Press, 1973.

_____, *Yields on Corporate Debt Directly Placed*. New York: National Bureau of Economic Research, 1967.

Fair, Ray C., and Burton G. Malkiel, "The Determination of Yield Differentials between Debt Instruments of the Same Maturity," *Journal of Money, Credit and Banking*, 3 (November, 1971), 733–749.

Fiedler, Edgar R., *Measures of Credit Experience and Risk*. New York: National Bureau of Economic Research, 1971.

Fisher, Lawrence, "Determinants of Risk Premiums on Corporate Bonds," *Journal of Political Economy*, 67 (June, 1959), 217–237.

Fraine, Harold G., and Robert H. Mills, "Effects of Defaults and Credit Deterioration on Yields of Corporate Bonds," *Journal of Finance*, 16 (September, 1961), 423–434.

Grier, Paul, and Steven Katz, "The Differential Effects of Bond Rating Changes Among Industrial and Public Utility Bonds by Maturity," *Journal of Business*, 49 (April, 1976), 226–39.

Hempel, George H., *The Postwar Quality of State and Local Debt*. New York: National Bureau of Economic Research, 1971.

Hickman, W. Braddock, *Corporate Bond Quality and Investor Experience*. New York: National Bureau of Economic Research, 1958.

Jaffee, Dwight M., "Cyclical Variations in the Risk Structure of Interest Rates," *Journal of Monetary Economics*, 1 (July, 1975), 309–325.

Joehnk, Michael D., and James F. Nielsen, "Return and Risk Characteristics of Speculative Grade Bonds," *Quarterly Review of Economics and Business*, 15 (Spring, 1975), 27–46.

Johnson, Ramon E., "Term Structures of Corporate Bond Yields as a Function of Risk of Default," *Journal of Finance*, 22 (May, 1967), 313–345.

Macaulay, Frederick R., *The Movement of Interest Rates, Bond Yields, and Stock Prices in the United States since 1856*. New York: National Bureau of Economic Research, 1938.

Merton, Robert C., "On the Pricing of Corporate Debt: The Risk Structure of Interest Rates," *Journal of Finance*, 29 (May, 1974), 449–470.

Reilly, Frank K., and Michael D. Joehnk, "The Association Between Market-Determined Risk Measures for Bonds and Bond Ratings," *Journal of Finance*, 31 (December, 1976), 1387–1403.

Robinson, Roland I., *Postwar Market for State and Local Government Securities*. New York: National Bureau of Economic Research, 1960.

Silvers, J. B., "An Alternative to the Yield Spread as a Measure of Risk," *Journal of Finance*, 28 (September, 1973), 933–955.

Sloane, Peter E., "Determinants of Bond Yield Differentials—1954–1959," *Yale Economic Essays*, 3 (Spring, 1963), 3–56.

Van Horne, James C., "Optimal Initiation of Bankruptcy Proceedings by Debt Holders," *Journal of Finance*, 31 (June, 1976), 897–910.

_____, "Implied Fixed Costs of Long-Term Debt Issues," *Journal of Financial and Quantitative Analysis*, 8 (December, 1973), 821–833.

_____, "Behavior of Default-Risk Premiums for Corporate Bonds and Commercial Paper," *Journal of Business Research*, forthcoming.

_____, and Samuel S. Stewart, "A Simultaneous Equations Analysis of the Bond Markets," *The Southern Economic Journal*, XXXVIII (April, 1972), 538–546.

West, Richard R., "Bond Ratings, Bond Yields and Financial Regulations: Some Findings," *Journal of Law and Economics*, 16 (April, 1973), 159–168.

logical to retire some of the bonds outstanding if there is any excess cash as a result of revenues exceeding projections. For general obligation issues, the percentage with a call feature is much less. In this case, callable bonds are the exception rather than the rule.[1] One reason for this may be the nature of political life. If a municipal security were made callable, in most cases the immediate interest cost to the municipality would rise. Gordon Pye suggests that the issuance of callable bonds would result in higher current taxes, with the possibility of tax savings some time in the future.[2] Because public officials may not be in office in the future, Pye reasons that they place a higher utility on lower taxes now than on possible savings in the future.

Another reason for state and local governments to issue noncallable bonds is the difference between their borrowing and lending rates. Because interest on municipal securities is exempt from federal income taxes, the borrowing rate is lower than the lending rate; the latter rate might be the return on a Treasury or corporate bond. Richard R. West theorizes that public officials may discount possible future interest savings by the lending, rather than the borrowing, rate. If that is true, the present value of expected cash savings from the exercise of the call privilege would usually be less than the cost of the privilege, and thereby its attractiveness would be reduced considerably.[3]

While most Treasury securities are noncallable, the call provision for those that are is geared to final maturity. For example, the 8 per cent bonds of August, 1996–2001 have a call feature which enables the Treasury to call the bonds anytime between August, 1996 and the final maturity five years later, August, 2001. The primary purpose of the call privilege is to give flexibility in refinancing to the Treasury. Unlike that of some corporations, the debt of the federal government generally is "rolled over" at maturity. The Treasury is primarily concerned with the tone of the market when it has to refinance its maturing obligations. By having five years in which to "roll over" the debt, the Treasury can be flexible in the timing of its refinancing. Thus, the principal purpose of the call privilege is not to achieve a savings in interest, but rather to obtain flexibility in financing near the final maturity of the existing obligation. The call feature is

---

[1] David S. Kidwell, in "The Inclusion and Exercise of Call Provisions by State and Local Governments," *Journal of Money, Credit and Banking*, 8 (August, 1976), 391–398, analyzes almost all municipal bond issues between 1959 and 1967. He found that 31 per cent of the general obligation issues contained call provisions, whereas 94 per cent of the revenue issues contained call provisions. The annual percentages ranged from 24 to 40 per cent and from 88 to 97 per cent for general obligation and revenue issues respectively.
[2] Gordon Pye, "The Value of the Call Option on a Bond," *Journal of Political Economy*, 74 (April, 1966), 200–201.
[3] Richard R. West, "On the Noncallability of State and Local Bonds: A Comment," *Journal of Political Economy*, 75 (February, 1967), 98–99.

basically restricted to long-term Treasury bonds; only about one-sixth of the bonds outstanding carry this feature. Because the maturity of the Treasury bond can be shortened by only five years, the call feature does not pose the same disadvantage to investors as does the call privilege for a corporate bond.[4]

A form of call privilege exists for mortgages. Unless otherwise specified in the contract, the borrower may pay the loan off at any time. In other words, the loan is callable immediately. Frequently, however, lenders demand a prepayment penalty if the loan is paid off before a certain date. For example, insurance companies usually require a prepayment penalty on residential mortgages, graduated downward through five years. After five years, the loan can be paid without penalty. In times of high interest rates, banks and savings and loan associations also impose prepayment penalties on their mortgage loans. However, it is important to recognize that the paying off of a residential mortgage usually is not motivated by the desire to refinance the mortgage at a lower interest rate. People move, and when they sell their houses they pay off their mortgages. As a result, the average life of a residential mortgage is about one-half its maturity.

Reverse Call Feature

In recent years, there have been a limited number of fixed-income security issues having a reverse call feature. With this feature, after a specified period of time the investor has the option to "put" the securities back to the borrower at a specified price. For example, in June, 1976, Beneficial Corporation issued $150 million of 8 per cent, 25-year debentures which gave the holder the option to have the company redeem the bonds at their face value anytime from the 7th to the 24th year. A second example of a reverse call feature is the Federal Home Loan Mortgage Corporation's guaranteed mortgage certificates. Here the investor has the option of requiring the corporation to repurchase the certificate at its face value at a specified date (usually 15 to 20 years from the date of issue). The advantage of the reverse call feature to the investor is obvious; in times of rising interest rates he may have his bonds redeemed and invest in other bonds providing higher yields. It is too early to tell whether the reverse call feature will find widespread use. As the principles of valuation are the mirror image of those for the regular call feature, we will confine our attention to call features where the option rests with the borrower.

---

[4]For callable Treasury bonds, yield to maturity is computed on the basis of final maturity when the market price of the bond is *below* its face value and on the basis of the earliest call date when its market price is *above* face value. When it is below face value, the implication is that the Treasury is unlikely to call the security.

The Value of the Call Provision

The call provision gives the borrower flexibility. Should interest rates decline significantly, the borrower can call the debt instrument and refinance at a lower interest cost. However, the decline in interest rates must be sufficient to offset the fact that the call price is above the face value of the instrument and the fact that there are flotation, legal, and inconvenience costs.[5] With a call provision, the borrower does not have to wait until final maturity to refinance. The optimal time for an issuer to call bonds is when the present value of the difference between the price at which the new, or refunding, bonds can be issued and the call price is greatest (holding constant the coupon rate and the final maturity).[6] In addition to flexibility, the call provision may be advantageous to a corporation with unduly restrictive protective covenants in its existing bond indenture. (The indenture is a legal document spelling out the conditions of the loan and the covenants under which default occurs.) By calling the bonds before maturity, the company can eliminate these restrictions.

The call privilege works to the benefit of the borrower but to the detriment of investors. If interest rates fall and the bond issue is called, they can invest in other bonds only at a sacrifice in yield to maturity. From the standpoint of an investor, bonds with the call feature have a different probability distribution of possible returns from bonds that have no call feature. To illustrate, suppose that for an investor the probability distribution of possible returns for a 20-year corporate bond with *no* call feature was that shown on the left-hand side of Fig. 7-1. The distribution is skewed to the left because of the possibility of default, an influence examined in the previous chapter. The most favorable outcome is that all principal and interest payments will be met on time, so that the realized rate of return equals the promised yield at the time of purchase. Should interest or principal payments not occur as scheduled, the realized yield will be less. (The deviation from promised yield depends on the degree of default.)

On the right-hand side of the figure, the likely consequence of the bond having a call feature is shown, assuming all other things are the

---

[5]For an analysis of the profitability of refunding by the borrower, see Oswald D. Bowlin, "The Refunding Decision: Another Special Case in Capital Budgeting," *Journal of Finance*, 21 (March, 1966), 55–68; and Aharon R. Ofer and Robert A. Taggart, Jr., "Bond Refunding: A Clarifying Analysis," *Journal of Finance*, 32 (March, 1977), 21–30. For articles dealing with the optimal timing of a refunding, see H. Martin Weingartner, "Optimal Timing of a Bond Refunding," *Management Science*, 13 (March, 1967), 511–524; Basil A. Kalymon, "Bond Refunding with Stochastic Interest Rates," *Management Science*, 18 (November, 1971), 171–183; and Alan Kraus,"The Bond Refunding Decision in an Efficient Market," *Journal of Financial and Quantitative Analysis*, 8 (December, 1973), 793–806.

[6]See Pye, *op. cit.*, 200–201.

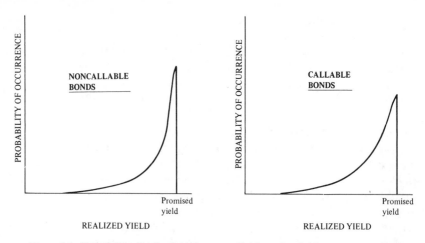

Figure 7-1. Probability distributions for noncallable and callable corporate bonds.

same. We see that there is still the strong possibility that the actual yield will equal the promised yield, although the probability is less. However, there is now a reasonable probability that the bond will be called and that the investor's actual return over the 20 years, including reinvestment, will be less than the promised yield. This negative factor is *in addition* to the possibility of default. In general, the extreme tail of the distribution is not altered materially because it depends on a severe default occurring and not on the bonds being called. It is the intermediate part of the distribution which is altered by the addition of the call feature.

Because of the disadvantage to the investor, the call privilege usually does not come free to the borrower. Its cost, or value, is measured by the difference in yield on the callable bond and the yield that would be necessary if the security were noncallable. In other words, the price of the callable bond would be such that the marginal investor would be indifferent between it and a noncallable bond. More fundamentally, this price is determined by supply and demand forces in the market for callable securities. In equilibrium, the value of the call feature will be just sufficient to bring the demand for callable securities by investors into balance with the supply of callable securities by borrowers.

Interest-Rate Expectations

In the equilibrating process, both borrowers and investors are influenced by expectations regarding the future course of interest rates. When interest rates are high and are expected to fall, the call feature is likely to have significant value. Investors are unwilling to invest in callable bonds unless such bonds yield more than bonds that are noncallable, all other things being the same. In other words, they must be compensated for the risk that the bonds might be called. On the other hand, borrowers are willing to pay a premium in yield for the call privilege in the belief that yields will fall and that it will be advantageous to refund the bonds. In equilibrium, both the marginal borrower and the marginal investor will be indifferent as to whether the bond is callable or noncallable.[7]

When interest rates are low and expected to rise, the call privilege may have negligible value, in that the borrower might pay the same yield if there were no call privilege. For the privilege to have value, interest-rate expectations must be such that there is a possibility that the issue will be called. If interest rates are very low and are not expected to fall further, there is little probability that the bonds will be called. The key factor is that the borrower has to be able to refund the issue at a profit. For him to do so, interest rates have to drop significantly, since the issuer must pay the call price, which usually is at a premium above par value, as well as flotation costs involved in the refunding. If there is no probability that the borrower can refund the issue profitably, the call feature is unlikely to have a value.

Empirical Evidence on Valuation

Because virtually all corporate bonds have call features, empirical studies of the differential in yield on a noncallable bond and a callable bond are not possible. However, it is possible to examine the yield differential between newly issued corporate bonds having an immediate call privilege and those of the same grade having a five-year or ten-year deferred call. For the immediate call privilege to have a value over the deferred call privilege, interest-rate expectations must be such that the immediately callable bond might be called during the deferment period. If there is no probability of its being called during this period, the value of the immediate over the deferred call privilege will be zero.

An examination of the yield differential between newly issued bonds of the same grade but with different call privileges reveals that the differential tends to increase in times of high interest rates and tight money, and to decline in periods of easy money and low interest rates. The differential for immediately callable and five-year deferred callable Aa public utility bonds over the period 1958–1970 is shown in Fig. 7-2.

[7]Pye, "*op. cit.*, 203.

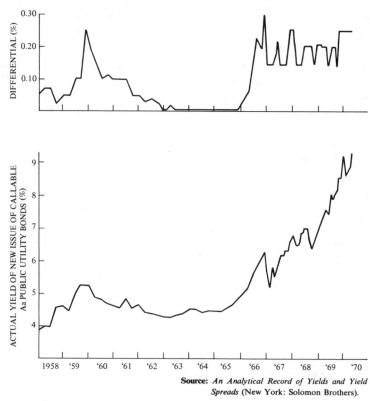

Figure 7-2. Yield differentials: new issues of callable and deferred callable
Aa public utility bonds, 1958-1970.

Source: *An Analytical Record of Yields and Yield Spreads* (New York: Solomon Brothers).

Unfortunately for empirical testing purposes, after the early 1970s utilities ceased to issue immediately callable bonds and issued only deferred callable bonds. In the figure, we see that for the 1959, 1966, and 1968–1970 periods of relatively high interest rates, the differential was fifteen to thirty basis points, whereas during the 1963–1965 period, an immediately callable bond offered no premium over a deferred callable bond.

Frank C. Jen and James E. Wert tested the offering yields of newly issued utility bonds over the 1960–1964 period and found the yield differential to be around zero when coupon rates were low, and positive when coupon rates were high.[8] In another test, Jen and Wert computed and

---

[8]Frank C. Jen and James E. Wert, "The Value of the Deferred Call Privilege," *National Banking Review*, 3 (March, 1966), 369–378. For an extension of this study, see Jen and Wert, "The Deferred Call Provision and Corporate Bond Yields," *Journal of Financial and Quantitative Analysis*, 3 (June, 1968), 157–169.

compared average callable yields and average call-free yields on 434 utility issues issued between 1956 and 1964.[9] The authors found that in periods of relatively high interest rates a number of issues were called. As a result, the average yield actually realized by investors on bonds issued in periods of high interest rates was only slightly higher than the average yield realized on bonds issued in moderate interest-rate periods.

In another study of callable corporate bonds, Mark W. Frankena analyzed yield spreads between low coupon ($2\frac{3}{4}$ to $2\frac{7}{8}$ per cent) and higher coupon ($3\frac{3}{4}$ to $5\frac{3}{4}$ per cent) public utility bonds rated Aaa and Aa.[10] The sample period was 1957–1967. The yield spread was regressed against: (1) the coupon rate on the higher coupon, (2) the level of yields on new issues of callable utility bonds, (3) a weighted average of changes in new issue yields the previous six months, and (4) a time trend variable. The first variable had a positive regression coefficient indicating that the higher the coupon rate, the greater the yield spread. This finding is consistent with low coupon bonds having much less of a possibility of being called than do high coupon bonds; hence they provide a lower yield to maturity.

The second variable had a negative sign, which indicates that when interest rates in general are low, yield spreads are wide. This is consistent with high coupon bonds being in danger of a call in the trough of an interest-rate cycle. As a result, the market price of the bond does not rise significantly above the call price, and this tends to increase yields on high coupon bonds relative to low coupon ones. A negative regression coefficient also was found for the third variable, which indicates that when interest rates in general have been falling yield spreads tend to be wide. Frankena reasons that as interest rates decline the expectation is that yields will continue to fall in the near term. Finally, the trend variable showed that yield spreads declined over the sample period. Frankena suggests that this may be due to the fact that with the rise in interest rates which occurred over the period studied, the possibility of higher coupon bonds being called lessened.

Frankena also studied deferred callable bonds. The hypothesis here was that the deferment period made such bonds more attractive than immediately callable bonds and, hence, resulted in a lower relative yield. Also, the attractiveness of the deferment was hypothesized to vary directly with the coupon rate and inversely with the overall level of interest rates. In general, these hypotheses were confirmed. Thus, the evidence is con-

[9]Jen and Wert, "The Effect of Call Risk on Corporate Bond Yields," *Journal of Finance*, 22 (December, 1967), 637–651.

[10]Mark W. Frankena, "The Influence of Call Provisions and Coupon Rate on Yields of Corporate Bonds," in Jack M. Guttentag, ed., *Essays on Interest Rates*, Vol. 2 (New York: National Bureau of Economic Research, 1971), pp. 134–186.

sistent with our evaluation of the data contained in Fig. 7-2, as well as with the evidence of Jen and Wert on the value of the deferred call feature relative to the value of immediately callable corporate bonds.

In a study of municipal securities, Kidwell analyzes 9,420 issues between 1959 and 1967 regarding the incidence and nature of a call feature.[11] Both general obligations and revenue issues were analyzed. Surprisingly, no statistically significant relationship was found between the percentage of issues which had a call provision and the level of interest rates. One might expect the percentage to be higher at the peak of an interest-rate cycle than it is at the trough. Another line of reasoning would suggest that if yields for callable bonds and noncallable bonds were in equilibrium with respect to the probability of a call, the municipality *should be* indifferent as to a call provision being used. Unfortunately, yield differentials between the two were not analyzed.

Of the bonds that were callable, Kidwell could find no relationship between the number of years to first call (12.2- to 13.2-year range for general obligation and 8.9- to 9.9-year range for revenue bonds) and the level of interest rates. One might expect the deferment period to lengthen as interest rates rose. In testing another hypothesis, Kidwell found that the observed exercise of the call provision by municipalities decreased with the level of interest rates. This makes sense, of course, because only when interest rates decline would we expect a significant number of bonds outstanding to be refunded at a lower interest cost. However, while the relationship was statistically significant, the explanatory power was relatively low, particularly for revenue issues. Kidwell suggests that refunding may not be the dominant motive for the exercise of the call feature by a municipality. All and all, this study represents the only recent analysis of the call feature for municipal securities and contains some interesting insights into the use of the call feature.

In general, the evidence on corporate bonds is consistent with the notion that the call privilege has the most value, and the most cost to the issuer, when interest rates are high and are expected to fall. By the same token, the call privilege has the greatest potential benefit to the corporation at this time. However, for this privilege the corporation must pay a cost at the time the bonds are sold. Moreover, the higher the coupon rate, the greater the danger to the investor of a call, if interest rates should decline. In contrast, a low coupon rate protects the investor because it lessens the probability of a call. However, the market for callable bonds of different coupon rates should equilibrate so that at a moment in time, the marginal investor is indifferent among the various issues. While some of these notions are apparent when municipal bond evidence is examined, there has

[11]Kidwell, *op. cit.*

been a lack of empirical work here. Virtually no work has been done on the call feature for Treasury bonds or on the value of the prepayment penalty for mortgages.

Summary

An additional factor that influences relative yields in the marketplace is callability. A call provision gives the issuer the ability to buy back the debt instrument prior to maturity. Almost all corporate bond issues have a call feature. Some municipal bonds, particularly revenue issues, have a call feature, and certain Treasury bonds have a call feature which is geared to the last five years of the investment. A form of call feature exists for mortgages in the prepayment penalty. Securities can be immediately callable or callable after a deferment period, usually five or ten years.

While the call feature gives the borrower flexibility in refinancing, it works to the disadvantage of the investor. If a security is called, the investor usually suffers an opportunity loss because he can invest in other bonds only at a sacrifice in yield. For this reason, the call feature has significant value when interest rates are high and expected to fall. By value, we mean that there is a differential between what the callable bond yields and what it would yield if it were noncallable. The call feature usually has value only as long as there is some probability that the issue might be called. In turn, this probability depends on interest-rate expectations. Empirical evidence on immediately callable and deferred callable corporate bonds is consistent with the call feature's having the most value when interest rates are relatively high, and little or no value when they are low. There has been little empirical testing of the value of the call feature for other issuers.

The call feature influences the valuation of bonds selling for less than their face value. The greater the discount, the less the probability that the bond will be called. To the extent that investors value this protection, it will influence upward the demand for discount bonds relative to that for other bonds. Another and more important factor influencing the valuation of discount bonds is taxability, which we will take up in the next chapter.

SELECTED REFERENCES

Cook, Timothy Q., "Some Factors Affecting Long-Term Yield Spreads in Recent Years," *Monthly Review of the Federal Reserve Bank of Richmond*, 59 (September, 1973), 2–14.

Elton, Edwin J., and Martin J. Gruber, "The Economic Value of the Call Option," *Journal of Finance*, 27 (September, 1972), 891–902.

Frankena, Mark W., "The Influence of Call Provisions and Coupon Rate on Yields of Corporate Bonds," in Jack M. Guttentag, ed., *Essays on Interest Rates*, Vol. 2, pp. 134–186. New York: National Bureau of Economic Research, 1971.

Jen, Frank C., and James E. Wert, "The Deferred Call Provision and Corporate Bond Yields," *Journal of Financial and Quantitative Analysis*, 3 (June, 1968), 157–169.

_____, "The Effect of Call Risk on Corporate Bond Yields," *Journal of Finance*, 22 (December, 1967), 637–651.

_____, "The Value of the Deferred Call Privilege," *National Banking Review*, 3 (March, 1966), 369–378.

Kidwell, David S., "The Inclusion and Exercise of Call Provisions by State and Local Governments," *Journal of Money, Credit and Banking*, 8 (August, 1976), 391–398.

Pye, Gordon, "The Value of the Call Option on a Bond," *Journal of Political Economy*, 74 (April, 1966), 200–205.

_____, "The Value of Call Deferment of a Bond: Some Empirical Results," *Journal of Finance*, 22 (December, 1967), 623–636.

Winn, Willis J., and Arleigh Hess, Jr., "The Value of the Call Privilege," *Journal of Finance*, 14 (May, 1959), 182–195.

The Effect of Taxes
on Yields

8 Another influence that we observe on the market yields is that of taxes. Up until now this effect has been ignored as we tried to explain the influences of maturity, default risk, and callability on yields. In this chapter we remedy this deficiency by extending our analysis to consider the consequences of a taxable world on yields and on yield differentials.

In the absence of taxes, the yield of a fixed-income security with a $1,000 face value and annual interest payments is found by solving the following equation for r:

$$P_0 = \sum_{t=1}^{n} \frac{C_t}{(1+r)^t} + \frac{\$1,000}{(1+r)^n} \qquad (8\text{-}1)$$

where P_0 is the current market price

C_t is the coupon payment at time t

n is the number of years to final maturity

The yield, or r, represents the promised rate of return applicable to all investors. Markets would be expected to equilibrate in terms of this rate, as it would be the relevant measure of return for all investors.

With taxes, r no longer represents the relevant return for all investors. The reason is that Eq. (8-1) does not take into account whether or not interest income is taxed and whether or not part of the yield to maturity is comprised of capital gains which are taxed at a different rate from that for interest income. Therefore, the equation does not allow one to determine the effective after-tax rate of return which, for the rational investor, is the relevant consideration. We would expect financial markets to equilibrate in terms of after-tax rates of return. Because of different tax situations, a financial instrument will imply different after-tax yields for different investors despite the fact that the before-tax yield [r in Eq. (8-1)] is the same for all of them.

The after-tax yield to maturity for a financial instrument can be expressed as the discount rate $\bar{r}$, which equates its current market price with the present value of after-tax cash returns. Thus,

$$P_0 = \sum_{t=1}^{n} \frac{C_t(1-T)}{(1+\bar{r})^t} + \frac{(\$1,000 - P_0)(1-G)}{(1+\bar{r})^n} + \frac{P_0}{(1+\bar{r})^n} \qquad (8\text{-}2)$$

where T is the marginal tax rate on ordinary income for the investor and G is his marginal tax rate on capital gains. We see that interest payments are taxed as ordinary income while any capital gain which occurs at final maturity, denoted by ($\$1,000 - P_0$), is taxed at the capital gains rate. In the past the capital gains tax rate on assets held more than six months was one-half the ordinary income tax rate, with a maximum tax rate of 25 per cent. However, the Tax Reform Act of 1976 has extended the time the asset must be held to qualify for a capital gain to one year and has increased the tax relative to that on ordinary income for high-income individuals.

In cases where a security is bought at a premium over its face value—i.e., where $P_0 > \$1,000$—a capital loss is involved. The investor has two options. He may amortize the premium over the remaining life of the instrument and deduct the prorated amount each year from ordinary income. For example, if a bond were purchased for $1,080 and it had a remaining life of 20 years, the investor would be entitled to deduct $4 each year.[1] The other option is to wait until maturity or until the instrument is sold and then declare a capital loss. As the former tax treatment usually is more favorable to the investor, it is typically employed.

Throughout the remainder of this chapter, Eq. (8-2) will serve as a focal point for the discussion of a number of tax issues. We assume that rational investors attempt to maximize their after-tax rates of return, as denoted by $\bar{r}$ in Eq. (8-2), relative to the perceived risk involved. As marginal tax rates for interest income and capital gains vary across investors, equilibration in financial markets is considerably complicated. In concept, prices should adjust so that in equilibrium the risk-adjusted after-tax yield to the marginal investor is the same for all financial instruments he might consider. This proposition may need to be modified for market imperfections. However, to the extent that it serves as an appropriate generalization of static equilibrium in financial markets, we

---

[1] If a bond is callable, the premium over the call price may be amortized to the first call date if this results in a smaller deduction than occurs if the full premium is amortized to maturity.

shall use it. In the remainder of the chapter, we wish to analyze the effect of taxes on yields and on yield differentials. We will be concerned with whether interest income is taxed, with the differential tax on interest income and capital gains, with the effect of depreciation and the investment tax credit on the expected return of a lease instrument, and with the effect of certain special tax considerations on yields.

Taxation of Interest Income

The tax treatment of interest income is different for different financial instruments. As a result, the after-tax rate of return computed with Eq. (8-2) is affected. Interest on state and local government securities is exempt from federal income taxes while that for other financial instruments is taxed at the ordinary income tax rate.[2] Consequently, observed before-tax yields are lower for municipal securities than they are for other securities of equivalent risk. The usual comparison is with corporate bonds. In Fig. 8-1, the yield differential between Aaa public utility bonds and Aaa municipal bonds is shown for the 1951–1976 period. It is seen that the yield differential is always positive, ranging between 0.70 per cent and 3.00 per cent.

We see also that the yield differential varies to some extent with the level of interest rates. This is because the tax benefit is proportional to level of interest rates. To illustrate, suppose the marginal tax rate for an investor were 40 per cent and the yield on taxable bonds were $7\frac{1}{2}$ per cent. The yield on the tax exempt security would then need to be $7\frac{1}{2}\%(1-0.4)=$ $4\frac{1}{2}$ per cent in order for the investor to be indifferent between the two securities on an after-tax basis. Under these circumstances, the yield differential would be 3 per cent. Suppose now that interest rates rose and that the taxable bond yields 10 per cent. The tax exempt security then would need to yield 6 per cent for the investor to be indifferent between the two, and the yield differential would be 4 per cent. Thus, the yield differential would be expected to vary with the overall level of interest rates.

As seen in Fig. 8-1, the spread between the two yields tends to rise and fall to some degree in keeping with rises and falls in the corporate rate. While the tax effect certainly is not the only explanation for the movement in the yield differential over time, it is an important one. If the marginal tax rate were constant over time, we might expect proportional changes in

---

[2]In addition, the interest income for municipal securities is usually not subject to state income taxes if the security is an obligation of the state involved or an obligation of a local government within the state. However, if the security is of another state, the interest is taxable.

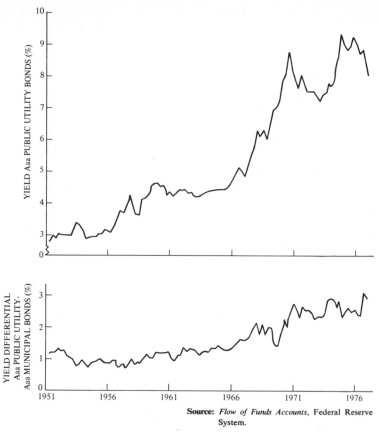

Figure 8-1. Aaa public utility bond yields and yield differentials with Aaa
municipal bond yields, 1951-1976.

yields for corporate and municipal bonds. We see that although the
marginal tax rate varies to some extent over time and other factors are *not*
held constant, there still is a close correspondence between movements in
the two series of yields.

The Segmented Nature of the Municipal Market

Because of the tax-exempt feature, municipal securities are
of interest mainly to individuals in high tax brackets and to financial
intermediaries paying taxes at or nearly at the full corporate tax rate. A
nonprofit organization which pays no taxes would have little reason to
invest in municipal securities, considering that yields on default-free

Treasury securities are higher. Similarly, life insurance companies, which pay only a limited tax, are able to take only partial advantage of the tax-exempt feature. As a result, the demand for municipals is relatively segmented. The market consists mainly of commercial banks, high income individuals, and fire and casualty companies. This segmentation is further characterized by the volatile participation by commercial banks. When banks experience a period of high loan demand and monetary restriction by the Federal Reserve, their relative commitment to municipal securities declines. Consequently, investment in new issues must be filled by other investors—individuals in particular. These investors can only be attracted by higher and higher yields. In contrast, in periods of low loan demand and easy money, banks bid aggressively for municipal bonds and the role of individuals becomes much less important. This usually corresponds to a period of falling interest rates.

The ebb and flow between commercial banks and households with respect to net investment in municipal securities is seen in Table 8-1. As shown, the investment behavior of commercial banks fluctuated widely over the 1960–1975 period. In the tight money eras of 1966, 1969, and 1974–1975, the net purchases by banks contracted considerably. During these periods, the household sector substantially expanded its holdings of municipals. In contrast, in periods like 1962, 1965, 1967–1968, and 1970–1971 banks increased dramatically their net purchases of municipal

Table 8-1. Net Changes in Holdings of Municipal Securities, 1960–1975 (in billions)

Year	Commercial Banks	Households	Fire and Casualty Companies	Other	Total Change
1960	$0.7	$3.5	$0.8	$3.0	$5.3
1961	2.8	1.2	1.0	1.0	5.1
1962	5.7	−1.0	0.8	−0.1	5.4
1963	3.9	1.0	0.7	0.1	5.7
1964	3.6	2.6	0.4	−0.6	6.0
1965	5.2	1.7	0.4	0	7.3
1966	2.3	3.6	1.3	−1.6	5.6
1967	9.1	−2.2	1.4	−1.5	7.8
1968	8.6	−0.8	1.0	0.7	9.5
1969	0.2	9.6	1.2	−1.1	9.9
1970	10.7	−0.8	1.5	−0.1	11.3
1971	12.6	−0.2	3.9	1.3	17.6
1972	7.2	1.0	4.8	1.4	14.4
1973	5.7	4.3	3.9	−0.2	13.7
1974	5.5	10.0	1.8	0.1	17.4
1975	1.7	7.0	2.1	4.6	15.4

Source: Flow of Funds Accounts, Federal Reserve System.

securities, and households correspondingly reduced their net purchases. In most of those years there was a net liquidation of municipals by the household sector.

Throughout this time frame, the investment behavior of fire and casualty companies was much more stable. However, in 1971–1973, fire and casualty companies were large purchasers of municipal securities on a relative basis.[3] The "other" sector was large in 1975 primarily because of the substantial purchase of New York City obligations by New York State and by City retirement funds and general funds. These purchases were made in conjunction with the near default of New York City described earlier. Because state or local governments do not pay taxes, they usually invest in taxable bonds where yields are more attractive.

By the mid 1970s, there was some question as to whether commercial banks would once again dominate the municipal market. Direct leasing as well as foreign operations competed with municipal bonds as tax sheltered investments. Both had grown considerably in importance and had lessened the appeal of municipals to commercial banks. In addition to these competing demands, commercial banks endeavored to restore their liquidity in 1975 and invested heavily in Treasury securities.

The segmented market for municipal securities, the fluctuating investment behavior of commercial banks, and the heavy and growing demand for funds by municipalities has caused yields in the municipal market to fluctuate somewhat more than yields in other markets. This is seen in Fig. 8-2, where yields on high coupon Aa public utility bonds and on the 20-bond municipal index are shown. While the two sets of yields tend to move together, the fluctuation in the municipal rate is greater on a relative basis when one considers the lower level of yields for municipals on which percentage changes are based. The greater relative fluctuation was more evident in the 1960s than it was in the 1970s. In the latter period, there was a considerable amount of absolute fluctuation in both corporate and municipal rates.

The importance of commercial banks in the municipal bond market on the demand side affects not only the variability of yields but also the term structure. Because of the nature of their deposit liabilities, banks are interested primarily in shorter maturities. Very seldom will a bank purchase a long-term municipal. As a result, there is greater relative demand for short-term securities than for long-term securities. Accordingly, the yield curve for municipals is almost always upward-sloping.

[3]For an excellent and extensive analysis of the pattern of demand for municipal bonds, see John Peterson, *Changing Conditions in the Market for State and Local Government Debt*, a study for the Joint Economic Committee, 94th Congress, 2d Session (Washington, D.C.: U.S. Government Printing Office, April 16, 1976), Chapter 5. See also his Chapter 2 for an analysis of the expanded supply of municipal securities embodying such nontraditional forms as moral obligation bonds, industrial revenue bonds, and pollution control bonds.

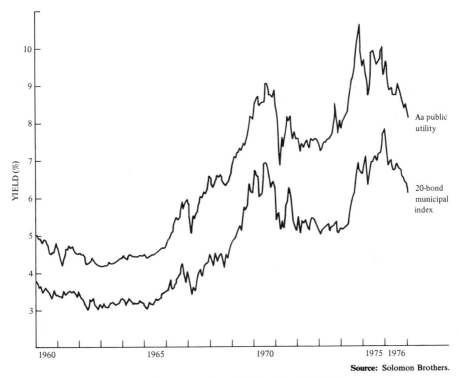

Source: Solomon Brothers.

Figure 8-2. Corporate and municipal yields, 1960-1976.

Value of the Tax Exemption Feature

One of the interesting aspects of the municipal market is the value placed on tax exemption. For an investor to be indifferent between a municipal security and, say, a corporate security of equal risk, the following would need to hold:

$$r_{\text{muni.}} = r_{\text{corp.}}(1 - T) \qquad (8\text{-}3)$$

where $r_{\text{muni.}}$ = the yield on the municipal security
$r_{\text{corp.}}$ = the yield on the corporate
T = the marginal tax rate of the investor .

We assume that the return on both securities is comprised solely of interest income, with no capital gains or losses. If $r_{\text{muni.}}$ were greater than $r_{\text{corp.}}(1 - T)$, the rational investor would invest in municipal securities; if it were less, he would invest in corporates. The implied marginal tax rate in the

market can be determined by

$$T_{\text{mkt.}} = 1 - \frac{r_{\text{muni.}}}{r_{\text{corp.}}} \qquad (8\text{-}4)$$

If a rational investor had a marginal tax rate (comprised of both federal and state and local income taxes) greater than $T_{\text{mkt.}}$, he would invest in municipals; if the marginal tax rate were less, he would invest in corporates.

If we regard Aaa municipal securities and Aaa corporate securities as comparable from the standpoint of risk, the implied marginal tax rate would be that shown in Fig. 8-3 for the 1950–1976 period. [The calculations involved use Eq. (8-4).] As seen in the figure, the implied tax rate fluctuated between 18 and 42 per cent over the period studied. This fluctuation is due in part to the segmented nature of the market which we discussed earlier. However, apart from this fluctuation, we see that the implied marginal tax rate averaged only about 30 per cent; yet the investors in municipal securities are usually individuals with high incomes and financial institutions whose marginal tax rate, when state and local income taxes as well as federal income taxes are taken into account, must surely be in the neighborhood of 50 per cent. This suggests that the tax exemption feature is not fully priced in the marketplace.[4] Put another way, municipalities are not obtaining the full benefit of the tax exemption feature. A sizable portion of it goes to investors.

Source: *Moody's Public Utility and Municipal and Government Manual.*

Figure 8-3 Implied marginal tax rate using Aaa public Utility and Aaa municipal bonds, 1951-1976

[4]This point was first made by Roland T. Robinson, *Postwar Market for State and Local Government Securities* (New York: National Bureau of Economic Research, 1960), Chapter 6.

It should be pointed out that this phenomenon is most evident in the long-term end of the market. For short- and intermediate-term maturities, yields on municipal securities are less in relation to corporate yields than they are for long-term maturities. Thus, a greater portion of the tax exempt feature is realized by the municipality vis à vis the investor. This is attributable primarily to commercial banks restricting their investment activities to the short- and intermediate-term end of the market. Thus, the degree to which tax exemption reduces municipal interest costs varies inversely with maturity. The longer the maturity, the greater the proportion of the tax exemption subsidy that is realized by the investor and the less that is realized by the municipality.

The portion of the tax exemption subsidy going to the investors also varies with the interest-rate cycle. When interest rates are high and credit is tight, municipalities have to offer sizable yield inducements to attract marginal investors. As a result, the investors' portion of the tax exempt feature increases and the portion going to the municipality declines. The opposite tends to occur in an interest-rate trough. Thus, when interest rates in general are high, the municipality's borrowing costs tend to be accentuated further by the fact that the tax exemption subsidy must be increasingly shared with investors. The reason for this occurrence is that only a limited number of investors are able to take advantage of the feature.

Broadening the Municipal Market

The tax exemption feature has been criticized because a sizable and fluctuating portion of the total tax revenues foregone by the Treasury goes to investors and not to the state and local governments for which the feature was intended. Rough estimates suggest that between 25 and 30 per cent of the tax revenues foregone go to investors.[5] In order to broaden the market for municipal securities and lower the interest portion of the tax exemption subsidy going to investors, a taxable bond option has been proposed for the municipality. This option would give the state or local government the ability to issue bonds in the taxable market and then receive a federal subsidy. In other words, the municipality would receive a subsidy from the federal government and would sell bonds without the tax exemption feature. To be sure, the interest cost would be higher, but the municipality would be appealing to a broader market. The *ex ante* higher interest cost would be more than offset by the subsidy; otherwise the municipality would elect to issue bonds in the tax-exempt market. In short,

[5]See Peterson, *op. cit.*, pp. 56–58.

the option would be that of the municipality in determining in which market—the taxable market or the tax-exempt market—it wished to borrow.[6]

The critical factor is the per cent of the municipality's interest cost the federal government would subsidize. Most proposals call for a subsidy of between 30 and 40 per cent of the interest cost. The higher the subsidy, of course, the greater the use that would be made of the taxable as opposed to the tax-exempt market. At a very high subsidy, of course, only taxable bonds would be employed.[7] Also, proposals call for a fixed percentage subsidy across maturities and over time. As the portion of the present tax exempt subsidy going to investors is greatest for long-term maturities, the taxable bond option would have the greatest benefit to the municipality for that end of the maturity structure. In fact, municipalities might issue bonds in the early maturities on a tax-exempt basis and bonds in the later maturities on a taxable basis. In addition, the fixed rate subsidy would be more valuable at the peaks of an interest-rate cycle than at the troughs. Therefore, municipalities would be expected to make greater use of the option to issue bonds in the taxable market at interest-rate peaks than they would at the troughs.

These are but some of the issues associated with the taxable bond option. The purpose is to allow municipalities to avoid some of the problems that arise from the segmented nature of the present municipal market by tapping a broader market. It would work to lower the portion of the tax-exempt feature that goes to investors. The proposal itself has surfaced twice during the last decade, but Congress has not enacted the option. Undoubtedly it will surface again, and that is the reason it is explored here.

Differential Taxes on Interest and Capital Gains

As discussed in the introduction, interest income and capital gains are taxed at different rates. While Congress has effectively raised the capital gains tax relative to that on ordinary income in recent years, there

---

[6]Mechanically, the best way to make the federal payment subsidy is to the interest paying agent. Only upon receipt of funds from the municipality for the balance of the interest payment would the subsidy funds be disbursed to investors. If the federal government paid investors directly, it would be underwriting a portion of the default risk of the municipality. If it paid the funds to the municipality, it would be a form of revenue sharing. Only if the payment of the subsidy is linked to the ability of the municipality to service its debt does the federal government avoid these problems. By restricting the interest paying agent in the manner described above, the federal government interferes least in the market process.

[7]For an analysis of the effect of this option on the portion of the subsidy realized by the municipality, see Harvey Galper and John Peterson, "An Analysis of Subsidy Plans to Support State and Local Borrowing," *National Tax Journal*, 24 (June, 1971), 205–234.

still is an advantage to capital gains that has an important effect on the yields we observe. Recall that the after-tax rate of return for a bond held to maturity is determined by solving the following equation for $\bar{r}$:

$$P_0 = \sum_{t=1}^{n} \frac{C_t(1-T)}{(1+\bar{r})^t} + \frac{(\$1,000 - P_0)(1-G)}{(1+\bar{r})^n} + \frac{P_0}{(1+\bar{r})^n} \tag{8-5}$$

where C_t is the interest payment at the end of year t,
$\qquad$ P_0 is the present market price,
$\qquad$ n is the number of years to final maturity, and
$\quad$ T and G are the marginal tax rates on interest income and capital gains respectively for the investor.

If T exceeds G, it is clear that a dollar of capital gains on a discounted present-value basis is more valuable than a dollar of interest income, again on a discounted present-value basis. This applies to all fixed-income securities other than municipals, which we will discuss shortly.

The favorable tax treatment of capital gains makes fixed-income securities selling at a discount from their face values attractive to investors.[8] As a result, their yield to maturity tends to be lower than the yield of comparable bonds with higher coupon rates. The greater the discount, the greater the capital gains attraction of the bond and the lower its yield relative to what it would be if the coupon rate were such that the bond sold at par. Another attraction of discount bonds, of course, is that they are less likely to be called. As this influence was discussed in the previous chapter, we will concentrate here on the tax effect alone.

The Attraction of Discount Bonds

The attractiveness of discount bonds can be visualized by comparing the yields for low coupon bonds already outstanding with yields for newly issued bonds where the coupon rate reflects the current level of interest rates. More specifically, we compare yields on Aa public utility bonds having a $4\frac{1}{8}$ to $4\frac{3}{8}$ per cent coupon with newly issued Aa public utility bonds having a five-year deferred call feature. The yield differential between the two sets of yields, as well as the yield on the newly issued bonds, are shown in Fig. 8-4 for the 1960–1976 period. As seen in the figure, the yield differential tends to widen as interest rates rise and

[8]Treasury bills and certain other money-market instruments are sold in the market without coupons. The yield is determined by the amount of discount. In these cases, the discount is taxed at the ordinary income tax rate despite the fact that the instrument might be held for a period longer than that required for capital gains purposes. The tax itself is payable in the year the instrument is sold by the investor or at maturity if held to that time.

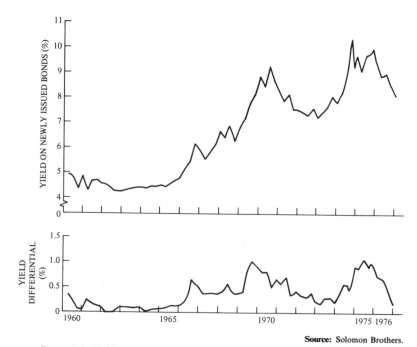

Source: Solomon Brothers.

Figure 8-4. Yields on newly issued Aa public utility bonds and differential with $4\frac{1}{8}$–$4\frac{3}{8}$ per cent coupon seasoned Aa public utility bonds, 1960-1976.

narrow as interest rates decline. In the early to mid-1960s the coupon rate on newly issued bonds was only slightly above the $4\frac{1}{8}$–$4\frac{3}{8}$ per cent coupon for the seasoned bonds used in comparison. As a result, the yield differential between the two sets of bonds was very small—sometimes zero. As interest rates began to rise in 1966, so too did the yield differential. This was as expected. Also, as the interest rate on newly issued bonds fluctuated from 1967 through 1969, so too did the yield differential.

The pattern of behavior of the yield differential from 1970 on also follows the pattern for the level of interest rates. However, the yield differential is lower relative to the level of interest rates than it was in earlier periods. Put another way, the $4\frac{1}{8}$–$4\frac{3}{8}$ per cent coupon bonds sell at a lesser discount in relation to the overall level of interest rates than they did in the 1960s. For example, in 1967 the yield differential averaged 0.33 per cent while the yield on five-year deferred callable Aa public utility new issues averaged 5.87 per cent. In 1972, the yield differential averaged 0.34 per cent while the average yield on new issues was 7.45 per cent, and in 1973 it averaged 0.28 per cent while the average yield on new issues was 7.74 per cent. Thus, the "value" of discount bonds would appear to have declined from the 1960s to the 1970s.

To probe into the reasons, suppose an investor were in a 40 per cent tax bracket with respect to interest income and 20 per cent with respect to capital gains. Suppose further that the coupon rate on a seasoned bond were $4\frac{1}{4}$ per cent with a maturity of 20 years. If the investor is interested in the before-tax yield necessary for a newly issued bond of 20 years to provide an after-tax yield equal to that of the seasoned bond, the relationships in Fig. 8-5 would hold.[9] On the horizontal axis we have after-tax yield and on the vertical axis before-tax yield. The diagonal lines represent

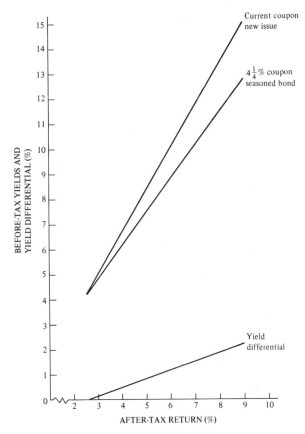

Figure 8-5. Yields on newly issued current coupon bonds, $4\frac{1}{4}$ per cent coupon seasoned bonds, and yield differential for various after-tax rates of return. Assumptions: 20-year maturity, 40% ordinary income tax applicable to interest income and 20% capital gains tax applicable to capital gains at maturity.

[9]The idea of this example came from Timothy Q. Cook, "Some Factors Affecting Long-Term Yield Spreads in Recent Years," *Monthly Review of the Federal Reserve Bank of Richmond,* 59 (September, 1973), 7.

the relationships between before- and after-tax yields for the new issue, for the $4\frac{1}{4}$ per cent coupon bond, and for the yield differential between the two. The after-tax yield for the new issue is simply $(1-0.4)$ times the before-tax yield. Because capital gains are involved for the seasoned bond, a variation of Eq. (8-4) is used to compute the after-tax yield. At $4\frac{1}{4}$ per cent of course, the after-tax yield for both securities is the same, 2.55 per cent, because there is no capital gain for the seasoned bond. For before-tax yields in excess of $4\frac{1}{4}$ per cent, however, the after-tax yields differ. We shall use Fig. 8-5 as a rough proxy for the relationship between the yield differential and the level of interest rates, based on tax considerations alone. This will be more or less true depending on how closely the tax rates of the marginal investor are 40 per cent and 20 per cent for interest income and capital gains respectively.

A comparison of Fig. 8-5 with Fig. 8-4 suggests that the actual yield differential shown in the former figure is roughly in line with new issues yields for most of the 1960s, but that this is not the case for the 1970s. Beginning in late 1969, the yield differential narrowed, and in mid-1970 yields on newly issued bonds began to decline. During 1972–1973, the differential fluctuated between 0.20 per cent and 0.40 per cent. Yet the new issue yield was around $7\frac{1}{2}$ per cent for most of this time which would suggest, according to Fig. 8-5, a yield differential of around 0.65 per cent. While at the peak 1974–1975 period the yield differential widened to about 1.05 per cent, it declined to a very low 0.20 per cent by the end of 1976. At that time, the yield on new issues was about 8 per cent, which would suggest a yield differential of about 0.75 per cent according to Fig. 8-5. A comparison of Fig. 8-5 with Fig. 8-4 then confirms our earlier suspicion that the behavior of the yield differential in Fig. 8-4 is *not* consistent over time with respect to taxes.

Several explanations are possible. First, the perception of a bond being called changes as interest rates rise. Whereas a $4\frac{1}{4}$ per cent coupon bond offered considerable perceived protection to investors in 1966, when interest rates rose to post-World War II highs of 6 per cent, investors gradually became accustomed to higher interest rates. If by the 1970s the perception was that there was little prospect of Aa newly issued public utility yields dropping below 7 per cent, the $4\frac{1}{4}$ per cent seasoned bonds would offer little more in the way of call protection than a seasoned bond with a $6\frac{1}{2}$ per cent coupon rate. To the extent that call protection is valued in discount bonds, it would be relatively more important for $4\frac{1}{4}$ per cent coupon bonds in the 1960s than it was in the 1970s. While this explanation is weakened by the fact that the newly issued bonds all had a five-year deferred call feature, we know from Chapter 7 that investors still take account of the likelihood of a call beyond the deferment period.

Another explanation might be that the composition of investors has changed over time, leaning toward those in lower tax brackets. To the extent that marginal investors exhibit declining tax brackets over time, the demand for current coupon new issues would increase relative to that for discount bonds, all other things the same. As a result, the yield differential would be expected to narrow. There is indication that the ownership pattern has changed from the 1960s to the 1970s. Using benchmark dates of 1963 and 1973, the percentage of ownership of corporate bonds in the United States was as follows:[10]

Investor Category	1963	1973
Commercial banks	0.8%	2.3%
Mutual savings banks	3.2	5.3
Life insurance companies	53.8	37.1
Property and liability insurance companies	1.7	2.9
Noninsured pension funds	16.8	11.0
State and local government retirement funds	11.5	19.8
Mutual investment companies	1.8	1.7
Individuals and others	10.4	19.8
	100.0%	100.0%

Clearly the increase in the importance of state and local government retirement funds is a movement toward lower tax bracketed investors, for these funds pay no taxes. Noninsured pension funds also pay no taxes for the most part, but there was a sizable decline in percentage of ownership here. Life insurance companies pay only limited taxes, and there was a substantial decline in ownership for these companies from 1963 to 1973. Individuals and others would be expected to pay taxes at regular rates, so the increased percentage of ownership here would probably be a movement toward higher tax bracketed investors. On balance, then, the evidence is mixed and we are unable to make the case that the ownership of corporate bonds has shifted toward lower tax bracketed investors.

Finally, and perhaps most important, there have been changes in the tax code which make capital gains less attractive relative to interest income than once was the case. In the Tax Reform Act of 1969, the maximum capital gains tax was increased from 25 per cent to 32.5 per cent for individuals and to 30 per cent for corporations.[11] In the Tax Reform Act of 1976, the length of the holding period was increased in steps from six months to one year, and changes in the minimum and maximum taxes effectively raised the capital gains tax rate for certain individuals. These tax changes lessen the attraction of discount bonds, all other things the

[10]The source is *Flow of Funds Accounts* of the Federal Reserve System.
[11]For an analysis of this change on yields, see Cook, *op. cit.*

same. As a result, the yield differential between current coupon new issues and lower coupon seasoned bonds would be expected to narrow. Some of the narrowing of the yield differential in late 1969 and 1970 as well as in late 1976 may be attributable to this cause. Indeed, if rationality prevails the yield differential would change with any tax change that makes capital gains less or more attractive.

Capital Gains Valuation for Municipal Bonds

While capital gains are attractive to taxable investors for most fixed-income securities, they are not for the investor in municipal bonds. Any capital gain realized upon the sale of a municipal security or upon its final redemption is subject to a capital gains tax. This contrasts with interest income, which is tax exempt. As a result, the yield behavior of discount bonds is exactly opposite to that which occurs for bonds in the taxable market. Municipal bonds selling at a discount typically provide a yield higher than that for comparable bonds selling at par. In other words, bonds selling at par are more attractive than discount bonds because their return is comprised entirely of interest and the final principal payment, neither of which are subject to taxation. Referring to our basic valuation formula for determining the after-tax rate of return, Eq. (8-5), it is clear that if $T=0$ and G is positive, the discount bond will provide a lower after-tax rate of return for the investor who is taxed than will a bond whose market price equals $1,000, all other things being the same. If market equilibration occurs in terms of after-tax rates of return, the discount bond must provide a higher yield than the municipal bond selling at par.

Estate Tax Bonds

For certain Treasury bonds, there is yet another phenomenon associated with discount bonds. Certain bonds issued prior to 1963 can be used in the payment of federal estate taxes, if they are owned by the deceased at the time of death. Known as "flower" bonds, these bonds count at their full face value in the settlement of estate taxes. For example, if a "flower" bond had a coupon rate below current prevailing interest rates such that its market price were $800, it could be purchased and at the time of death would be worth $1,000 in the payment of federal estate taxes. This advantage was reduced but not eliminated by the Tax Reform Act of 1976. Beginning in 1977, the estate must pay capital gains taxes based on the original cost of the security or upon its market value at

December 31, 1976, whichever is higher. Moreover, the holding period necessary to qualify for a capital gains tax treatment was extended from six months to one year, beginning in 1978. Thus, the difference in price between what is paid for a "flower" bond and its face value when used in the settlement of estate taxes will be subject to taxation, whereas before it was not. Moreover, the security must be purchased at least one year before death to qualify for the more favorable capital gains tax treatment. As a result of these tax changes, "flower" bonds are less attractive than before but they still retain some estate tax benefits.

The Value of "Flower" Bonds

Because of these benefits and the resulting demand for them, "flower" bonds tend to sell at lower yields than do other Treasury bonds of roughly the same maturity. In Fig. 8-6, bid-ask quotations on January 26, 1977 are shown for longer-term Treasury securities. The asterisks before the bonds denote estate tax bonds. In particular, we see that the longest-term "flower" bonds have the lowest yields relative to surrounding issues. The 3s of 1995 yield 4.77 per cent while the $3\frac{1}{2}$s of 1998 yield 5.14 per cent. Yields on bonds with current coupons and approximately the same maturity are about $7\frac{1}{2}$ per cent. Therefore, there is a substantial yield sacrifice associated with these "flower" bonds. To be sure there would be a yield sacrifice associated with bonds having low coupon rates even if they were not "flower" bonds. Figure 8-5 can be used as a rough gauge of the capital gains attraction for an investor with marginal tax rates of 40 per cent on ordinary income and 20 per cent on capital gains. From the figure, we see that the yield differential between a 20-year bond with a current coupon rate of $7\frac{1}{2}$ per cent and one with a $4\frac{1}{4}$ per cent coupon rate is about 0.65 per cent. While the two longer term "flower" bonds have somewhat lower coupon rates, it is clear that considerably more than capital gains attraction is involved in their valuation.

We see also in Fig. 8-6 that for "flower" bonds with longer maturities, the yield sacrifice tends to be greater. For example, the 4s of 1980 yield 6.26 per cent while the $7\frac{1}{2}$s of 1980 yield 6.43 per cent—a modest yield differential. In contrast, the $3\frac{1}{2}$s of 1998, the longest-term "flower" bonds, yield 5.14 per cent compared with 7.22 per cent for the 7s of 1993–1998—a substantial yield spread. If a "flower" bond were bought for its estate tax value rather than its current yield, the purchaser would favor the bonds with the lowest coupon rate and the longest time to maturity. These are the 3s of 1995 and the $3\frac{1}{2}$s of 1998, and indeed they have the lowest yields to maturity of the "flower" bonds outstanding.

As "flower" bonds are used to pay federal estate taxes, they are

Wednesday, January 26, 1977
Over-the-Counter Quotations: Source on request.
Decimals in bid-and-asked and bid changes represent
32nds 101.1 means 101 1-32. a-Plus 1-64. b-Yield to
call date. d-Minus 1-64.

U.S. TREASURY BONDS

			Bid	Asked	Bid Chg.	Yld.
*4s,	1980 Feb	......	93.10	93.26–	.2	6.26
7 1/2s,	1980 Mar n	.....	102.24	103	.....	6.43
6 7/8s,	1980 May n	.....	100.31	101.7.	...	6.46
7 5/8s,	1980 Jun n	.....	103.2	103.10	. ..	6.53
9s,	1980 Aug n	.....	107.14	107.22–	.2	6.54
6 7/8s,	1980 Sep n	.....	100.23	100.31–	.2	6.56
*3 1/2s,	1980 Nov	......	90.8	91.8 –	.2	6.12
5 7/8s,	1980 Dec n	.....	97.20	97.24–	.1	6.53
7s,	1981 Feb n	.....	100.30	101.6 –	.1	6.67
7 3/8s,	1981 Feb n	.....	102.5	102.13	. ..	6.69
7 3/8s,	1981 May n	.....	102.6	102.14	. ..	6.71
7 5/8s,	1981 Aug n	.....	103.1	103.9 –	.2	6.78
7s,	1981 Aug	......	101.1	102.1 –	.1	6.47
7s,	1981 Nov n	.....	100.25	101.1.	...	6.74
7 3/4s,	1981 Nov n	.....	103.23	103.31–	.1	6.76
6 1/8s,	1982 Feb n	.....	97.11	97.13–	.1	6.73
6 3/8s,	1982 Feb	......	98.12	98.28	. ..	6.64
8s,	1982 May n	.....	104.22	104.30–	.2	6.87
8 1/8s,	1982 Aug n	.....	105.6	105.14–	.2	6.93
7 7/8s,	1982 Nov n	.....	104.5	104.13+	.1	6.94
8s,	1983 Feb n	.....	104.24	105 –	.2	6.97
*3 1/4s,	1978-83 Jun	....	81.10	82.10–	.2	6.70
7s,	1983 Nov n	.....	100.1	100.5 –	.1	6.97
6 3/8s,	1984 Aug	......	97.10	98.10+	.2	6.66
*3 1/4s,	1985 May	......	78.10	79.10–	.14	6.52
*4 1/4s,	1975-85 May	....	82.28	83.28–	.4	7.01
7 7/8s,	1986 May n	.....	103.23	103.31–	.3	7.28
8s,	1986 Aug n	.....	104.23	104.27–	.4	7.28
6 1/8s,	1986 Nov	......	96.4	97.4 –	.4	6.53
*3 1/2s,	1990 Feb	......	77.24	78.24–	.6	5.85
8 1/4s,	1990 May	......	106.24	107.8 –	.2	7.38
*4 1/4s,	1987-92 Aug	....	78.22	79.22–	.8	6.32
*4s,	1988-93 Feb	....	78.18	79.18–	.4	6.00
6 3/4s,	1993 Feb	......	95.24	96.24.	..	7.09
7 1/2s,	1988-93 Aug	....	100.14	101.14–	.4	7.31
*4 1/8s,	1989-94 May	....	78.12	79.12–	.4	6.07
*3s,	1995 Feb	......	77.22	78.22–	.6	4.77
7s,	1993-98 May	....	96.22	97.22	. ..	7.22
*3 1/2s,	1998 Nov	......	77.22	78.22–	.14	5.14
8 1/2s,	1994-99 May	....	107.22	108.6 –	.8	7.64
7 7/8s,	1995-00 Feb	....	102.18	102.26–	.4	7.59
8 3/8s,	1995-00 Aug	....	106.28	107.12–	.4	7.63
8s,	1996-01 Aug	....	103.18	103.26–	.2	7.63
8 1/4s,	2000-05 May	....	106.8	106.24–	.4	7.63

n– Treasury notes.
*Estate tax bonds

Source: *Wall Street Journal*, January 27, 1977.

Figure 8-6. Estate tax bonds and other longer-term Treasury securities.

retired by the Treasury. As a result, the supply of "flower" bonds constantly diminishes over time. Table 8-2 shows the two longest-term issues in two-year intervals from 1962 to 1976. The amounts of bonds held by the public are shown in millions of dollars.[12] With the rise in interest rates which occurred beginning in the mid-1960s, these bonds sold at increasing discounts and became increasingly attractive as vehicles by which to reduce the estate tax burden. As a result, increasing numbers were so used and their supply diminished accordingly. It is quite likely that the 3s of 1995 will entirely disappear before their final maturity, and the same thing

---

[12]The source for these data is the *Treasury Bulletin*.

*Table 8-2. Estate Tax Bonds Amounts Outstanding
(in millions)*

May 31	3s 1995	$3\frac{1}{2}$s 1998	May 31	3s 1995	$3\frac{1}{2}$s 1998
1962	$2,472	$3,562	1970	1,183	3,257
1964	2,290	3,526	1972	876	2,613
1966	1,951	3,509	1974	670	2,141
1968	1,560	3,433	1976	500	1,677

may occur for the $3\frac{1}{2}$s of 1998. Diminishing supply in the face of what is likely to be relatively constant demand exerts upward pressure on prices and downward pressure on yields. As no new "flower" bonds will be issued and have not been issued since 1963, existing "flower" bonds will be increasingly sought in the years to come.

Discount Bonds: Some Reflections and Additional Considerations

In Chapters 5 and 7, and in this chapter, we have considered several things that bear on the valuation of discount bonds. It is useful now to review them prior to looking at some related issues. With respect to the mathematics of finance, we saw in Chapter 5 that the deeper the discount the longer the duration of a bond. To the extent that the term structure of interest rates is upward-sloping with respect to duration, this proposition implies a higher yield for the discount bond than for a bond with the same maturity but with a current coupon rate. The opposite would occur in the case of a downward-sloping yield curve. Another factor influencing the valuation of discount bonds is callability. Discount bonds are particularly attractive in times of falling interest rates, because of the protection they afford the investor against being called. While this influence is most applicable to corporate bonds, it applies also to other fixed-income securities that are subject to call. Discount bonds are also attractive because of the favorable tax treatment of capital gains relative to that of interest income. Finally, estate tax bonds that sell at a discount have a special demand.

With the exception of the duration argument,[13] all of these factors work to make taxable bonds selling at a discount more attractive in the market than comparable bonds selling at par. In general, the deeper the

---

[13]Even here the term *structure* with respect to duration must be upward-sloping for discount bonds to provide higher yields than bonds selling at par, all other things remaining the same.

discount the greater the attraction of a discount bond and the lower its yield relative to comparable bonds selling at par. However, beyond a point, the discount affords little incremental call protection to the investor. Put another way, if interest rates on corporate bonds are never expected to fall below 6 per cent, it makes little difference from the standpoint of call protection whether an investor holds a bond with a $3\frac{1}{2}$ per cent coupon rate or one with a 5 per cent coupon rate. While sorting out the separate influences on the value of discount bonds is difficult, we know that the capital gains tax influence and the estate tax consideration, when applicable, are the most important. The duration factor is relatively unimportant and the callability factor is important primarily in times of falling interest rates.

Discount Bonds and Investor Behavior

As with tax-exempt municipal securities, discount bonds appeal only to certain investors. As a result, the market for these bonds is somewhat limited. Their basic appeal of course is to taxable investors. The investor that pays no taxes would be indifferent between a dollar of interest on a discounted present-value basis and a dollar of capital gains on the same basis if all other things were the same. However, if taxable investors bid up the price of discount bonds, the tax-exempt investor is better off investing in high coupon bonds. In this way, yield need not be sacrificed for a feature, namely the prospect of a capital gain, which has no tax value to him. The same applies to a lesser extent to other institutional investors which pay limited taxes, such as life insurance companies.

While commercial banks typically are in high tax brackets, they are unable to avail themselves of the favorable tax rate on capital gains. Unfortunately for them, capital gains are treated as ordinary income when it comes to paying taxes. Therefore, commercial banks do not seek discount bonds but rather bonds selling more nearly at par or above.[14] As before, the reason is simply that yields on these bonds are more attractive. By the process of elimination, discount bonds are primarily attractive to higher income individuals and to fire and casualty companies. Thus, the capital gains tax feature associated with discount bonds results in a segmented market for these bonds. This market in turn is determined by the tax status of the investor and by an institutional restriction on the tax treatment of commercial banks.

[14]For an analysis of the investment behavior of institutional investors with respect to taxes and likely future reinvestment rates on coupon payments, see Robert H. Cramer and Stephen L. Hawk, "The Consideration of Coupon Levels, Taxes, Reinvestment Rates, and Maturity in the Investment Management of Financial Institutions," *Journal of Financial and Quantitative Analysis*, 10 (March, 1975), 67–84.

The Effect of Discount Bonds on Yield Curves

Bonds selling at a discount can distort the drawing of the yield curve, a subject considered in Chapter 4. For example, if a particular maturity range consisted only of discount bonds, while observations for other ranges consisted of bonds selling around par, the yield curve would be pulled downward in the former range. This type of distortion is illustrated in Fig. 8-7, where the observations in the long-term area are low coupon bonds which bend the yield curve downward. With rising interest rates, bonds issued in the past sell at increasing discounts, and such distortions of the yield curve become even more of a problem.

Several approaches to reducing the problem have been advanced. If a sizable portion of total observations is represented by current coupon bonds, one can simply ignore the low coupon bonds in the drawing of the yield curve. For example, the Treasury ignores deep discount bonds in fitting yield curves to the observations shown in the *Treasury Bulletin*. However, there remains a problem if there are maturity areas where no bonds are selling near par. This occurred from the mid-1960s to the early 1970s when the Treasury was precluded from issuing bonds by the $4\frac{1}{4}$ per cent interest-rate ceiling imposed by Congress. As interest rates rose, long-term bonds with coupon rates of $4\frac{1}{4}$ per cent or less sold at increasing discounts. As there were no higher coupon bonds being issued, the lower coupon levels had to be used in drawing the yield curve.

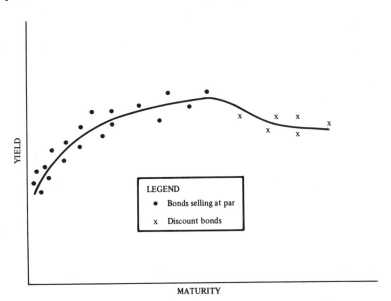

Figure 8-7. Illustration of yield-curve distortion introduced by discount bonds.

Another method of adjustment is to assume tax rates on ordinary income and on capital gains for investors at the margin. These rates then are inserted into Eq. (8-5), or a variation thereof, and after-tax rates of return or adjusted before-tax returns are estimated. The yield curve can then be drawn on the basis of the adjusted data. Alexander A. Robichek and W. David Niebuhr used various pairs of Treasury bonds with different coupons, but roughly the same maturity, to derive implied tax rates.[15] These estimates varied widely, but the median for September 23, 1968, was roughly 44 per cent for ordinary income taxes. One half of this, or 22 per cent, was assumed as the capital gains tax rate. These tax rates then were used to derive adjusted before-tax yields for all Treasury bonds on September 23, 1968, and March 26, 1969. Although yield curves were not drawn, the results were still rather striking. Because prevailing yields in the market on the two dates were above the coupon rates on all of the bonds (maximum of $4\frac{1}{4}$ per cent), tax adjusted yields were higher than observed yields. The greatest adjustments occurred for the deep discount bonds with coupon rates of $2\frac{1}{2}$ per cent. Over all, the adjustment process considerably smoothed differences in yield observed for bonds of like maturity.

While the adjustment of yields for taxes using a variation of Eq. (8-5) goes a long way toward making yield observations more consistent, some problems still remain. For one thing, tax rates for the marginal investor must be estimated and these estimates are subject to rather wide error. In addition, effective tax rates of the marginal investor can and probably do change over time. Moreover, the tax adjustment process ignores other factors which affect the valuation of discount bonds. These include duration, the call protection afforded, and the use of certain Treasury bonds for the settlement of federal estate taxes. The latter bias was particularly evident in the Robichek and Niebuhr results.

J. Huston McCulloch uses a more sophisticated variation of Eq. (8-5) to adjust for taxes for discount bonds.[16] He also makes adjustments for bonds selling above par and for Treasury bills, where all of the appreciation is treated as ordinary income for tax purposes. Estate tax, or "flower," bonds are analyzed after tax adjustments are made. As in the case of Robichek and Niebuhr, McCulloch endeavors to estimate the coupon rate necessary to issue new debt at par. Using Treasury security data from 1965 to 1973, he estimates the discount function with respect to maturity using an instrumental variables approach. Given estimates of the discount rates, the value of a specific security is estimated on the same basis as other securities in the regression study. The largest errors in estimate were found

[15]Alexander A. Robichek and W. David Niebuhr, "Tax-Induced Bias in Reporting Treasury Yields," *Journal of Finance*, 25 (December, 1970), 1081–1090.

[16]J. Huston McCulloch, "The Tax-Adjusted Yield Curve," *Journal of Finance*, 30 (June, 1975), 811–830.

for the two longest term "flower" bonds, and these errors were attributed to the estate tax effect. McCulloch fitted yield curves to the coupon rates which the bonds would have had to have had in order to sell at par. He also used the data to fit forward rate curves under the assumption that the bonds were pure discount ones, with appreciation taxed at the ordinary income tax rate. Finally, McCulloch estimated an implied tax rate for investors in Treasury securities and concluded that it fell somewhere in the range of 22 to 30 per cent.

In summary, there are several ways for adjusting yield observations for the differential impact of taxes on interest income and capital gains. All of the approaches have their difficulties, so estimates are subject to error. However, the goal is to more nearly compare "apples" with "apples" as opposed to "apples" with "oranges." The yield curves which are fitted to the adjusted data give a more accurate and consistent picture of the relationship between yield and maturity than is the case when raw yield observations are used.

Depreciation and the Investment Tax Credit

Depreciation and the investment tax credit have an effect on the valuation of a lease instrument and thereby on the implicit interest rate embodied in the lease payments. By way of definition, a lease is a means by which a party can acquire the economic use of an asset over a stated period of time. A financial lease is a noncancellable contract whereby the lessee agrees to make a series of payments to the lessor for use of the asset. The lease period generally corresponds to the economic life of the asset, and the total payments the lessee agrees to make must exceed the purchase price of the asset. While the lessor owns the asset, the lessee acquires the economic use of it.

Assuming that lease payments are made at the beginning of each year, the implicit rate of interest to the lessee may be found by solving the following equation for r:

$$C = \sum_{t=0}^{n-1} \frac{L}{(1+r)^t} \tag{8-6}$$

where C is the cost of the asset whose use is being acquired, n is the length in years of the lease contract, and L is the amount of annual lease payment. To illustrate, suppose an asset costing $200,000 were leased for ten years with annual lease payments of $28,600 due at the beginning of each year. The implicit interest rate then would be found by solving the following for r:

$$\$200,000 = \sum_{t=0}^{9} \frac{\$28,600}{(1+r)^t} \tag{8-7}$$

which is found to be 9 per cent. This then would be used as the interest-rate cost of the lease instrument.

The Valuation of the Lease Instrument

Because of the contractual nature of a financial lease obligation, it must be evaluated in the same manner as other forms of financing. An alternative is to purchase the asset and finance this acquisition with debt. Both the lease payment and the payment of principal and interest are fixed obligations that must be met. One might ask, then—why is lease financing used? Under assumptions of perfect financial markets and the implied competition among financial markets that results from this idealized and taxless world, it can be shown that the debt and lease obligations of an economic unit will be valued by lenders and lessors in the same manner.[17] As a result, the interest rates will be the same and the economic unit would be indifferent between the two methods of financing. In other words, the two instruments would differ in name only.

When we relax the assumptions of perfect financial markets, however, debt and lease instruments may not be valued in the same manner. As a result, their costs to the firm may differ. The introduction of transaction costs, information costs, and less than infinite divisibility of securities results in impediments to arbitraging between financial instruments. However, these imperfections do *not* have a systematic effect in the sense that they favor leasing or favor debt financing all of the time. Rather, arbitrage between the markets is impeded, and consequently it may be possible for the firm to take "advantage" of the situation by issuing one type of instrument or the other. However, the advantage is likely to be small and extremely difficult to predict in practice. Therefore, we do not concentrate on these imperfections.

The dominant economic reason for the existence of leasing is differences in the tax benefits associated with the ownership of an asset among companies, financial institutions, and individuals. The greater the

---

[17]These assumptions include no transaction costs; a situation where information is costless and readily available to all and securities are infinitely divisible; there are no bankruptcy costs; and there are no taxes. In James C. Van Horne, "The Cost of Leasing with Capital Market Imperfections," *Engineering Economist* (forthcoming), this indifference is demonstrated using a state-preference model. As the model is complicated, it is not presented here.

divergence in tax benefits from owning an asset among economic units in an economy, the greater the attraction of lease financing overall, all other things the same. The tax benefits associated with owning an asset are the investment tax credit, which is realized when the asset is placed into service, and the tax shield afforded by the deduction of depreciation over the depreciable life of the asset.

If the effective tax benefits associated with owning an asset were the same for all economic units in the economy, and if financial markets were perfect in every other way, debt and lease obligations would be valued in the same manner. As a result, their interest-rate costs would be the same. If the lessor did not pass on all of the tax benefits associated with the ownership of the asset to the prospective lessee in the form of lower lease payments than would otherwise be the case, the prospective lessee could simply purchase the asset and finance it with debt. In this way, it could avail itself of all of the tax benefits. Therefore, it is not the existence of taxes *per se* which gives rise to leasing being a thing of value, but it is due to a situation where different companies, financial institutions, and individuals have different abilities to realize the tax benefits associated with owning an asset.

Such differences are due to (1) different tax rates among economic units in the economy and (2) different levels of past and current income among economic units. Examples of the former include differences in personal and corporate income tax rates, as well as differences in tax rates among various individuals and corporations. An example of the latter is a company with a tax-loss carry forward which pays little or no taxes on profits. Another example is a situation where the investment tax credit is so large that it exceeds the taxes that the firm otherwise would pay. As a result, part of the tax credit goes unutilized.

To the extent that one party that pays little or no taxes is able to lease an asset from another party that pays high taxes, it may be able to avail itself of part of the tax benefits associated with ownership through lease payments that are lower than they would otherwise be. In turn, the lessor is able to use the full tax credit which might not otherwise be available to it. As a result, both parties gain.

The Market for Lease Financing

Again, the reason for this occurrence is differences among the economic units within society in their ability to realize the tax benefits associated with owning an asset. Leasing permits the economic unit with little such ability to realize a greater portion of these benefits than it is able to do on its own. As a result, a yield differential will exist between the debt obligations of an economic unit and its lease obligations. The lease obligation will have a lower effective interest rate, all other things the same, as the economic unit first begins to employ lease financing as opposed to debt. If rationality prevails, the economic unit will substitute lease financing for debt financing up to the point where the marginal costs are the same. In the overall market for lease financing, differences among economic units in their ability to realize the economic benefits associated with owning an asset become the basis for negotiation. As we demonstrated in Chapter 3, the equilibrating process in financial markets depends upon the behavior of individual economic units in maximizing their expected utility, which in turn arises from holding financial and real assets, from issuing financial liabilities including lease obligations, and from consuming—all subject to wealth and income constraints. Savings-surplus economic units in high tax brackets and with large amounts of taxable income would be expected to be lessors, while savings-deficit economic units with relatively low taxes to be paid would be expected to be lessees. The greater the correlation between savings surpluses and high taxes on the one hand and savings deficits and low taxes among economic units on the other, the greater the role leasing is likely to play in channeling funds from savings-surplus economic units to ultimate users of funds in society.

In the United States, a sophisticated market has developed for the leasing of such assets as airplanes, ships, railroad cars, and computers. With respect to lessors, commercial banks have come to dominate the field, owing to their profitability and relatively high tax brackets. The lessees of such assets are largely companies which either have relatively low profitability and are unable to take full advantage of the tax benefits available, particularly those associated with the investment tax credit, and other economic units which have a low tax rate. An interesting and understandable extension of leasing is into that of equipment to municipalities, which of course pay no taxes.

The principal *raison d'etre* for leasing, then, is differences among economic units in their abilities to realize the tax benefits associated with owning an asset.[18] Leasing permits economic units with little ability to realize such tax benefits on their own to realize part of them through

---

[18]A second "advantage" or reason for lease financing is the lessor's superior position in liquidation, relative to that of the lender. Even with a secured position, a lender finds it more difficult and costly to gain possession of the asset in case of default than does a lessor with a lease. As a result, *ex ante* bankruptcy costs will be higher. This factor too can be embodied in the valuation of a lease instrument. See Van Horne, *op. cit.* Another alledged "advantage" of leasing is that it represents "off balance" sheet financing. However, accounting principle changes in recent years have resulted in enough disclosure that the financial statement user is able to judge the impact of a lease obligation in the same way as he is the impact of debt financing. There is no empirical evidence to support the notion that leasing, as opposed to debt financing, enhances the value of a corporation because investors and creditors at the margin are fooled and do not recognize the full impact of the lease obligations.

leasing. The fact that taxes fall unevenly on different economic units in the economy impedes the efficient flow of savings to the most promising investment opportunities. Leasing reduces the impact of this inefficiency and thereby improves the flow of savings to efficient investment opportunities.

The economic advantage of leasing varies among economic units in the economy. For the economic unit in a high tax bracket which is very profitable, lease financing holds little or no advantage over debt financing. In contrast, for the economic unit which is in a low tax bracket and is marginally profitable, lease financing is likely to hold great attraction.

Some Implications for Financial Intermediation

As already discussed, leasing provides a means for circumventing certain market imperfections. By reducing the opportunity cost of the tax benefits foregone by the economic unit unable to take advantage of such benefits on its own and by reducing liquidating costs, financial markets become more efficient. By more efficiently allocating savings to the most promising investment opportunities, lease financing enhances both capital formation in the economy and overall want satisfaction. However, it is important to recognize that the foundation for its existence rests largely on the tax imperfection discussed.

Offsetting in some measure the advantages of lease financing is the cost of operation. To the extent that an additional financial intermediary is introduced which buys assets, leases them, and borrows in the capital markets to finance these acquisitions, there are costs associated with the process. In particular, third-party lessors add a costly degree of intermediation. Their justification for existence is only the presence of the imperfections described earlier. Prior to 1963, commercial banks were precluded from the direct leasing of real assets. With this barrier to entry broken in 1963, banks have come to dominate the leasing of large expensive equipment. The banks' entry into this market has reduced the role of third-party lessors and thereby eliminated the costs associated with this additional step of intermediation (third-party leasing). As a result, the taxes received by the government may be less than otherwise would be the case. Offsetting this is the increased ability of firms and individuals to invest in the most promising investment opportunities, which in turn enhances the efficient allocation of savings and tax revenues in the economy. Troubling, however, is the incentive to lease given certain parties in low or zero brackets. A case in point is the incentive to lease capital assets by municipalities, which pay no taxes.

The fact that tax benefits associated with leasing are likely to be shared between the lessor and the lessee suggests that the allocative efficiency of leasing in channeling savings in the economy to the most productive uses leaves something to be desired. Indeed, the intermediation process is costly. Allocative efficiency could be improved by reform of the factors which give rise to the leasing. Suppose that instead of the present tax system, the government introduced one where all economic units derived the same benefits from depreciation of an asset, either in the form of lower taxes or cash payment (in cases where taxes to be paid were less than the total benefits available). Suppose the same were to occur for the investment tax credit. If these reforms *were* undertaken, the advantages of leasing would largely cease to exist. The efficiency with which savings are channeled to productive investment opportunities in an economy would be improved and the cost of lease intermediation eliminated.

Summary

Taxes affect yields in a variety of ways. Because interest income on municipal securities is tax exempt, yields are lower than they are on other fixed-income securities. Moreover, the higher the level of interest rates, the wider the differential should be between yields on the two types of bonds. The tax-exempt feature has caused the municipal market to be relatively segmented on the demand side, consisting primarily of commercial banks, fire and casualty companies, and high income individuals. This segmentation, together with the fluctuating participation by commercial banks, causes municipal yields to be somewhat more volatile than Treasury or corporate yields and causes the yield curve to be almost always upward-sloping. The value of the tax exemption feature is shared between the municipality and the investors. The portion realized by the municipality tends to vary inversely with the level of interest rates and with the degree of monetary restriction. In order to broaden the market for municipal financing, an option has been proposed whereby the municipality could elect to finance with bonds whose interest is taxable and to receive a subsidy from the federal government.

A differential tax on interest income and on capital gains affects the valuation of discount bonds. Because part of the yield to maturity is comprised of a capital gain, discount bonds are attractive and accordingly provide lower yields than do bonds with coupon rates which result in their selling at par. The attractiveness of discount bonds can be studied by comparing yields on bonds having low coupon rates with those having current coupon rates. The yield differential moves in keeping with changes in the level of interest rates. However, on a relative basis the differential was narrower in the 1970s than it was in the 1960s, and possible reasons for this were explored. While discount bonds are attractive relative to bonds selling at par for taxable issues, the opposite is true for municipal securities. Here capital gains are taxed, whereas interest income is not. Certain Treasury bonds can be used in the settlement of federal estate taxes, where they count at their full face value. As a result of this feature these bonds, known as "flower" bonds, are in special demand when they are selling at a discount.

Because of the tax consequences, discount bonds are attractive to only a limited number of investors. In a sense the market is segmented in much the same way as the municipal market is segmented. The presence of a number of discount bonds in a particular maturity range can distort downward the drawing of the yield curve. Several methods were explored for adjusting yields for the capital gains effect so that the yield observations were more consistent with each other. In addition to the capital gains and estate tax effects, we endeavored to integrate considerations of call protection and duration into our examination of the valuation of discount bonds.

In the final section the impact of depreciation and the investment tax credit on the cost of lease financing was explored. The principal reason for the existence of lease financing is differences in the tax benefits associated with the ownership of an asset among economic units in society. The economic unit in a low tax bracket or without sufficient taxable income can lease finance and realize some of the tax benefits associated with owning an asset through lower lease payments than otherwise would be the case. In this sense, leasing improves the flow of savings to efficient investment opportunities. However, the financial intermediation involved with leasing is not without its costs, and allocative efficiency might be improved with another tax policy concerning investment.

SELECTED REFERENCES

Colin, J. W., and Richard S. Bayer, "Calculation of Tax Effective Yields for Discount Instruments," *Journal of Financial and Quantitative Analysis*, 5 (June, 1970), 265–273.

Cook, Timothy Q., "Some Factors Affecting Long-Term Yield Spreads in Recent Years," *Monthly Review of the Federal Reserve Bank of Richmond*, 59 (September, 1973).

Cramer, Robert H., and Stephen L. Hawk, "The Consideration of Coupon Levels, Taxes, Reinvestment Rates and Maturity in the Investment Management of Financial Institutions," *Journal of Financial and Quantitative Analysis*, 10 (March, 1975), 67–84.

Federal Tax Course. Englewood Cliffs, N.J.: Prentice-Hall, Inc., 1977.

McCollum, John S., "The Impact of the Capital Gains Tax on Bond Yields," *National Tax Journal*, 26 (December, 1973), 575–583.

McCulloch, J. Huston, "The Tax-Adjusted Yield Curve," *Journal of Finance*, 30 (June, 1975), 811–830.

Peterson, John, *Changing Conditions in the Market for State and Local Government Debt*, a study for the Joint Economic Committee, 94th Congress, 2d Session. Washington, D.C.: U.S. Government Printing Office, April 16, 1976.

Pye, Gordon, "On the Tax Structure of Interest Rates," *Quarterly Journal of Economics*, LXXXIII (November, 1969), 562–579.

Robichek, Alexander A., and W. David Niebuhr, "Tax-Induced Bias in Reporting Treasury Yields," *Journal of Finance*, 25 (December, 1970), 1081–1090.

Van Horne, James C., "The Cost of Leasing with Capital Market Imperfections," *Engineering Economist*, forthcoming.

_____, and Samuel S. Stewart, "A Simultaneous Equations Analysis of the Bond Markets," *The Southern Economic Journal*, XXXVIII (April, 1972), 538–546.

The Social Allocation
of Capital

9 Stated early in this book was the proposition that funds flow from savings-surplus economic units to savings-deficit ones *primarily* on the basis of expected return and risk. We then looked at various factors affecting risk and return and analyzed their impact on the yields we observe in the marketplace. Factors considered included maturity, duration, inflationary expectations, default risk, callability, taxability, and certain market imperfections. In examining each of these factors, we held constant the influence of other factors. We also saw that the more efficient the financial markets of a society, the less the cost and inconvenience with which funds flow from ultimate savers to ultimate investors in real assets. Greater efficiency results in a higher level of capital formation, economic growth, and want satisfaction, all other things the same. The efficient channeling of savings requires competition among financial intermediaries and continual financial innovation. When profit opportunities arise, new intermediaries, financial instruments, or methods come into being to exploit these opportunities and, ultimately, to drive out the excess profits previously available. Thus, competition leads to financial innovation, which in turn leads to a reduction in the cost of financial intermediation and, from an economic standpoint, to a more efficient allocation of savings in society.

Market imperfections impede the efficiency with which financial markets operate. In Chapters 4 through 8 we investigated some of the more important imperfections. Such things as institutional restrictions on investor and borrower behavior, transaction costs, and taxes were examined. Where empirical evidence *was* available, these imperfections were found to have only a modest effect in hampering market efficiency. Still, in certain

217

instances significant effects were found over what would have been the case if interest rates were allowed to seek their own levels in free and competitive financial markets.

In this chapter we wish to examine another influence on the flow of funds and on interest rates—the influence of the government. This influence is one apart from its taxing power and certain other government restrictions already discussed. Our focus will be on attempts by the government to direct the flow of funds in our society toward socially desirable goals or to lower the interest-rate cost to socially desirable borrowers. These attempts fall under a broad heading which we will call the *social allocation of capital*. Because of the nature of the topic, our consideration of it will be somewhat more conceptual in orientation than was true of former topics.

The Issues Involved

By social allocation of capital, we mean any action by the government that attempts to direct the flow of savings in our society toward some specific objective. This objective might be housing (through mortgages), inner cities, low-income families, pollution and environmental control, minority enterprises, consumer cooperatives, small businesses, a failing corporation, or what have you. The essential thing is that savings flows are directed in ways that would not occur if market forces alone were allowed to prevail. In other words, the "socially desirable" project does not attract the financing that the government would like it to attract at an interest rate that is sufficiently low from a social standpoint. To remedy the perceived deficiency, the government steps into the savings allocation process to redirect flows toward socially desirable projects at appropriate interest rates (presumably low).

At the time the program is initiated, the perceived social benefits exceed the social costs in the eyes of the initiators—Congress, the executive branch, state legislatures, or others. The benefits are readily apparent; one category or group in our society is able to borrow at favorable interest rates where before credit was either unavailable or available only at a higher interest cost. As a result of a program to socially allocate capital they move to the head, or nearly to the head, of the credit line. However, seldom are the social and economic costs of a program evaluated in their totality. These costs involve not only the *out-of-pocket cost* to the government in administering the subsidy, but also the *opportunity cost* of the restrictions imposed on the efficiency of financial markets, the opportunity cost of lessened economic growth which in turn results from directing savings toward projects on the basis of social return as opposed to economic return, and, in certain cases, the redistributional effects which work to the detriment of low-income families. As this chapter unfolds, we will identify these costs as we explore various methods for socially allocating capital in our society.

Our purpose is not to suggest that the social allocation of capital is bad *per se*. Rather we suggest the need for a more encompassing cost-benefit-type of analysis before a plan is undertaken. Too often the costs of a method to socially allocate capital are not considered in their entirety, or they are ignored altogether because of their "hidden" nature. It is not surprising then that proposals to socially allocate capital are so popular. The political appeal is irresistible. The benefits to a disadvantaged constituency are perceived to be abundant and the costs negligible. Is it any wonder that proposals to socially allocate capital are so popularly received? In this chapter we hope to make a case for a more objective appraisal of such plans so that the need, the benefits, and the costs can be realistically appraised, and, when a decision to "go ahead" is made, the most efficient and equitable method can be chosen.

A number of methods have been used to socially allocate capital to a desired cause and/or to lower the interest rate that otherwise would be paid. We endeavor to evaluate these methods with respect to their conceptual underpinnings. The methods examined include: (1) a ceiling rate of interest on loans; (2) the use of a government guarantee or "moral obligation" to enhance a borrower's appeal in the market; (3) a government interest subsidy to the borrower or lender; (4) the government borrowing in the financial markets and relending to the socially desirable project; and (5) the imposition of various government regulations to divert the flow of savings to a social project. We investigate each of these in turn.

Ceilings on Interest Costs

Many states have usury laws which govern the maximum interest rate a lender can charge. The intent of these laws is to lower the cost of borrowing, particularly to lower income families, and to protect those less educated in the mathematics of compound interest. Whereas once usury laws were religious in conception, this has not been the case since Martin Luther caused lending to be tolerable if not respected. The greatest concentration of usury laws occurs in the areas of consumer credit and residential mortgages. The critical question we wish to address is, what is the effect of interest-rate ceilings on the supply of loans and on noninterest costs?

The Effect of Usury Laws

When the equilibrium market rate of interest is below the interest-rate ceiling imposed under a usury law, there is no effect on either the supply of loans or on noninterest costs. Borrowing and lending occur in free and competitive markets. However, when the ceiling is below what otherwise would be a market clearing rate, there usually is an effect. The notion that interest rates can be held down by government mandate without an adverse effect on loan flows rests on a proposition of complete segmentation, or unsubstitutability, between markets. In other words, the supply of loans is interest inelastic. The situation is illustrated in Fig. 9-1. At the market clearing rate of r_c, the supply of loans is $d*$ while at the lower rate determined by usury laws, r_u, the supply is still $d*$. However, at a rate of interest of r_u desired demand is d', so there is excess demand of $d' - d*$. In the face of this excess demand, lenders would be expected to: (1) increase the quality of their loan portfolios by raising credit standards and screening out riskier borrowers, frequently low-income families; and/or (2) seek additional compensation through various noninterest devices such as closing fees, servicing fees, and discounts from the face value of the debt instrument.[1] Thus, even with completely segmented markets and an inelastic supply curve, the presence of excess demand

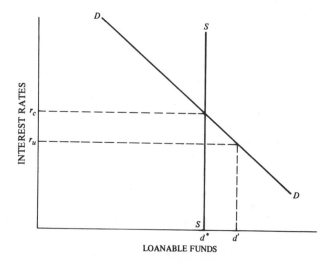

Figure 9-1. Illustration of interest-rate ceiling with an inelastic supply curve.

[1] A discount from face value enables the lender to obtain a higher effective yield. If the face value were $1,000, the usury rate ceiling were 10 per cent and the lender advanced only $940, his yield would be higher than 10 per cent because the borrower would need to repay the full $1,000 plus compound interest of 10 per cent.

results in some side effects which are adverse from the standpoint of the framers of usury law legislation.

In the case of an interest elastic supply curve, the amount of loanable funds available will be less if the usury rate is below what would otherwise be the market clearing rate of interest. From all that we know about the competitive nature of financial markets we would have to say that an assumption of an elastic supply curve is reasonable. The situation is illustrated in Fig. 9-2.

We see that at a ceiling rate of interest of r_u, lenders will supply loans in the amount of d'', which of course is less than would occur with a market clearing rate of r_c. The presence of excess loan demand, $d' - d''$, will result in the same incentives as before—namely, for lenders to upgrade the quality of their loans and to seek other compensation which falls outside the usury law. To the extent this occurs, the supply of loans at r_u may be greater than d''. What we have done then is to introduce dimensions other than interest payments to the supply of loanable funds. As a result, the supply curve in Fig. 9-2 would no longer hold, but in some measure would shift to the right. It is conceivable the shift might be sufficient to provide d^* or even more loanable funds at the lower than market clearing rate, r_u. However, this does not mean that the usury law is working for its intended purpose—only that it is being circumvented and the lender is receiving payment by other means.

Are usury laws harmful then? For the most part the answer is *yes*. For

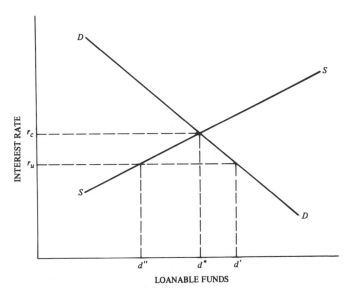

Figure 9-2. Illustration of interest-rate ceiling with an elastic supply curve.

one thing, they affect the efficiency with which financial markets operate. Inherently, the mechanisms for circumventing usury laws are less efficient than the simple use of interest rates to allocate credit. To the extent that a financial market is less efficient, there is greater cost and/or inconvenience associated with the channeling of savings in our society. Moreover, circumvention around usury laws results in less "truth in lending." Borrowers may not fully recognize the true cost of a loan. To the extent they are deceived relative to what they would be if interest charges alone were the only cost, this too is counter to the intentions of those advocating social measures to allocate capital. Finally, and perhaps most importantly, usury rates below market clearing rates of interest usually result in credit being rationed. The larger the gap of excess demand in Fig. 9-2, the more lenders will try to increase the quality of their loans and seek alternative forms of compensation. In upgrading quality, riskier loan applicants will be increasingly rejected. To the extent that these applicants are low-income people or the poor, their ability to borrow is foreclosed. As the formulation of most usury laws is with a concern for the cost of borrowing by the poor, ironically the end result may be that there is no cost for them because they are unable to obtain credit at the ceiling rate. Thus, there should be concern not only with the impact of usury laws on the total amount of credit extended but on the composition of borrowers as well.

Empirical Studies of Usury Laws

In general, various empirical studies on consumer credit and mortgages support the idea that when interest-rate ceilings are binding, the volume of loans declines, lenders try to upgrade quality to the detriment of lower income individuals, and noninterest methods of compensation increasingly are employed. Studies of consumer credit have shown that risk acceptance by finance companies is directly related to the level of the interest-rate ceiling. These studies suggest that in those states with high interest-rate ceilings, finance companies are less stringent in their credit standards, as evidenced by loan rejection rates. This also is manifested in higher bad debt losses.[2] In addition, there is some evidence that the supply of personal loans is adversely affected by binding interest-rate ceilings. However, the empirical evidence here is mixed, owing to certain data

[2]See Douglas F. Greer, "Rate Ceilings and Loan Turndowns," *Journal of Finance*, 30 (December, 1975), 1376–1383; Greer, "Rate Ceilings, Market Structure, and the Supply of Finance Company Personal Loans," *Journal of Finance*, 29 (December, 1974), 1363–1382; Robert P. Shay, "Factors Affecting Price, Volume and Credit Risk in the Consumer Finance Industry," *Journal of Finance*, 25 (May, 1970), 503–515; and Maurice B. Goudzwaard, "Price Ceilings and Credit Rationing," *Journal of Finance*, 23 (March, 1968), 177–185.

problems. In one of the more comprehensive studies, which was based on an extensive sample survey, Greer found that the supply of personal loans was directly related to the legal rate ceiling.[3] As the ceiling decreased, small personal loans in particular were curtailed.

For mortgage loans, empirical studies have shown that binding interest-rate ceilings cause lenders to upgrade credit standards and to increase closing fees and discounts. Increased credit standards are reflected in such things as the percentage of downpayment required, the ratio of family income to debt, and the maturity of that debt. As explained in footnote 1, a discount is the amount by which the loan advanced is less than the face value of the instrument: The lower the discount, the higher the effective yield on the loan. These studies also have shown that the volume of mortgage loans decreases as the market clearing rate rises above the interest rate ceiling.[4]

On balance then, the empirical evidence on usury laws suggests that they can result in reductions in the supply of loans and increases in the number and types of loan applicants rejected. Also, there is indication that noninterest forms of compensation are increasingly being employed. All of this is in accord with our previous conceptual discussion of usury laws in financial markets characterized by elastic supply curves.

Government Guarantees and Moral Obligations

The government also can socially allocate capital through a guarantee of a borrower's obligation. The federal government's guarantee, of course, reduces the default risk of a loan to zero for the duration of the guarantee. With this risk reduction, the debt obligation is made more attractive to investors. The potential borrower may now be able to attract lenders where before there were none, or it may simply pay a lower interest cost. In all cases, the debt instrument becomes a more desirable substitute relative to other financial instruments in the marketplace.

The situation is illustrated in Fig. 9-3. In this case, the demand curves represent those of a single borrower. Without a guarantee, the demand curve D–D and supply curve S–S intersect at point X, which results in a market clearing rate of interest of r_c. With the guarantee, however, the

---

[3]Greer, "Rate Ceilings, Market Structure, and the Supply of Finance Company Personal Loans."

[4]See James R. Ostas, "Effects of Usury Ceilings in the Mortgage Market," *Journal of Finance*, 31 (June, 1976), 821–834; and Jack M. Guttentag, "Changes in the Structure of the Residential Mortgage Market: Analysis and Proposals," in Irwin Friend, ed., *Study of the Savings and Loan Industry* (Washington, D.C.: Federal Home Loan Bank Board, 1969), pp. 1479–1561.

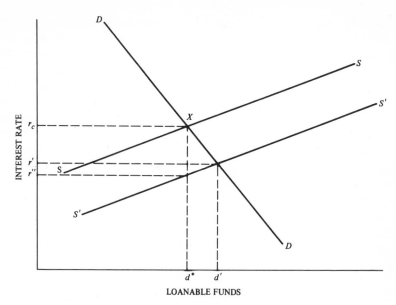

Figure 9-3. Illustration of the effect of a government guarantee.

supply curve shifts to the right—to $S'-S'$. This occurs because the financial instrument now is more attractive due to the reduction in risk. If the borrower is unrestricted by the government in the amount it is able to borrow, it will seek d' in financing at an interest rate of r'. Thus, the interest rate will decline and the amount borrowed will increase. If, however, the government restricts the amount that can be borrowed, the effective supply curve shortens. Suppose for purposes of illustration the restriction were set at the amount borrowed before the guarantee, d^*. Instead of a supply curve of $S'-S'$, the supply curve would be $S'-d^*$ in Fig. 9-3. As a result, the interest rate would be r''. Thus, the entire effect of the guarantee would be on interest cost and not on the amount of financing.

Use of Guarantees and Moral Obligations

There are a number of instances where loan guarantees have been used, although over all this method for socially allocating capital is not as widespread as other methods. The Veterans Administration guarantees mortgages for qualified veterans. During World War II and on occasion thereafter, the federal government guaranteed bank loans of certain defense manufacturers. This program was called the Victory Loan, or V-Loan, program and it endeavored to assure credit being availiable to essential defense contractors. Perhaps the largest recent example of a government guarantee was that of the Lockheed Corporation in 1971. This guarantee was passed by Congress in order to keep the company alive with its L1011 airplane, which in its development had exerted a huge cash drain on the company. While defense and national security considerations may have been a motivating factor, most of the debate in Congress was over the preservation of jobs. In 1975, initial discussion concerning the federal government coming to the aid of New York City was in terms of a guarantee of the City's obligations. This ultimately did not come to pass, and another method to socially allocate capital was used, which we will discuss shortly. There are other instances of government guarantees. For example, the Export-Import Bank guarantees certain financing incurred in the export of U.S. goods and services. We will not try to list all guarantees, if indeed that were possible, because our concern is with the principle and not the specifics.

In recent years, various state governments have set up special corporations which borrow money with the "moral obligation" of the state. While this backing is not legally enforceable, there nonetheless is an implied backing, and this works to make the debt instruments of the borrower more attractive than otherwise would be the case. The most controversial example of the use of moral obligations was by New York State with their housing authority corporations. These were set up to finance low-to moderate-income housing. When many of the authorities experienced financial difficulty in 1975 and 1976, this unfortunately coincided with the difficulty experienced by New York City. It became clear to investors that the state would not necessarily honor the housing authority's obligations. As a result, the "value" of New York State's "moral obligation" declined appreciably in the minds of investors. (Similar problems occurred in the state of Massachusetts.) The original purpose was to find a way to socially allocate capital to urban development and low-income housing at favorable interest costs without taking on a contingent legal obligation. It worked, if you would call it that, for a while, until the moral obligation was put to the test and found lacking.

The Transfer of Underlying Risk

The use of a guarantee or moral obligation obviously has great appeal. The borrower is able to avail himself of financing which otherwise might not be available or available only at a significantly higher interest cost. In many instances, the government receives a guarantee fee. Proponents of this method of socially allocating capital will argue that everyone gains and no one loses. The apparent implication is pareto optimality with no boundaries. However, when one analyzes the situation a little more closely one finds that there is a cost and that someone must bear this cost.

The crux of this issue is that underlying risk does not go away with a government guarantee. The borrower can still default, particularly if there is a limit to the amount of government guarantee. The underlying risk is simply shifted from the investor to the federal government and to taxpayers at large. If default occurs, the federal government will need to make good on the obligation. In final analysis, this will result in foregoing federal programs, increasing taxes, or increasing the federal debt. Therefore, there is a cost to the guarantee, though admittedly it is largely a hidden one. It is the contingent or potential cost to present and future taxpayers. As taken up in Chapter 6, which dealt with default risk, the cost is represented by the left-hand side of the probability distribution of possible returns where actual returns are less than the promised return. This probabilistic cost is absorbed by the government in order to make credit available at a lower cost to a socially desirable project.

Thus, the government supplants the marketplace in judging the risk-return tradeoff, and return is broadened to include not only the project's economic return but its social return as well. More will be said about this supplanting later in the chapter once we have considered other methods for socially allocating capital. Unfortunately, there has been virtually no empirical work done on the effect of government guarantees and moral obligations on yields and risk.

Interest-Rate Subsidies

A third method for socially allocating capital is for the government to pay an interest-rate subsidy to either the lender or to the borrower. When it goes to the lender, the government typically subsidizes a category of loans—such as mortgages or loans to cities. This approach tends to be "shotgun" in that it benefits all borrowers in a particular category. While this may be appropriate if one is trying to stimulate housing or construction overall, it is not effective if the purpose is to enable low-income families to purchase housing. Here a subsidy to the borrower, or to the lender where the subsidy is tied to a loan to a specific borrower, is better. Note that in either case the lender receives the market clearing rate of interest on his loan. The borrower pays this rate minus the subsidy. For the most part, interest-rate subsidies have been used to subsidize the mortgage payments of low income families.

The Effect of the Subsidy

With an interest-rate subsidy, the demand for that type of financing presumably will increase. Whether or not the supply of financing increases, however, depends on the elasticity of supply. In turn, this depends on the substitutability between the type of debt instrument or market involved and other financial instruments.[5] If the supply curve is reasonably interest elastic, the amount of financing will increase. The situation is illustrated in Fig. 9-4. Before the subsidy, the demand for financing is depicted by $D-D$. With a supply curve of $S-S$, financing in the amount of d^* will occur at a market clearing rate of r_c. With a subsidy of $R-r_c$, the demand curve shifts to $D'-D'$. In turn, this causes the amount of financing to increase to d', and the market clearing rate to increase to r'_c. However, the interest rate the borrower pays is the new market clearing rate minus the subsidy, or $r'_c - (R - r_c) = r_s$. Thus, the amount of financing increases, and the effective interest rate paid by the borrower declines.

If the supply curve were inelastic, however, there would be no increase

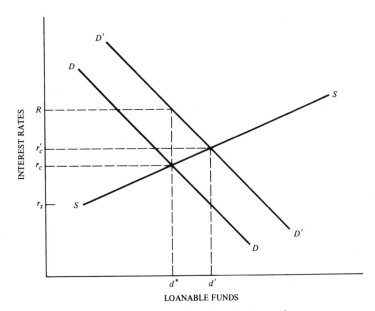

Figure 9-4. Interest-rate subsidy with an elastic supply curve.

[5]For an analysis of this point, see Rudolph G. Penner and William L. Silber, "The Interaction between Federal Credit Programs and the Impact on the Allocation of Credit," *American Economic Review*, LXIII (December, 1973), 839–842.

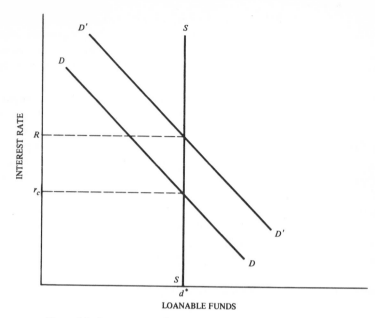

Figure 9-5. Interest-rate subsidy with an inelastic supply curve.

in the amount of financing. This situation is illustrated in Fig. 9-5. Here a subsidy of $R - r_c$ shifts the demand curve to $D'-D'$. However, because of the inelastic supply curve, the amount of financing does not increase. The shift in the demand curve is reflected entirely in an increase in the market clearing rate, namely from r_c to R. Thus, this increase exactly offsets the subsidy, so the effective rate of interest to the borrower is the same as before. Put another way, all of the subsidy goes to the lender.

Thus, the degree of substitutability between the financial instrument or market involved in the subsidy arrangement and other financial instruments and markets determines the success of the arrangement. With an inelastic supply curve, neither the amount of financing is raised, nor is the effective rate paid by the borrower lowered. Given all we know about financial markets, however, the case for a completely inelastic supply curve of loanable funds for a particular financial instrument seems weak. We would expect supply curves to be reasonably elastic, and the situation to resemble that depicted in Fig. 9-4.

One important feature of the interest-rate subsidy approach to socially allocate capital is that the government does not intercede directly into the marketplace. It pays a subsidy, but financial markets then equilibrate on the basis of expected return and risk. Therefore there is a minimum of interference in the workings of financial markets. However, indirect pressure on financial markets can result if the subsidy is raised by increasing the amount of government debt. By issuing securities in the Treasury or municipal markets, the supply curve for the particular market to which the government is trying to socially allocate capital would be adversely affected if there were substitutability between the markets. Put another way, it is final general equilibrium in financial markets which is important in judging the success of a plan to socially allocate capital. If the secondary effects offset the initial action, this must be considered before a decision can be made. Instead of an increase in government debt to pay for the subsidy, the capital may be raised by an increase in general taxes. In this case, there is little effect on other financial markets and this offsetting factor can be safely ignored when judging the merits of the subsidy arrangement.[6] More will be said about the relative merits of an interest-rate subsidy approach once we have considered all of the methods for socially allocating capital.

Financial Intermediation Through Borrowing and Relending

Another means for socially allocating capital is for the government, or an agency thereof, to borrow in the financial markets and then to relend to a savings and loan association, a corporation, a housing authority, a municipality, or what have you, at either the same rate at which it borrows or at a higher rate. In either case, the rate charged is lower than what the ultimate borrower would pay in the market. Examples of this type of arrangement include the federal government's revolving credit to New York City (1976), where the ultimate source of these funds was an increase in the federal debt; the Federal Home Loan Bank borrowing in the financial markets and relending to savings and loan associations; and the Federal National Mortgage Association (Fannie Mae) and the Federal Home Loan Mortgage Corporation borrowing in the financial markets in order to buy mortgages.

The Situation Illustrated

In all of these cases the government becomes a financial intermediary for purposes or redirecting the flow of savings toward socially desirable projects. In so doing, the credit worthiness of the government or agency thereof is substituted for that of the party involved. Because of the credit worthiness of the government, the rate the borrower pays is lower. The situation is illustrated in Fig. 9-6. Before the government program to

[6]See Penner and Silber, *ibid.*

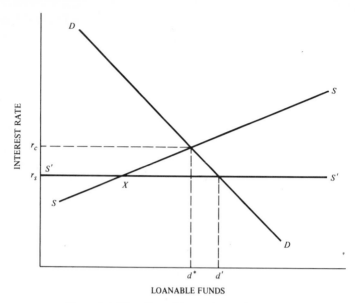

Figure 9-6. The effect of borrowing and relending.

borrow and relend to the socially desirable project, the intersection of the supply, S–S, and demand, D–D, curves results in a market clearing rate of r_c and in a total amount borrowed of d^*. When the government steps in, it replaces the previous supply curve with a new supply curve, S'–S'. We assume that the interest rate charged, r_s, is the same regardless of the amount borrowed, although this need not be the case.

It is possible that part of the funding of the project will be fulfilled by private sources if a discriminating auction takes place. In the case of Fig. 9-6, this would result in a kinked supply curve of S–X–S', with the former portion coming from private sources. If the subsidy rate charged is low enough, however, the government will end up displacing entirely the financing of the project through private sources. Another qualification to Fig. 9-6 is that the government may not wish to provide unlimited amounts of financing at a rate of r_s. Rather, it may simply agree to provide up to so much financing, in which case the supply curve S'–S' in Fig. 9-6 would be a horizontal line which would stop abruptly at some point.

The Effect of Government Intermediation

The effect of this form of socially allocating capital is somewhat the same as that which occurs in the case of a government guarantee. In whole or in part, the government absorbs the risk of default. As before, the underlying risk of the project does not go away but it is merely shifted from private investors to the government and, ultimately, to taxpayers at large. In addition, the amount borrowed will be larger than would occur under free market conditions, unless the government limits the amount it is willing to lend. In Fig. 9-6, equilibrium borrowings occur at d' where before they were at the lower d^*.

What happens of course is that the government borrows at a favorable interest rate and then relends to the project involved. Again the equilibrating mechanism in financial markets is distorted. Funds no longer flow on the basis of expected return and risk. One set of potential borrowers moves to the head of the credit line and capital is allocated to those borrowers on the basis of government decree, not by the marketplace. To the extent that substitutability exists between the financial instrument or market involved in the social allocation process and other financial markets and, to the extent that the amount of financing for the social project is larger than would otherwise be the case, the supply function for the other markets is adversely affected from the standpoint of borrowers. In other words, the supply curves for the other markets would shift to the left. In general equilibrium, then, other borrowers may pay somewhat higher interest rates as a result of the government borrowing and relending for the social project. This would also affect the government in its borrowing, so part of the expected advantage would be offset. However, if the amount of capital socially allocated is relatively small, there will be little offset.

Another way of looking at the matter is that as long as a project is able to obtain a social allocation of capital from the government and relatively few others are able to do so, significant advantage accrues to it. However, if a large number of other borrowers have similar access to the government, the advantage diminishes. Beyond a point, essentially all financial flows would be determined by social criteria as opposed to economic criteria, and there would be no private financial markets as we know them. Savings would not flow to investment projects that appear to be most productive from an economic standpoint. They would flow on the basis of government determined priorities. To the extent that these priorities differed significantly from economic priorities, the economic growth of the country would lessen and the wherewithal to address social problems would be reduced. The point of all this is simply to show that while some borrowing and relending by the government for social purposes may be beneficial to the favored parties and not significantly detrimental to other borrowers, as more and more action takes place the advantage quickly disappears. In an era of economic scarcity, it takes a relatively rich nation to deal effectively with its social problems. The tradeoffs are ever present and must be recognized. This issue will be discussed further in the closing section of the chapter.

Regulations Affecting Investor
and Lender Behavior

The last method for socially allocating capital which we will examine is the use of government regulations to divert the flow of savings toward socially desirable projects. In this case, artificial restraints are established to affect the flows. The best known and most important example of this method has to do with mortgage financing. By forcing certain financial institutions to engage primarily in mortgage lending, by establishing ceilings on the savings rates that these mortgage lending institutions can pay, and by creating certain barriers to the saver with respect to investing elsewhere, i.e., by restricting competition, the hope is to increase mortgage financing at rates of interest lower than what would otherwise be the market clearing rates. Unlike other approaches for socially allocating capital, the government's role is indirect, sometimes bordering on the obscure, but nonetheless powerful.

The Effectiveness of this Approach

The success of this approach depends on the degree of substitutability between markets. The more isolated the mortgage market is relative to other markets and the less the substitutability between mortgages and other financial instruments, the greater will be the flow of savings to mortgages and the lower the rate of interest, all other things remaining the same. However, if mortgages and other financial instruments are perfect substitutes, lenders who are unrestricted by the government will simply substitute other securities for mortgages whenever the risk-adjusted rate of return falls below that which is available in other financial markets. The actions of these unrestricted investors will offset actions by financial institutions, which are restricted in their investment behavior to mortgages. Therefore, within limits, government efforts to lower mortgage rates and increase the supply of mortgage funds will be for naught.[7] Increases in mortgage purchases by restricted lenders will merely replace the exit of unrestricted lenders. However, if there are no unrestricted investors and only restricted lenders make mortgage loans, the government's efforts to increase the flow of savings to these institutions will be successful in increasing the amount of mortgage loans.

Let us turn now to the situation where mortgages and other securities are less than perfect substitutes and there are unrestricted lenders present in the mortgage market. Here there would be a less than one-for-one offset by unrestricted lenders in selling mortgages for other securities when the risk-adjusted return was forced below that available in other markets. In

[7]For further analysis of this point, see Penner and Silber, *ibid.*, 841–843.

the extreme case of zero substitutability between markets, there would be no offset. As long as the degree of substitutability is less than perfect, there will be a "stickiness" on the part of unrestricted lenders in selling mortgages, even though risk-adjusted rates may be more attractive elsewhere. As a result, this approach to socially allocate capital will be only partially successful. In summary, this approach is essentially one which advances the government imposing restrictions to thwart competition so that the flow of savings to mortgage lending institutions can be enhanced.

On Whom the Costs Fall

With this approach there is no direct cost to the government and to taxpayers, with the exception of the costs associated with initiating the restrictions and with enforcing them. Therefore, the approach is viewed by some as "costless." However, there are costs, although admittedly they are largely hidden. For one thing, artificial restrictions result in a less efficient functioning of the financial markets of society. They impede the effectiveness with which financial markets channel savings from savings-surplus economic units to savings-deficit ones. Moreover, there is a cost to savers who must accept lower interest rates on their savings than otherwise would prevail. By placing limits on the maximum savings rate that a mortgage lending institution can pay and by establishing barriers to investing elsewhere, such as the $10,000 minimum denomination purchase of Treasury bills initiated in 1970, savers must accept lower rates of interest than the market clearing rates which would occur in the absence of these restrictions. This is particularly true in times of rising interest rates.

Moreover, the cost falls unevenly on different savers. Higher income individuals with larger amounts of savings typically are able to take advantage of alternative investment opportunities, such as money-market instruments, which pay higher rates of interest. Because of minimum denomination problems and transaction, information, and inconvenience costs, low- to medium-income families usually are unable to take advantage of these alternatives. Even here, however, the forces of competition and financial innovation are not long shackled. In the 1974–1975 era of high interest rates, there developed money-market funds which enabled individuals to invest in money-market instruments in smaller denominations than is possible with a direct purchase of Treasury bills, commercial paper, bank certificates of deposit, or bankers' acceptances. This financial innovation has given the traditional saver alternatives. Still the money-market funds require a minimum denomination of $500 or $1,000, and certain inconvenience costs are involved. Therefore, this alternative is not available to all.

In the final analysis, one of the costs of socially allocating capital to mortgages by regulations falls on low- to medium-income families who do not have alternative investment opportunities for their savings. They must accept lower savings rates than would be possible in competitive markets, unhampered by ceiling deposit rates and other restrictions. The beneficiaries of this social allocation of capital are home buyers, residential building buyers, and, to a much lesser extent, commercial building buyers. These owners typically are medium- to high-income individuals. Very few low-income families own homes. Therefore, we have an equity or income redistribution problem. Those individuals that benefit most from available mortgages at favorable interest rates usually are able to avail themselves of alternative investments for their savings when money-market rates rise significantly above deposit rates. Those that are least able to take advantage of such alternatives are not home buyers, so they do not benefit directly from the social allocation of capital to mortgages. In this sense, there is discrimination against the small saver. While not deliberate, there is nonetheless a regressive income redistributional effect.[8]

Empirical Studies of Mortgages and Housing

Of all the areas involving the social allocation of capital, mortgage financing has received the most attention empirically. In a comprehensive study of federal credit programs designed to spur housing, Penner and Silber categorize the various programs as to the approach used.[9] Also, the interrelationships between programs were studied to determine if they were reinforcing, negatively correlated, or neutral. A key factor for both subsidy-type programs and regulatory-type programs is the degree of substitutability between mortgages and other financial instruments. Penner and Silber suggest that actions undertaken to increase the attractiveness of mortgages and their substitutability with other financial instruments are compatible with subsidy-type programs but not with regulatory-type programs. This point was examined in previous sections. While Penner and Silber do not analyze actual mortgage data, their contribution lies in carefully synthesizing the various programs for socially allocating capital to mortgages.

In a provocative article, Allan H. Meltzer questions whether federal programs have any positive effect on stimulating housing.[10] In examining

[8]For further development of this charge, see Edward J. Kane, "Short-Changing the Small Saver: Federal Government Discrimination against the Small Saver during the Vietnam War," *Journal of Money, Credit and Banking*, 2 (November, 1970), 513–522. The point also was raised independently by James C. Van Horne, "The Liability Structure of Deposit Institutions," A Position Paper for the Presidential Commission on Financial Structure and Regulation, 1970.

[9]Penner and Silber, *op. cit.*

[10]Allan H. Meltzer, "Credit Availability and Economic Decisions: Some Evidence from the Mortgage and Housing Markets," *Journal of Finance*, 29 (June, 1974), 763–777.

the long-run relationship between housing and mortgage credit, he finds no relation between changes in the composition of credit (toward mortgages) and changes in the ratio of housing to total assets. In further analyzing other economic studies, Meltzer finds that the demand for mortgage loans is highly interest elastic. He argues that the main effect of government programs to stimulate housing through greater availability of mortgage financing is to increase the owner's per cent of equity as opposed to increasing the relative amount of housing. The contention here is that as individuals increase their relative proportion of mortgage debt, they decrease their relative proportions of other debt, particularly security loans. In other words, there *is* significant substitution between various forms of borrowing. Asset purchases are largely independent of the form of financing, since there is no matching of specific assets with specific liabilities. This agrees with our discussion in Chapter 3, where economic units were depicted as maximizing their utility associated with owning various types of assets and with the overall issuing of financial liabilities. This argument suggests that when mortgage credit is made available on favorable terms by the government, individuals substitute mortgage borrowing for other forms of borrowing. As a result, the relative increase in mortgage credit does not give rise to a like increase in housing.

There have been several studies dealing with the effectiveness and cost of government efforts to protect the flow of savings to savings and loan associations as well as to mutual savings banks during periods of sharply rising interest rates. During these times, interest rates on money-market instruments rise significantly in excess of deposit rates. Given attractive yields elsewhere, thrift institutions experience a slowdown, and sometimes even a decline, in their deposit growth. Called disintermediation, this phenomenon causes concern for many in government, due to the important role these institutions play in mortgage lending. To thwart disintermediation during the 1966 period of rapidly rising interest rates, the Interest Rate Adjustment Act was enacted. This bill extended deposit rate ceilings to thrift institutions and established a positive rate differential between thrift deposit rates and deposit rates at commercial banks. The apparent desire was to limit competition among thrift institutions and to protect them from commercial bank competition.

In studying the 1966 period, Peter Fortune developed an econometric model of the household sector with particular emphasis on their allocation of liquid assets, including savings deposits.[11] Among other things, Fortune found that flows of new savings were more sensitive to interest rates than were existing savings deposits. This held for both commercial banks and thrift institutions. In studying the effect of commercial bank competition

[11]Peter Fortune, "The Effectiveness of Recent Policies to Maintain Thrift-Deposit Flows," *Journal of Money, Banking and Credit*, 7 (August, 1975), 297–315.

on thrift deposit flows during 1966, Fortune discovered that only about 20 per cent of the decrease in such flows could be attributed to commercial bank competition. Most of the disintermediation was attributable to competition from money-market instruments. He suggests that this evidence does not provide strong support for restricting competition by commercial banks as a means for preserving the flow of savings to thrift institutions. Fortune also studied the effect of the $10,000 minimum denomination purchase of Treasury bills, which was initiated in 1970, as a means for protecting thrift deposit flows. In contrast to the previous results, he found that this action was highly effective in protecting such flows during 1970. In effect, it thwarted the ability of savers to invest directly in money-market instruments, which Fortune suggests is the most important source of competition for thrift institutions.

While these results indicate that variation in the minimum denomination of Treasury bills was a more effective means for socially allocating capital to mortgages in 1970 than was variation in deposit-rate ceilings, Fortune recognizes that the former was an innovation in 1970. Its future effectiveness is in doubt, owing in no small measure to the development of money-market funds in the 1974–1975 era of high interest rates. As previously discussed, the forces of competition are not long shackled as evidenced by this innovation. Also, active use of variation in the minimum denomination of Treasury bills as a policy variable will no longer take people by surprise as it did in 1970. They will come to anticipate changes and endeavor to buy Treasury bills before a change occurs. Indeed, a theory of rational expectations would suggest that these anticipatory moves will completely offset the effectiveness of a policy change.

In another study of the effect of competition from money market instruments on savings deposit flows, Donald J. Mullineaux analyzes Treasury bill purchase behavior by noncompetitive bidders.[12] A noncompetitive bidder is one who places a tender with the Treasury at its Monday auction for an amount of bills less than $200,000 (at the time of the study). These tenders are awarded at the average price paid by competitive bidders in the auction. Mullineaux uses noncompetitive bids as a proxy for the behavior of smaller investors in bidding for Treasury bills. The volume of noncompetitive bids is made a function of a number of variables including the opportunity cost of holding deposit-type assets as measured by their ceiling rate. Using auction data from January, 1963, to February, 1970, the model was tested. The opportunity cost measure for deposit-type assets was found to be negative and significant, indicating that the higher the deposit rate, the lower the participation of small investors in Treasury bill auctions. When the sample period was partitioned into 1963–1968 and 1969–February, 1970, the regression coefficient for this variable was found to be substantially higher in absolute terms during the latter period.

[12]Donald J. Mullineaux, "Deposit-Rate Ceilings and Noncompetitive Bidding for U.S. Treasury Bills," *Journal of Money, Credit and Banking,* 5 (February, 1973), 201–212.

Mullineaux suggests that this is consistent with small savers shifting substantial amounts of funds to Treasury bills and other open market instruments during the high interest-rate period of 1969–1970.

In keeping with the previous study, this study suggests that there is a high degree of substitutability between savings deposits and money-market instruments. When interest rates rise significantly, savings flows to deposit institutions are affected adversely, and disintermediation occurs. Mullineaux estimates that if savings and loan associations and mutual savings banks had been allowed to raise their deposit rates competitively, significantly fewer smaller bids would have been received for Treasury bills. Instead, competition was thwarted by raising the minimum denomination on Treasury bills to $10,000 on February 25, 1970. As discussed earlier, the purpose was to stem disintermediation which was occurring at the time, and the move was regarded as successful. Mullineaux reports that noncompetitive bids for Treasury bills dropped by over 75 per cent in March, 1970 from January levels. Thus, the change in the minimum denomination for purchase of Treasury bills had a powerful effect in curtailing savings deposit outflows in 1970. However, as we discussed, changes in this variable are unlikely to be as successful in the future as they were in 1970. Also, there are serious questions as to the effect on market efficiency, which we will discuss shortly.

Another question regarding the use of regulations to redirect savings flows to mortgages is that of income redistribution. As we studied earlier, the cost of socially allocating capital in this way falls primarily on low-to medium-income families who are forced to accept lower than market clearing rates on their savings. David H. Pyle endeavors to estimate the overall size of the opportunity loss to savers.[13] In so doing, he devised a model to estimate the deposit rates that would have been paid during 1968–1970 in the absence of these restrictions. Separate estimates were made for savings and loan associations, for commercial banks, and for mutual savings banks, based on 1952–1967 data. The parameters derived then were used to predict deposit rates for 1968, 1969, and 1970. Comparisons of predicted rates with actual rates for each of the years were as follows:

Year	SAVINGS AND LOAN ASSOCIATIONS		COMMERCIAL BANKS		MUTUAL SAVINGS BANKS	
	Predicted	Actual	Predicted	Actual	Predicted	Actual
1968	4.88%	4.68%	4.46%	4.25%	4.88%	4.76%
1969	5.22	4.80	4.96	4.34	5.17	4.89
1970	5.61	5.06	5.49	4.72	5.53	5.01

[13]David H. Pyle, "The Losses on Savings Deposits from Interest Rate Regulation," *Bell Journal of Economics and Management Science*, 5 (Autumn, 1974), 614–622.

In all three years, predicted rates were above actual rates, and Pyle attributes this to binding interest-rate ceilings. Using the differential between predicted and actual rates as an estimate of the interest income lost by savers due to restrictions, he multiplied these differentials times the stocks of savings deposits at each institution for each of the years. For the three years, his overall estimate of the interest income loss was in excess of $5 billion. This represents an opportunity loss in the sense of what savers would have received if market clearing savings rates had been paid and what they actually were paid. As discussed earlier, the burden of this opportunity loss would be expected to fall heavily on low- to medium-income families.

Policy Implications

In this chapter we have examined a number of means by which the government can influence the flow of savings to a desired cause and/or reduce the rate of interest paid by a designated borrower. In all cases, there is intervention into the marketplace; hence we have in whole or in part a social allocation of capital as opposed to a pure market allocation. There is little question that the social allocation of capital has become increasingly popular in recent years. Special interest groups and politicians see it as a means for improving the condition of a particular sector of society, enabling it to borrow funds which might not otherwise be available or might be available only at a significantly higher interest cost. The political appeal is irresistible—there appears to be enormous benefits and, on the surface at least, few costs. However, we know from our previous discussion that there are costs. For one thing, the function of financial markets is altered. This function is to efficiently channel savings in our society to the most productive investment opportunities. These opportunities may be private sector investments, where there are private rates of return, or public sector investments with social rates of return. The mechanism by which funds are channeled is the tradeoff between expected return and risk. When the government explicitly directs funds to certain investments which would either not be able to attract funds on their own or would attract them only at a higher rate of interest, it tampers with the workings of the marketplace. This tampering can lead to less efficient financial markets with the result that savings are allocated at higher costs and/or with greater inconvenience. This has adverse implications for us all.

Funds no longer flow on the basis of expected return and risk. Certain borrowers—namely those whom the government decides are socially deserving—no longer must justify their investment's private or social rate of return in relation to a market determined standard of efficiency. The result is that some investments are undertaken which would be rejected if the borrower had to compete directly in the financial markets for funds. Put another way, in society as a whole investments are undertaken which are not optimal in the sense of economic efficiency. As a result, there may be an adverse effect on real economic growth. Moreover, if distortions in risk-return relationships lead to less efficient financial markets, this also may have an adverse effect on economic growth. Financial markets simply become less efficient in channeling savings to investment opportunities on a risk-adjusted return basis. For these reasons, economic growth and want satisfaction in society may be less than otherwise would be the case. This is not to say that savings flows should be allocated on the basis of economic considerations alone. Without question there are unmet social needs, and some of these needs may be satisfied by the social allocation of capital. The problem is that methods for socially allocating capital are seldom evaluated in their totality. Usually the benefits are readily apparent and always cited. However, the "true costs" are seldom considered. As a result, the idea is often given that the social allocation of capital is either without cost or that the costs are unimportant. As we have shown, however, there is a cost, not only to the government and to taxpayers, but to society as a whole, in having less efficient financial markets and lower than possible economic growth.

Unfortunately, the more hidden the cost, the more tempting it is to socially allocate capital. More disturbing is the fact that usually the more hidden the cost of a method, the less efficient the process by which capital is socially allocated. A case in point is the use of regulations to divert the flow of savings toward mortgages. In this and other cases, there is a serious question of equity as well as of allocative efficiency. The beneficiaries are mortgage borrowers in general as opposed to a particular subset. Moreover, the opportunity cost falls primarily on low- to medium-income families who must accept lower than market clearing rates of interest on their savings. Also, there is serious question as to whether housing is actually stimulated or whether people simply substitute mortgage borrowing, on attractive terms, for other forms of borrowing. This has led many to advocate government subsidies for housing as opposed to subsidies for mortgages.[14]

These problems as well as others which we have discussed throughout this chapter are sufficient to give insight into the costs of socially allocating capital. It is extremely important that these costs be recognized and evaluated before a decision is made. The benefits of a plan to socially

[14]See Meltzer, *op. cit.*; and Dwight M. Jaffee, "What To Do about Savings and Loan Associations? A Review Essay," *Journal of Money, Credit and Banking*, 6 (November, 1974), 546–548.

allocate capital must be judged in relation to the opportunity cost to taxpayers, to other borrowers, to savers, to the efficiency of financial markets, and to the economic and/or social contribution foregone by the rejection of other projects. While there is little question that the decision-making process is easier if these costs can somehow be ignored, they represent the very crux of the issue. As they ultimately must be borne by society in one way or another, these costs should be analyzed at the time of a decision.

In those cases where Congress or some other part of government deems it appropriate on the basis of a cost-benefit-type of analysis to socially allocate capital, a strong case can be made that it be in the form of an interest-rate subsidy to the borrower. Assuming a high degree of substitutability and competition between various financial instruments —and most evidence seems to confirm this—the subsidy is likely to be the most effective way to socially allocate capital, provided it comes from general tax revenues. With an interest-rate subsidy, financial markets are able to perform their function in terms of market clearing rates of interest as opposed to some artificial ceiling rate of interest imposed by government. With an absence of such restrictions, we would expect financial markets to perform as efficiently as possible under the circumstances. Also, the cost of socially allocating capital in the case of mortgages would not fall on low- to medium-income families who are forced to accept lower than market clearing rates of interest on their savings. With a removal of deposit rate ceilings, they would receive market clearing rates of interest on their savings. The subsidy would come from the federal government at the expense of taxpayers in general rather than a subset of them as now occurs. The advantage of such an arrangement would be that savings would be more efficiently channeled in society. While there still exists the question of social priorities versus economic priorities,[15] once these are resolved a free market mechanism would allocate savings in a competitive environment on the basis of risk and return.

Summary

The social allocation of capital involves efforts by the government to direct the flow of savings in our society toward socially desirable projects and/or to lower the interest cost for these projects. A number of methods for socially allocating capital were analyzed. These include: (1) a ceiling or usury rate of interest on loans; (2) the use of a

[15]The use of a subsidy may result in overconsumption of certain commodities relative to others. Consideration of this issue in an overall framework of public choice is beyond the scope of this book.

government guarantee or "moral obligation"; (3) an interest-rate subsidy; (4) government's borrowing in the financial markets and relending to the socially desirable project; and (5) the use of regulations to divert the flow of savings toward socially desirable projects. Each of these methods was examined regarding its effect in increasing the flow of financing and in lowering interest costs. A key ingredient was found to be the substitutability of the financial instrument in question with other financial instruments. In our analysis, available empirical evidence was examined and examples were presented.

In most cases, the costs of socially allocating capital are not understood. These costs include such things as the probabilistic cost of making good on a guarantee by the government, the less efficient functioning of financial markets, the lessened allocative efficiency of real resources, and the opportunity cost to low- and medium-income savers in being forced to accept less than market clearing interest rates on their deposits. It is critical that these costs be considered in relation to their benefits before a decision to socially allocate capital is made. Too often this does not occur due to the "hidden" nature of many of the costs. When it is deemed appropriate to socially allocate capital, a strong case can be made for the use of an interest-rate subsidy, because it has the least disruptive influence on the functioning of financial markets. Use of this method implicitly assumes a reasonably high degree of substitutability among financial instruments.

SELECTED REFERENCES

Fortune, Peter, "The Effectiveness of Recent Policies to Maintain Thrift-Deposit Flows," *Journal of Money, Credit and Banking,* 7 (August, 1975), 297–315.

Greer, Douglas F., "Rate Ceilings, Market Structure, and the Supply of Finance Company Personal Loans," *Journal of Finance,* 29 (December, 1974), 1363–1382.

Meltzer, Allan H., "Credit Availability and Economic Decisions: Some Evidence from the Mortgage and Housing Markets," *Journal of Finance,* 29 (June, 1974), 763–777.

Penner, Rudolph G., and William L. Silber, "The Interaction between Federal Credit Programs and the Impact on the Allocation of Credit," *American Economic Review,* LXII (December, 1973), 838–852.

Pyle, David H., "The Losses on Savings Deposits from Interest Rate Regulation," *Bell Journal of Economics and Management Science,* 5 (Autumn, 1974), 614–622.

Van Horne, James C., "The Liability Structure of Deposit Institutions," A Position Paper for the Presidential Commission on Financial Structure and Regulation, 1970.

Index